PHILOLOGICAL INQUIRIES:

PART THE FIRST.

Vol. II.   N n

PHILOLOGICAL

INQUIRIES

ADDREST TO MY MUCH ESTEEMED RELATION AND FRIEND,

EDWARD HOOPER, Esq.

OF HURN-COURT, IN THE COUNTY OF HANTS.

DEAR SIR,

BEING yourself advanced in years, you will the more easily for-give me, if I claim *a Privilege of Age*, and pass from PHILO-SOPHY to PHILOLOGY.

You may compare me, if you please, to some weary Traveller, who, having long wandered over craggy heights, descends at length to the Plains below, and hopes, *at his Journey's End*, to find a smooth and easy Road.

FOR MY WRITINGS (such as they are) they have answered a *Pur-pose* I always wished, if they have led men to inspect *Authors, far su-perior to myself, many* of whose Works (like hidden Treasures) have lain *for years* out of sight.

N n 2

Be

Be that however as it may, I shall at least enjoy the pleasure of thus *recording* our mutual Friendship; a *Friendship*, which has lasted for *more than fifty* years, and which I think so much for my honour, *to have merited so long.*

But I proceed to my Subject.

As the *great Events of* Nature* led Mankind to *Admiration:* so Curiosity *to learn the Cause,* whence such Events should arise, was that, which by due degrees formed Natural Philosophy.

What happened in the *Natural* World, happened also in the *Literary. Exquisite Productions* both in Prose and Verse induced men *here* likewise *to seek the Cause;* and *such Inquiries,* often repeated, gave birth to Philology.

Philology should hence appear to be of a most *comprehensive* character, and to include not only all Accounts both of *Criticism* and *Critics,* but of every thing connected with *Letters,* be it *Speculative* or *Historical.*

The Treatise, which follows, is of this Philological kind, and will consist of three Parts, properly distinct from each other.

The

()

---

* *Some of these great Events are enumerated by* Virgil—*the Course of the Heavens—Eclipses of the Sun and Moon—Earthquakes—the Flux and Reflux of the Sea—the quick Return of Night in Winter, and the flow Return of it in Summer.* Virg. Geor, II. 475, &c.

THE FIRST will be an *Investigation of the Rise and different Species of* CRITICISM *and* CRITICS.

THE SECOND will be AN ILLUSTRATION OF CRITICAL DOCTRINES AND PRINCIPLES, *as they appear in* DISTINGUISHED AUTHORS, *as well Ancient as Modern.*

THE THIRD AND LAST PART will be rather HISTORICAL than *Critical,* being AN ESSAY ON THE TASTE AND LITERATURE OF THE MIDDLE AGE.

THESE subjects of Speculation being dispatched, we shall here conclude THESE PHILOLOGICAL INQUIRIES.

First therefore for the *First,* THE RISE AND DIFFERENT SPECIES OF CRITICISM AND CRITICS.

CHAPTER I.

Concerning the Rise of CRITICISM *in its* FIRST SPECIES, *the* PHILO-
SOPHICAL — *eminent perfons,* GREEKS *and* ROMANS, *by whom this
Species was cultivated.*

Part I. THOSE, who can imagine that the Rules of Writing were firft
eftablifhed, and that men then wrote in conformity to them, as
they make conferves and comfits by referring to receipt-books, know
nothing of *Criticifm*, either as to its origin or progrefs. The truth is,
they were Authors, who made the firft good Critics, and not Critics,
who made the firft good Authors, however writers of later date may
have profited by critical Precepts.

IF this appear ftrange, we may refer to other fubjects. Can we
doubt that men had Mufic, fuch indeed as it was, before the principles of Harmony were eftablifhed into a Science? that Difeafes
were healed, and Buildings erected, before Medicine and Architecture were fyftematized into Arts? that men reafoned and harangued
upon matters of fpeculation and practice, long before there were
profeft teachers either of Logic or of Rhetoric? To return therefore to our fubject, the rife and progrefs of Criticifm.

ANCIENT GREECE in its happy days was the feat of Liberty, of
Sciences, and of Arts. In this fair region, fertile of wit, the *Epic*
Writers came firft; then the *Lyric*; then the *Tragic*; and laftly the
Hiftorians,

Hiſtorians, the *Comic* Writers, and the *Orators,* each in their turns delighting whole multitudes, and commanding the attention and admiration of all. Now, when wiſe and thinking men, the ſubtle inveſtigators of principles and cauſes, obſerved the wonderful effect of theſe works upon the human mind, they were prompted to inquire *whence this ſhould proceed;* for that it ſhould happen *merely from Chance,* they could not well believe.

HERE therefore we have the RISE and ORIGIN of CRITICISM, which in its beginning was " a deep and philoſophical Search into " the primary Laws and Elements of good Writing, as far as they " could be collected from the moſt approved Performances."

IN this contemplation of Authors, the firſt Critics not only attended to the Powers, and different Species of WORDS; the Force of *numerous Compoſition* whether in proſe or verſe; the Aptitude of *its various kinds to different ſubjects;* but they farther conſidered that, which is the baſis of all, that is to ſay in other words, the MEANING or the SENSE. This led them at once into the moſt curious of ſubjects; the nature of *Man* in general; *the different characters of men,* as they differ in rank or age; their *Reaſon* and their *Paſſions;* how the one was to be perſuaded, the others to be raiſed or calmed; the *Places* or *Repoſitories,* to which we may recur, when we want proper matter for any of theſe purpoſes. Beſides all this they ſtudied *Sentiments* and *Manners;* what conſtitutes a Work, *One;* what, a *Whole* and *Parts;* what the Eſſence of probable, and even of natural *Fiction,* as contributing to conſtitute a *juſt Dramatic Fable.*

MUCH

Much of this kind may be found in different parts of Plato. But Aristotle his Disciple, who may be called *the Systematizer of* his Master's Doctrines, has in his two Treatises of *Poetry* and *Rhetoric*[*], with such wonderful penetration, developed every part of the subject, that he may be justly called THE FATHER OF CRITICISM, both from the age when he lived, and from his truly transcendent genius. The *Criticism*, which this capital writer taught, has so intimate a correspondence and alliance with *Philosophy*, that we can call it by no other name, than that of PHILOSOPHICAL CRITICISM.

To *Aristotle* succeeded his Disciple *Theophrastus*, who followed his master's example in the study of *Criticism*, as may be seen in the catalogue of his writings, preserved by † *Diogenes Laertius*. But all the *critical* works of *Theophrastus*, as well as of many others, are now lost. The principal authors of the kind now remaining in *Greek*, are *Demetrius* of *Phalera*, *Dionysius* of *Halicarnassus*, *Dionysius Longinus*, together with *Hermogenes*, *Aphthonius*, and a few others.

Of these the most masterly seems to be *Demetrius*, who was the earliest, and who appears to follow the Precepts, and even the Text of *Aristotle*, with far greater attention, than any of the rest. His Examples, it must be confessed, are sometimes obscure, but this we rather

---

[*] To such as read not this Author in the Original, we recommend the French Translation of his *Rhetoric* by *Cassandre*, and that of his Art of *Poetry* by *Dacier*; both of them elaborate and laudable performances.

† Vid. Diog. Laert. L. V. ſ. 46, 47, &c.

rather impute to the destructive hand of time, which has prevented us from seeing many of the original authors.

Dionysius of *Halicarnassus,* the next in order, may be said to have written with judgment upon the force of *Numerous Composition,* not to mention other tracts on the subject of *Oratory,* and those also *critical,* as well as *historical.* *Longinus,* who was in time far later than these, seems principally to have had in view the *Passions,* and the *Imagination,* in the treating of which he has acquired a just applause, and expressed himself with a dignity suitable to the subject. The rest of the *Greek Critics,* tho' they have said many useful things, have yet so minutely multiplied the rules of Art, and so much confined themselves to the Oratory of the Tribunal, that they appear of no great service, as to good writing *in general.*

AMONG the ROMANS, the first Critic of note was CICERO, who, tho' far below *Aristotle* in depth of philosophy, may be said, like him, to have exceeded all his countrymen. As his celebrated Treatise *concerning the Orator** is written in dialogue, where the Speakers introduced are the greatest men of his nation, we have incidentally an elegant sample of those manners, and that politeness, which were peculiar to the leading characters during the *Roman* Commonwealth. There we may see the behaviour of free and accomplished men,
before

---

* This Treatise, being the Work of a *capital* Orator on the subject of his own Art, may fairly be pronounced a *capital* Performance.

The *Proem* to the third Book, both for language and sentiment, is perhaps as *pathetic,* and in that view as *sublime,* as any thing remaining among the Writings of the Antients.

 before a bafer addrefs had fet that ftandard, which has been too often taken for good-breeding ever fince.

'Next to *Cicero* came *Horace*, who often in *other* parts of his writings acts the *Critic* and Scholar, but whofe *Art of Poetry* is a ftandard of its kind, and too well known to need any encomium. After *Horace* arofe *Quinctilian*, *Cicero's* admirer, and follower, who appears by his works not only learned and ingenious, but (what is ftill more) an honeft and a worthy man. He likewife dwells too much upon the Oratory of the Tribunal, a fact no way furprifing, when we confider the age in which he lived; an age, when tyrannic Government being the fafhion of the times, that *nobler Species of Eloquence*, I mean the *popular* and *deliberative*, was, with all things truly liberal, degenerated and funk. The latter *Latin* Rhetoricians there is no need to mention, as they little help to illuftrate the fubject in hand. I would only repeat that the fpecies of Criticifm here mentioned, as far at leaft as handled by the more able Mafters, is that which we have denominated CRITICISM PHILOSOPHICAL. We are now to proceed to another fpecies.

CHAP. II.

Concerning the Progress of Criticism *in its* Second Species, *the* Historical—Greek *and* Roman Critics, *by whom this Species of Criticism was cultivated.*

AS to the *Criticism* already treated, we find it *not confined to any one particular* Author, but containing *general* Rules of Art, either for judging or writing, confirmed by the example not of *one* Author, but of *many.* But we know from experience that, in process of time, Languages, Customs, Manners, Laws, Governments, and Religions infensibly change. The *Macedonian* Tyranny, after the fatal battle of *Chæronea,* wrought much of this kind in *Greece;* and the *Roman* Tyranny, after the fatal battles of *Pharsalia* and *Philippi,* carried it throughout the known world*. Hence therefore of *Things* obsolete, the *Names* became obsolete also; and authors, who in their own age were intelligible and easy, in after days grew difficult and obscure. Here then we behold *the rise of a second race of Critics,* the tribe of *Scholiasts, Commentators,* and *Explainers.*

These naturally attached themselves to *particular* authors. *Aristarchus, Didymus, Eustathius,* and many others bestowed their labours upon *Homer; Proclus,* and *Tzetzes* upon *Hesiod;* the same *Proclus* and *Olympiodorus* upon *Plato; Simplicius, Ammonius,* and *Philoponus*

upon

* See Vol. I. p. 439.

 upon *Ariſtotle*; *Ulpian* upon *Demoſthenes*; *Macrobius* and *Aſconius* upon *Cicero*; *Calliergus* upon *Theocritus*; *Donatus* upon *Terence*; *Servius* upon *Virgil*; *Acro* and *Porphyrio* upon *Horace*; and ſo with reſpect to others, as well Philoſophers, as Poets and Orators. To theſe Scholiaſts may be added the ſeveral Compoſers of Lexicons; ſuch as *Heſychius*, *Philoxenus*, *Suidas*, &c. alſo the Writers upon Grammar, ſuch as *Apollonius*, *Priſcian*, *Soſipater*, *Chariſius*, &c. Now all theſe pains-taking men, conſidered together, may be ſaid to have completed another ſpecies of Criticiſm, a ſpecies which, in diſtinction to the former, we call Criticism Historical.

And thus things continued, tho' in a declining way, till, after many a ſevere and unſucceſsful plunge, the *Roman Empire* ſunk through the *Weſt of Europe*. *Latin* then ſoon loſt its purity; *Greek* they hardly knew; *Claſſics*, and their *Scholiaſts* were no longer ſtudied; and an Age ſucceeded of Legends and Cruſades.

CHAP. III.

MODERNS, *eminent in the two Species of Criticism before mentioned, the PHILOSOPHICAL and the HISTORICAL—the last Sort of Critics more numerous—those, mentioned in this Chapter, confined to the Greek and Latin Languages.*

AT length, after a long and barbarous period, when the shades of Monkery began to retire, and the light of Humanity once again to dawn, the Arts also of CRITICISM insensibly revived. 'Tis true indeed, the Authors of THE PHILOSOPHICAL SORT (I mean that which respects the Causes and Principles of good writing *in general*) were not many in number. However of this rank among the *Italians* were *Vida*, and the elder *Scaliger*; among the *French* were *Rapin*, *Bouhours*, *Boileau*, together with *Bossu*, the most methodic and accurate of them all. In our own Country our *Nobility* may be said to have distinguished themselves; Lord *Roscommon*, in his *Essay upon translated Verse*; the Duke of *Buckingham*, in his *Essay on Poetry*; and Lord *Shaftesbury*, in his Treatise called *Advice to an Author*: to whom may be added our late admired Genius, *Pope*, in his truely elegant poem, *the Essay upon Criticism*.

THE Discourses of *Sir Joshua Reynolds* upon *Painting* have, after a philosophical manner, investigated the Principles of an Art, which no one in *Practice* has better verified than himself.

WE

WE have mentioned these Discourses, not only from their merit, but as they incidentally teach us, that to write *well upon a liberal Art*, we must write *philosophically* — that all *the liberal Arts* in their Principles are *congenial* — and that these *Principles*, when traced to their *common Source*, are found all to terminate in the FIRST PHILO-SOPHY[*].

BUT to pursue our subject — However small among *Moderns* may be the number of these *Philosophical* Critics, the Writers of HISTO-RICAL or EXPLANATORY CRITICISM have been in a manner innu-merable. To name, out of many, only a few — of *Italy* were *Be-roaldus, Ficinus, Victorius,* and *Robertellus;* of the Higher and Lower *Germany* were *Erasmus, Sylburgius, Le Clerc,* and *Fabricius;* of *France* were *Lambin, Du Vall, Harduin, Capperonerius;* of *England* were *Stanley* (editor of *Æschylus) Gataker, Davis, Clarke* (editor of *Homer)* together with multitudes more from every region and quarter,

> *Thick as autumnal leaves, that strow the brooks*
> *In Vallombrosa* — — — —

BUT I fear I have given a strange catalogue, where we seek in vain for such illustrious personages, as *Sesostris, Cyrus, Alexander, Cæsar, Attila, Tottila, Tamerlane,* &c. The Heroes of my Work (if I may be pardoned for calling them so) have only aimed *in retirement* to present us with *Knowledge.* *Knowledge only* was *their Object*, not Havock, nor Devastation.

.AFTER

---

[*] See Vol. I. p. 235, and *Philosoph. Arrang.* p. 205; also the words, *First Philosophy,* in the Index to those *Arrangements.*

AFTER Commentators and Editors, we must not forget the Compilers of *Lexicons* and *Dictionaries*, such as *Charles* and *Henry Stevens*, *Favorinus*, *Conflantine*, *Budæus*, *Cooper*, *Faber*, *Voffius*, and others. To these also we may add the Authors upon *Grammar*; in which subject the learned *Greeks*, when they quitted the *East*, led the way; *Mofchopulus*, *Chryfoloras*, *Lafcaris*, *Theodore Gaza*; then in *Italy*, *Laurentius Valla*; in *England*, *Grocin* and *Linacer*; in *Spain*, *Sanctius* *; in the *Low Countries Voffius*; in *France*, *Cæfar Scaliger* by his refidence, tho' by birth an *Italian*, together with those able Writers *Meff. de Port Roial.* Nor ought we to omit the Writers of *Philological Epiflles*, fuch as *Emanuel Martin* †; nor the Writers of Literary Catalogues (in French called *Catalogues Raifonnées)* fuch as the account of the Manufcripts in the Imperial Library at *Vienna*,

by

---

* SANCTIUS, towards the end of the Sixteenth Century, was Profeffor of Rhetoric, and of the Greek Tongue, in the Univerfity of *Salamanca.* He wrote many works, but his moft celebrated is that, which bears the name of *Sanctii Minerva, feu de Caufis Lingua Latinæ.* This invaluable Book (to which the Author of thefe Treatifes readily owns himfelf indebted for his *firft* rational Ideas of *Grammar* and *Language)* was publifhed by *Sanctius* at Salamanca in the Year 1587. Its fuperior merit foon made it known thro' *Europe*, and caufed it to pafs thro' many Editions in different places. The moft common Edition is a large octavo printed at *Amfterdam* in the year 1733, and illuftrated with Notes by the learned *Perizonius.*

† EMANUEL MARTIN was Dean of *Alicant* in the beginning of the prefent Century. He appears from his writings, as well as from his hiftory, to have been a perfon of pleafing and amiable manners; to have been an able antiquarian, and as fuch, a friend to the celebrated *Montfaucon*; to have cultivated with eagernefs the various ftudies of Humanity, and to have written Latin with facility and elegance. His Works, containing twelve Books of Epiftles, and a few other pieces, were printed in *Spain* about the year 1735, at the private expence of that refpectable ftatefman and fcholar, Sir *Benjamin Keene*, the *Britifh* Ambaffador, to whom they were inferibed in a Claffical Dedication by the learned Dean himfelf, then living at *Alicant.* As Copies of this Edition foon became fcarce, the Book was reprinted by *Weffelingius*, in a fair Quarto (the two Tomes being ufually bound together) at *Amfterdam* in the year 1738.

Part I.   by *Lambecius*; or of the *Arabic* Manuscripts in the *Efcurial* Library, by *Michael Cafiri* *.

---

* MICHAEL CASIRI, the learned Librarian of the *Efcurial*, has been enabled by the Munificence of the laft and the prefent Kings of *Spain*, to publifh an accurate and erudite Catalogue of the *Arabic* Manufcripts in that curious Library, a Work well becoming its Royal Patrons, as it gives an ample Exhibition of *Arabic* Literature in all its various Branches of Poetry, Philofophy, Divinity, Hiftory, &c. But of thefe Manufcripts we fhall fay more in *the Appendix*, fubjoined to *the End of thefe Inquiries.*

CHAP. IV.

Modern Critics of the Explanatory kind, commenting Modern Writers — Lexicographers — Grammarians — Tranflators.

THO' much HISTORICAL EXPLANATION has been beftowed on the *antient* Claffics, yet have the Authors *of our own Country* by no means been forgotten, having exercifed many Critics of *Learning* and *Ingenuity*.

Mr. *Thomas Warton* (befides his fine Edition of *Theocritus*) has given a curious Hiftory of *Englifh* Poetry during the *middle* Centuries; Mr. *Tyrwhit*, much accurate and diverfified Erudition upon *Chaucer*; Mr. *Upton*, a learned Comment on *the 'Fairy Queen of Spencer*; Mr. *Addifon*, many polite and elegant *Spectators* on the Conduct and Beauties of *the Paradife Loft*; Dr. *Warton*, an *Effay on the Genius and Writings of Pope*, a work filled with Speculations, in a tafte perfectly pure. The Lovers of Literature would not forgive me, were I to omit that ornament of her Sex and Country, *the Critic* and *Patronefs* of our illuftrious *Shakfpeare*, Mrs. *Montagu.* For the honour of CRITICISM not only the *Divines* already mentioned, but others alfo, of rank ftill fuperior, have beftowed their labours upon our *capital* Poets *, fufpending for a while their feverer ftudies, to relax in thefe Regions of Genius and Imagination.

THE

---

* *Shakfpeare, Milton, Cowley, Pope.*

 THE *Dictionaries* of *Minsheu, Skinner, Spelman, Sumner, Junius,* and *Johnson,* are all well known, and justly esteemed. Such is the Merit of *the last,* that *our Language* does not possess a more copious, learned, and valuable Work. For *Grammatical Knowledge* we ought to mention with distinction the learned prelate, *Dr. Lowth,* Bishop of *London;* whose admirable tract on the *Grammar* of the *English Language,* every Lover of that Language ought to study and understand, if he would write, or even speak it, with purity and precision.

LET my Countrymen too reflect, that in studying a Work upon this subject, they are not only studying *a Language,* in which it becomes them to be knowing, but a *Language,* which can boast of as many *good Books,* as any among the living, or modern Languages of *Europe.* The Writers, born and educated in a *free* Country, have been left for years to their *native Freedom.* Their Pages have been never defiled with an *Index expurgatorius,* nor their Genius ever shackled with the terrors of an Inquisition.

MAY this invaluable Privilege never be impaired either by the hand of Power, or by licentious Abuse.

PERHAPS with the Critics *just described* I ought to arrange TRANSLATORS, if it be true that *Translation* is a Species of *Explanation,* which differs no otherwise from *explanatory* Comments, than that these attend *to Parts,* while *Translation* goes *to the Whole.*

Now

Now as *Tranſlators* are infinite, and many of them (to borrow a
phraſe from Sportſmen) *unqualified Perſons*, I ſhall enumerate only
a few, and thoſe, ſuch as for their merits have been deſervedly
eſteemed.

Ch. IV.

Of this number I may very truly reckon MERIC CASAUBON, the
Tranſlator of *Marcus Antoninus*; MRS. CARTER, the Tranſlator of
Epictetus; and MR. SYDENHAM, the Tranſlator of many of *Plato's*
Dialogues.   All theſe ſeem to have *accurately underſtood* the original
Language, from which they tranſlated.   But that is not all.   The
Authors tranſlated being Philoſophers, the Tranſlators appear to have
ſtudied *the Style* of their Philoſophy, well knowing that in antient
Greece every Sect of Philoſophy, like every Science and Art, had *a
Language of its own* *.

To theſe may be added the reſpectable names of *Melmoth* and of
Hampton, of *Franklyn* and of *Potter*; nor ſhould I omit a few others,
whoſe labours have been ſimilar, did I not recollect the trite, tho'
elegant admonition,

> ——— *fugit irreparabile tempus,*
> *Singula dum capti circumvectamur amore.*   VIRG.

YET one Tranſlation I can by no means forget, I mean that of
Xenophon's Cyropædia, or the *Inſtitution of Cyrus*, by the Honourable
MAURICE

---

* See Vol. I. p. 361, 362.

Part I. MAURICE ASHLEY COWPER, fon to the fecond Earl of *Shaftefbury*, and brother to the third, who was Author of the *Characterifics*. This Tranflation is made in all the *Purity* and *Simplicity* of the Original, and to it the Tranflator has prefixed a truly philofophical Dedication, addreffed to my Mother, who was one of his Sifters.

I ESTEEM it an honour to call this Author my Uncle, and that not only from his Rank, but much more from his *Learning*, and unblemifhed *Virtue*; Qualities, which the Love of *Retirement* (where he thought they could be beft cultivated) induced him to *conceal*, rather than to produce in public.

THE firft Edition of this Tranflation, confifting of two octavo Volumes, was publifhed foon after his deceafe, in the year 1728. Between this time and the year 1770, the Book has paft thro' a fecond and a third Edition, not with the eclat of popular Applaufe, but with the filent approbation of the ftudious Few.

CHAP. V.

Rife of the THIRD SPECIES *of* CRITICISM, *the* CORRECTIVE—*prac-tifed by the Antients, but much more by the Moderns, and* WHY.

BUT we are now to inquire after ANOTHER SPECIES OF CRI-TICISM. All antient books, having been preferved by *Tran-fcription,* were liable thro' *Ignorance, Negligence,* or *Fraud,* to be cor-rupted in three different ways, that is to fay, by *Retrenchings,* by *Additions,* and by *Alterations.*

To remedy thefe evils, a *third* Sort of *Criticifm* arofe, and that was CRITICISM CORRECTIVE. The Bufinefs of this *at firft* was painfully to *collate* all the various Copies of authority, and then, from amidft the variety of Readings thus *collected,* to eftablifh by good reafons either *the true,* or *the moft probable.* In this fenfe we may call fuch CRITICISM not only CORRECTIVE, but AUTHORITATIVE.

As the number of thefe Corruptions muft needs have increafed by length of time, hence it has happened that *Corrective Criticifm* has become much more neceffary in thefe *latter* ages, than it was in others more antient. Not but that even in *antient* days *various Read-ings* have been noted. Of this kind there are a multitude in the Text of *Homer;* a fact not fingular, when we confider his great anti-quity. In the Comments of *Ammonius* and *Philoponus* upon *Ariftotle,*
there

 there is mention made of several in the text of that Philosopher, which these his Commentators compare and examine.

WE find the same in *Aulus Gellius*, as to the *Roman* Authors; where it is withal remarkable, that, even in that *early* period, much stress is laid upon the authority of *antient* Manuscripts *, a Reading in *Cicero* being justified from a Copy made by his learned freedman, *Tiro*; and a Reading in *Virgil's Georgics*, from a Book, which had once belonged to *Virgil's* Family.

BUT since the revival of Literature, TO CORRECT has been a business of much more latitude, having continually employed, for two centuries and a half, both the Pains of the most laborious, and the Wits of the most acute. Many of the learned men before enumerated were not only famous as *historical* Critics, but as *corrective* also. Such were the two *Scaligers* (of whom one has been † already mentioned) the two *Casaubons*, *Salmasius*, the *Heinsii*, *Grævius*, the *Gronovii*, *Burman*, *Kuster*, *Wasse*, *Bentley*, *Pearce*, and *Markland*. In the same Class, and in a rank highly eminent, I place Mr. TOUPE *of Cornwall*, who, in his *Emendations upon Suidas*, and his Edition of *Longinus*, has shewn a *critical* acumen, and a compass of learning, that may justly arrange him with the most distinguished scholars. Nor must I forget Dr. TAYLOR, Residentiary of St. Paul's, nor Mr. UPTON, Prebendary of Rochester. The former, by his Edition of *Demosthenes*

(as

---

* See *Aulus Gellius*, Lib. I. c. 7. and 21. *Macrob. Saturn.* Lib. I. c. 5.

† Pag. 285.

(as far as he lived to carry it), by his *Lyfias*, by his comment on the   Ch. V.
Marmor Sandvicenfe, and other critical pieces; the latter, by his correct and elegant Edition, in Greek and Latin, of *Arrian's Epictetus*
(the firft of the kind that had any pretenfions to be called complete),
have rendered themfelves, as Scholars, lafting ornaments of their
Country. Thefe two valuable men were the Friends of my youth;
the companions of my focial, as well as my literary hours. I admired them for their Erudition; I loved them for their Virtue; they
are now no more—

> *His faltem accumulem donis, et fungar inani*
> *Munere——*   Virg.

CHAP. VI.

CRITICISM may have been ABUSED.—Yet DEFENDED, as of the last Importance to the Cause of Literature.

Part I. BUT here was the misfortune of this last species of *Criticism.* The best of things may pass into abuse. There were numerous Corruptions in many of the finest authors, which neither antient Editions, nor Manuscripts could heal. What then was to be done?— Were Forms so fair to remain disfigured, and be seen for ever under such apparent blemishes?—" No (says a Critic), CONJECTURE can " cure all—*Conjecture*, whose performances are for the most part " *more certain* than any thing, that we can exhibit from the autho- " rity of Manuscripts *."—We will not ask, upon this wonderful assertion, *how, if so certain, can it be called Conjecture?*—'Tis enough to observe (be it called as it may) that this spirit of *Conjecture* has too often past into an intemperate excess; and then, whatever it may have boasted, has done more mischief by far than good. Authors have been taken in hand, like anatomical subjects, only to display the skill and abilities of the Artist; so that the end of many an Edition seems often to have been no more, than to exhibit the great sagacity and erudition of an Editor. The Joy of the task was the Honour of mending, while Corruptions were sought with a more
than

---

* *Plura igitur in Horatianis his curis ex Conjectura exhibemus, quam ex Codicum subfidio; et, nisi me omnia fallunt, plerumque certiora.* Bentleii Prefat. ad Horat.

than common attention, as each of them afforded a testimony to the Ch. VI.
Editor and his Art.

AND here I beg leave, by way of digression, to relate a short story concerning a noted Empiric. " Being once in a ball-room crowded " with company, he was asked by a gentleman, *what he thought of* " *such a lady? was it not pity that she squinted?—Squint! Sir!* replied " the doctor, *I wish every lady in the room squinted; there's not a man* " *in Europe can cure squinting but myself.*"

BUT to return to our subject—Well indeed would it be for the cause of letters, were this bold *conjectural* spirit confined to works of *second* rate, where let it change, expunge, or add, as happens, it may be tolerably sure to leave matters as they were; or if not much better, at least not much worse. But when the divine Geniuses of *higher* rank, whom we not only applaud, but in a manner revere, when these come to be attempted by petulant Correctors, and to be made the subject of their wanton caprice, how can we but exclaim with a kind of religious abhorrence,

——*procul! O! procul este profani!*

THESE sentiments may be applied even to the celebrated *Bentley*. It would have become that able writer, tho' in literature and natural abilities among *the first* of his age, had he been more temperate in his Criticism upon *the Paradise lost*; had he not so repeatedly and injuriously offered violence to its Author, from an affected superiority, to which he had no pretence. But the rage of *Conjecture* seems to

VOL. II.   Q q   have

 have seized him, as that of *Jealousy* did *Medea* *; a rage, which she confest herself unable to resist, altho' she knew the mischiefs, it would prompt her to perpetrate.

AND now to obviate an unmerited Censure, (as if I were an enemy *to the thing, from being an enemy to its abuse)* I would have it remember'd, 'tis not either with *Criticism* or *Critics*, that I presume to find fault. The Art, and its Professors, while they practise it with temper, I truly honour; and think, that, were it not for their acute and learned labours, we should be in danger of degenerating into an age of dunces.

INDEED CRITICS (if I may be allowed the metaphor) are a sort of *Masters of the ceremony* in the Court of letters, thro' whose assistance we are introduced into some of the first and best company. Should we ever, therefore, by idle prejudices against pedantry, verbal accuracies, and we know not what, come to slight their art, and reject them from our favour, 'tis well we do not slight also those *Classics*, with whom Criticism converses, becoming content to read them in translations, or (what is still worse) in translations of translations, or (what is worse even than that) not to read them at all. And I will be bold to assert, if that should ever happen, we shall speedily return into those days of darkness, out of which we happily emerged upon the revival of *antient* Literature.

---

* See the *Medea* of *Euripides*, v. 1078. See also *Philosoph. Arrangements*, p. 238.

CHAP. VII.

Conclufion—Recapitulation—Preparation for the Second Part.

AND fo much at prefent for *Critics*, and learned Editors. So Ch. VII. much alfo for the *Origin* and *Progreſs* of CRITICISM; which has been divided into three *ſpecies*, the PHILOSOPHICAL, the HISTO-RICAL, and the CORRECTIVE; the PHILOSOPHICAL, *treating of the principles, and primary cauſes of good writing in general;* the HISTO-RICAL, *being converſant in particular facts, cuſtoms, phraſes, &c.* and the CORRECTIVE being divided into the AUTHORITATIVE and the CONJECTURAL; the AUTHORITATIVE, *depending on the Collation of Manuſcripts and the beſt Editions;* the CONJECTUBAL, *on the Sagacity and Erudition of Editors* *.

As *the Firſt Part* of thefe Inquiries ends here, we are now to pro-ceed to *the Second Part, a* SPECIMEN OF THE DOCTRINES AND PRINCIPLES OF CRITICISM, *as they are illuſtrated in the Writings of the moſt diſtinguiſhed Authors.*

---

* For the FIRST SPECIES OF CRITICISM, fee p. 278. For the SECOND SPECIES, fee p. 283. For the THIRD SPECIES, fee p. 293, to the end of the Chapter following, p. 298.

There are a few other Notes befides the preceding; but as fome of them were *long,* and it was apprehended for that reafon that they might too much interrupt the *Conti-nuity* of the Text, they have been joined with other pieces, *in the forming of an* AP-PENDIX.

END OF THE FIRST PART.

Qq2

PHILOLOGICAL

INQUIRIES:

PART THE SECOND.

PHILOLOGICAL

INQUIRIES.

PART THE SECOND.

INTRODUCTION.

WE are, in the following Part of this Work, to give a Specimen Part II
of thofe Doctrines, which, having been *flightly* touched in *the
Firſt Part*, we are now to illuftrate more amply, by referring to Examples, as well antient as modern.

IT has been already hinted, that among Writers THE EPIC CAME
FIRST [*]; it has been hinted likewife, that NOTHING EXCELLENT IN
A LITERARY WAY HAPPENS MERELY BY CHANCE [†].

MENTION alfo has been made of NUMEROUS COMPOSITION [‡],
and the force of it fuggefted, tho' little faid farther.

To

---

[*] p. 278.   [†] p. 279.   [‡] Ibid.

 To this we may add the THEORY OF WHOLE AND PARTS*, so essential to the very being of a *legitimate* Composition; and THE THEORY also of SENTIMENT and MANNERS†, both of which naturally belong to *every Whole*, called *Dramatic*.

NOR can we on this occasion omit a few Speculations on THE FABLE or ACTION; Speculations necessarily connected with every Drama, and which we shall illustrate from Tragedy, its most striking Species.

AND here, if it should be objected that we refer to *English* Authors, the Connection should be remembered between *good* Authors of *every* Country, as far as they all draw from *the same* Sources, the Sources I mean of *Nature* and of *Truth*. A like Apology may be made for Inquiries concerning the ENGLISH TONGUE, and how far it may be made susceptible of *Classic Decoration*. *All* Languages are in some degree *congenial*, and, both in their *Matter* and their *Form*, are founded upon *the same Principles*‡.

WHAT is here said, will, we hope, sufficiently justify the following DETAIL; *a Detail* naturally arising from the *former* part of the Plan, by being founded upon expressions, *not sufficiently there developed*.

FIRST, therefore, for the First; that THE EPIC POETS LED THE WAY, and that NOTHING EXCELLENT IN A LITERARY VIEW HAPPENS MERELY BY CHANCE.

---

* p. 279.   † Ibid.   ‡ See Vol. I. p. 404.

CHAPTER I.

THAT THE EPIC WRITERS CAME FIRST, *and that* NOTHING EXCEL-LENT IN LITERARY *Performances happens merely from* CHANCE —*the* CAUSES, *or* REASONS *of such Excellence, illustrated by Examples.*

IT appears, that not only in GREECE, but in *other* Countries, more barbarous, the *first* Writings were in *Metre*[*], and of an *Epic* Cast, recording Wars, Battles, Heroes, Ghosts; the Marvellous always, and often the Incredible. Men seemed to have thought, that the higher they soared, the more important they should appear; and that the common Life, which they *then* lived, was a thing too contemptible to merit Imitation.

HENCE it followed, that it was not till *this Common Life* was rendered respectable by more *refined* and *polished Manners*, that Men thought it might be copied, so as to gain them applause.

EVEN in GREECE itself, *Tragedy* had attained its maturity[†] many years before *Comedy*, as may be seen by comparing the age of *Sophocles* and *Euripides* with that of *Philemon* and *Menander*.

FOR

---

[*] Temple's Works, Vol. I. p. 239. Fol. Edit.

[†] Aristot. Poet. c. 4. p. 227. Edit. Sylb. Also Characteristics, Vol. I. p. 244.

  FOR *ourselves*, we shall find most of our *first Poets* prone to a *turgid Bombast*, and most of our *first Prosaic Writers* to a *pedantic Stiffness*, which rude Styles gradually improved, but reached not a Classical Purity sooner than *Tillotson, Dryden, Addison, Shaftesbury, Prior, Pope, Atterbury*, &c. &c.

As to what is asserted soon after upon the Efficacy of Causes *in Works of Ingenuity and Art*, we think in general, that the *Effect* must always be proportioned to its *Cause*. 'Tis hard for him, who reasons attentively, to refer to CHANCE any *superlative* Production*.

EFFECTS indeed strike us, when *we are not thinking about the* CAUSE; yet may we be assured, if we reflect, *that* A CAUSE THERE IS, and that too a CAUSE INTELLIGENT, and RATIONAL. Nothing would perhaps more contribute to give us a *Taste truly critical*, than on every occasion *to investigate* this Cause; and to ask ourselves, upon feeling any uncommon Effect, *why* we are thus delighted; *why* thus affected; *why* melted into Pity; *why* made to shudder with Horrour?

TILL this WHY is well answered, all is Darkness, and our *Admiration*, like that of the *Vulgar*, founded upon *Ignorance*.

To explain by a few Examples, that are *known* to all, and for that reason here alleged, *because they are known.*

I AM

---

* Vol. I. (Philosoph. Arrang.) p. 172. 242.

I am struck with the Night-scene in Virgil's *fourth* Æneid—
" the *universal* Silence throughout the Globe—*the sweet Rest* of its
" various Inhabitants, soothing their Cares and forgetting their La-
" bours—the unhappy Dido alone *restless;* restless and agitated
" with impetuous Passions *."

I am affected with the Story of Regulus, as painted by West.
—" The crowd of *anxious* Friends, persuading him not to return—
" his Wife, *fainting* thro' sensibility and fear—Persons, the least con-
" nected, appearing to feel for him—yet himself *unmoved,* inexor-
" able and stern †."

Without referring to these deeply tragic Scenes, what Charms
has Music, when a masterly Band pass unexpectedly from *loud* to
soft, or from *soft* to *loud?*—When the System changes from the
greater Third to the *less;* or reciprocally, when it changes from this
last to the former?

All these Effects have a similar, and well-known Cause, *the
amazing Force which* Contraries *acquire, either by* Juxta-position,
or by Quick Succession ‡.

BUT

---

* Æn. IV. 522, &c.   † Horat. Carm. L. III. Od. 5.

‡ This Truth is not only obvious, but antient. *Aristotle* says,—Παράλληλα τὰ Ἐναντία
μάλιστα φαίνεται—*that* Contraries, *when set beside each other, make the strongest appearance.* Παράλληλα γὰρ μάλιστα τὰ Ἐναντία γνωρίζεται—*that* Contraries *are better known, when
set beside each other.* Arist. Rhetor. Lib. III. p. 120, & p. 152. *Edit. Sylb.* The same
author often makes use of this Truth in other places; which Truth, *simple as it seems,*
is the source of many capital Beauties in all the Fine Arts.

R r 2

Part II.   BUT we aſk ſtill farther, *why have* CONTRARIES *this Force?*—We
anſwer, becauſe, *of all things which differ, none differ ſo widely.* Sound
differs from Darkneſs, but *not ſo much* as from Silence; Darkneſs
differs from Sound, but *not ſo much* as from Light. In the ſame
intenſe manner differ Repoſe and Reſtleſſneſs; Felicity and Miſery;
dubious Solicitude and firm Reſolution; the Epic and the Comic;
the Sublime and the Ludicrous *.

And, *why differ* CONTRARIES *thus widely?* — Becauſe while *Attri-
butes, ſimply different,* may *co-exiſt* in the ſame ſubject, CONTRARIES
cannot *co-exiſt,* but always deſtroy one another †. Thus the ſame
Marble may be both *white* and *hard*; but the ſame Marble cannot
be both *white* and *black.* And hence it follows, that as their *Difference is more intenſe,* ſo is our *Recognition* of them *more vivid,* and
our *Impreſſions more permanent.*

THIS

---

* From theſe inſtances we perceive the meaning of thoſe *deſcriptions* of CONTRARIES,
that they are τὰ πλεῖςον διαφέρονΙα τῶν ἐν τῷ αὐτῷ γένει—ἐν τῷ αὐτῷ δεκτικῷ—τῶν ὑπὸ τὴν αὐτὴν δύναμιν
—*things which differ moſt widely; among things exiſting in the ſame Genus—in the ſame
Recipient—comprehended under the ſame Power or Faculty.* *Ariſt. Metaph.* Δ. 1. p. 82.
Edit. Sylb. *Cicero,* in his Topics, tranſlates *the firſt deſcription—*quæ in eodem genere
plurimum differunt. S. 70.

Ariſtotle reaſons as follows. 'Επεὶ δὲ διαφέρειν ἐνδέχεται ἀλλήλων τὰ διαφέρονΙα πλεῖον καὶ ἔλαττον,
ἔςι τις καὶ μεγίςη διαφορά, καὶ ταύτην λέγω ENANTIΩΣIN. *It being admitted that things differing from one another, differ* MORE *and* LESS, *there muſt be alſo a certain* DIFFERENCE,
which is MOST, *and this I call* CONTRARIETY. *Metaph.* p. 163. *Edit. Sylb.*

† *Ammonius,* commenting the doctrine of CONTRARIES, (as ſet forth in *Ariſtotle's
Categories*) informs us, that *they not only do not imply one another (as a Son neceſſarily
implies a Father) but that they even* DESTROY ONE ANOTHER, *ſo that, where one is preſent, the other cannot remain—*ἃ μόνον οὐ ſυνειςφέρει ἄλληλα, ἀλλὰ καὶ φθείρει· τὰ γὰρ ἥ ἐ παρουσίᾳ
οὐκ ἐᾷ μένειν τὸ ἕτερον. *Ammon. in Categ.* p. 147. *Edit. Venet.* The *Stagirite* himſelf
deſcribes them in the ſame manner, τὰ μὴ δυνατὰ ἅμα τῷ αὐτῷ παρεῖναι, *things that cannot
be preſent at once in the ſame ſubject.* *Metaph.* Δ. p. 82. *Edit. Sylb.*

This Effect of Contraries is evident even in objects of *Senfe*, where Imagination and Intellect are not in the leaft concerned. When we pafs (for example) from a Hot-houfe, we feel the common Air *more intenfely* cool; when we pafs from a dark Cavern, we feel the common light of the Day *more intenfely* glaring.

But to proceed to Inftances of another and a very different kind.

Few Scenes are *more affecting* than the taking of Troy, as defcribed in the *fecond Eneid*—" the Apparition of *Hector* to *Eneas*, " when afleep, announcing to him the Commencement of that direful Event—the diftant Lamentations, heard by *Eneas*, as he " awakes—his afcending the Houfe-top, and viewing the City in " flames—his Friend *Pentheus*, efcaped from deftruction, and relat- " ing to him their wretched and deplorable condition—*Eneas*, with " a few Friends, rufhing into the thickeft danger—their various " fuccefs, till they all perifh, but himfelf and two more—the affect- " ing Scenes of Horror and Pity at *Priam's* Palace—a Son, flain at " his Father's feet; and the immediate Maffacre of the old Monarch " himfelf—*Eneas*, on feeing this, infpired with the memory of *his* " own Father—his refolving to return home, having now loft *all* his " Companions—his feeing *Helen* in the way, and his Defign to dif- " patch fo wicked a woman—*Venus* interpofing, and fhewing him " (by removing the film from his Eyes) the *moft fublime*, tho' *moft* " *direful*, of all fights; the Gods themfelves bufied in *Troy's* Deftruc- " tion; *Neptune* at one employ, *Juno* at another, *Pallas* at a third—

" 'Tis

 " *'Tis not Helen (says Venus) but the Gods, that are the Authors of*
" *your Country's Ruin—'tis their Inclemency, &c."*

Nor less solemn and awful, tho' less leading to *Pity*, is the Commencement of the *sixth Eneid.*—" the *Sibyl's* Cavern—her frantic
" Gestures, and Prophecy—the Request of *Eneas* to descend to the
" Shades—her Answer, and Information about the Loss of one of
" his Friends—the Fate of poor *Misenus*—his Funeral—the Gold-
" en Bough discovered, a preparatory Circumstance for the Descent
" —the Sacrifice—the Ground bellowing under their Feet—the
" Woods in motion—the Dogs of *Hecate* howling—the *actual* De-
" scent in all its particulars of *the marvellous*, and *the terrible."*

If we pass from an antient Author to a modern, what Scene more
striking, than *the first Scene in* HAMLET?—" The Solemnity of the
" Time, a severe and pinching Night—the Solemnity of the *Place*, a
" Platform for a Guard—the Guards themselves; and their ap-
" posite Discourse—*yonder Star in such a Position; the Bell then beat-*
" ing one—when *Description* is exhausted, the thing *itself* appears,
" the Ghost enters."

From SHAKESPEAR the Transition to MILTON is natural. What
Pieces have ever met a more just, as well as universal applause, than
his *L'Allegro* and *Il Penseroso?*—The first, a Combination of every
incident that is *lively* and *chearful*; the second, of every incident
that is *melancholy* and *serious*; the Materials of each collected, according to their character, from Rural Life, from City Life, from
Music,

Muſic, from Poetry; in a word, from every part of *Nature*, and every part of *Art*.

To paſs from POETRY to PAINTING—*the Crucifixion of Polycrates* by SALVATOR ROSA * is " a moſt affecting Repreſentation of various " human Figures, ſeen under different modes of Horror and Pity, " as they contemplate a dreadful Spectacle, the Crucifixion above " mentioned." *The Aurora of* GUIDO on the other ſide is " one 'of " thoſe joyous Exhibitions, where nothing is ſeen but Youth and " Beauty, in every attitude of Elegance and Grace." *The former* Picture in Poetry would have been a deep *Penſeroſo; the latter*, a moſt pleaſing and animated *Allegro*.

AND to what Cauſe are we to refer theſe *laſt* Enumerations of ſtriking Effects?

To a very different one from the former—not *to an* OPPOSITION *of contrary Incidents*, but *to a* CONCATENATION *or* ACCUMULATION *of many, that are ſimilar and congenial*.

AND why have CONCATENATION and ACCUMULATION ſuch a Force?—From theſe moſt ſimple and obvious Truths, that *many* things *ſimilar, when added together*, will be more in *Quantity*, than *any one* of them *taken ſingly*;—conſequently, that *the more* things are thus added, *the greater* will be their Effect †.

WE

---

* See Vol. I. (Treatiſes,) p. 38.

† QUINCTILIAN obſerves, that the man who tells us, a *City was formed*, includes, in what he ſays, *all things which ſuch a diſaſter implies*; and yet for all, that ſuch a brief Information

Part II.

WE have mentioned at the same time both *Accumulation* and *Concatenation*, because in *Painting*, the Objects, by *existing at once*, are accumulated; in *Poetry*, as they *exist by succession*, they are not accumulated but concatenated. Yet, *thro'* *Memory* and *Imagination* *, even these also derive an *accumulative* Force, being *preserved* from passing away by those admirable Faculties, till, like many Pieces of Metal melted together, they collectively form one common Magnitude.

IT must be farther remembered, there is an Accumulation of things *analogous*, even when those things are the objects of *different Faculties*.

Information *less affects us than a Detail, because 'tis less striking, to deliver the whole at once, than it is to enumerate the several particulars.* His words are—*minus est* TOTUM *dicere, quam* OMNIA. *Quinct. Institut.* VIII. 3.

The whole is well worth reading, particularly his Detail of the various and horrid Events, which befal the storming of a City. *Sine dubio enim, qui dicit expugnatam esse Civitatem,* &c.

ARISTOTLE reasons much after the same manner.—καὶ διαιρούμενα δὲ εἰς τὰ μέρη, τὰ αὐτὰ μείζω φαίνεται· πλειόνων γὰρ ὑπεροχὴ φαίνεται—*the same things, divided into Parts, appear* GREATER, *for then there appears an Excess or an Abundance of* MANY *things.*

By way of proof, he quotes HOMER on the same subject, I mean the taking of a City by storm,

    'Οσσα κακ' ἀνθρώποισι πέλει, τῶν ἄστυ ἁλώῃ·
    'Ἄνδρας μὲν κτείνουσι, πόλιν δέ τε πῦρ ἀμαθύνει,
    Τέκνα δέ τ' ἄλλοι ἄγουσι, βαθυζώνους τε γυναῖκας.   Iliad. IX. v. 588.

    The dire disasters of a City stormed;
    The Men they massacre; the Town they fire;
    And others lead the Children and the Wives
    Into Captivity—

See *Arist. Rhetor. Lib.* I. p. 29. *Edit. Sylb.* where the above Lines of *Homer* are quoted; and tho' with some variation from the common Reading, yet with none, which affects the Sense.

* See Vol. I. p. 407, &c.

Faculties. For example—As are paſſionate *Geſtures* to the Eye, ſo are paſſionate *Tones* to the Ear; ſo are paſſionate *Ideas* to the Imagination. To feel the amazing force of an Accumulation *like this,* we muſt ſee ſome capital *Actor,* acting the *Drama* of ſome capital *Poet,* where all the Powers of *Both* are *aſſembled at the ſame inſtant.*

AND thus have we endeavoured, by a few obvious and eaſy examples, to explain what we mean by the words, *ſeeking the Cauſe or Reaſon, as often as we feel works of Art and Ingenuity to affect us**.

IF I might adviſe a *Beginner* in this elegant purſuit, it ſhould be, as far as poſſible, to recur *for Principles* to the *moſt plain and ſimple Truths,* and to *extend* every Theorem, as he advances, to *its utmoſt latitude,* ſo as to make it *ſuit,* and *include,* the greateſt number of poſſible Cafes.

I WOULD adviſe him farther, *to avoid ſubtle and far-fetched Refinement,* which, as it is for the moſt part adverſe to *Perſpicuity* and *Truth,* may ſerve to make an able *Sophiſt,* but never an able *Critic.*

A WORD more—I would adviſe a young Critic, in his Contemplations, to turn his Eye rather to *the Praiſe-worthy* than *the Blameable;* that is, *to inveſtigate the Cauſes of Praiſe,* rather than the Cauſes of *Blame.* For tho' an uninformed Beginner may in a ſingle inſtance
happen

---

* See p. 275. 278. 279. 305. 306.

Part II. happen to *blame properly,* 'tis more than probable, that in the next
he may fail, and incur the Cenfure paft upon the criticizing Cobler,
Ne futor ultra crepidam *.

WE are now to inquire concerning NUMEROUS COMPOSITION.

---

* Thofe, who wifh to fee the origin of this ingenious Proverb, may find it in *Pliny,*
L. XXV. f. 12, and in *Valerius Maximus,* L. VIII. c. 12.

CHAP. II.

NUMEROUS COMPOSITION—*derived from* QUANTITY SYLLABIC—*antiently essential both to Verse and Prose*—*Rhythm*—*Peans and Cretics, the Feet for Prose*—QUANTITY ACCENTUAL—*a Degeneracy from the* SYLLABIC—*Instances of it*—*first in Latin*—*then in Greek*—*Versus Politici*—*Traces of Accentual Quantity in Terence*—*essential to Modern Languages, and among others to English, from which last Examples are taken.*

AS NUMEROUS COMPOSITION arises from *a just* Arrangement of *Words*; so is that *Arrangement just*, when formed upon their VERBAL QUANTITY. Ch. II.

Now if we seek for this VERBAL QUANTITY in *Greek* and *Latin*, we shall find that, while *those two Languages* were in Purity, their *Verbal Quantity* was in Purity also. *Every Syllable* had a measure of *Time*, either long or short, defined with precision either by its *constituent Vowel*, or by *the Relation* of that Vowel to other Letters adjoining. SYLLABLES thus characterized, when combined, made A FOOT; and FEET thus characterized, when combined, made A VERSE; so that, while a *particular* Harmony existed in every *Part*, a general Harmony was diffused thro' the *Whole*.

PRONUNTIATION at this period being, like other things, perfect, ACCENT and QUANTITY were accurately *distinguished*; of which distinction, familiar *then*, tho' *now* obscure, we venture to suggest the

S s 2

following

 following Explanation. We compare QUANTITY to *Mufical Tones differing* IN LONG AND SHORT, as, upon whatever Line they ſtand, *a Semibreif* differs from *a Minim*. We compare ACCENT to *Mufical Tones differing* IN HIGH AND LOW, as D upon the *third* line differs from G upon the *firſt*, be its length the ſame, or be it longer or ſhorter.

AND thus things continued for a ſucceſſion of Centuries, from *Homer* and *Heſiod* to *Virgil* and *Horace*, during which interval, if we add a trifle to its end, all the truly claſſical POETS, both *Greek* and *Latin*, flouriſhed.

NOR was PROSE at the ſame time neglected. Penetrating Wits diſcovered THIS ALSO to be capable of NUMEROUS COMPOSITION, and founded their Ideas upon the following Reaſonings.

THO' they allowed, that PROSE ſhould *not* be *ſtrictly* metrical (for then it would be no longer *Proſe*, but Poetry); yet at the ſame time they aſſerted, *if it had no Rhythm at all*, ſuch a vague Effuſion would of courſe fatigue, and the Reader would ſeek in vain for thoſe returning Pauſes, ſo helpful to his reading, and ſo grateful to his Ear[*].

Now as FEET were found an Eſſential to that *Rhythm*, they were obliged, as well as Poets, to conſider FEET under their ſeveral characters.

IN

---

[*] See *Ariſtot. Rhetor.* L. III. p. 129. *Edit. Sylb.* Τὸ δὲ ſχῆμα τῆς λέξεως δεῖ μήτε ἔμμετρον εἶναι, μήτε ἄρρυθμον, κ. τ. λ. So *Cicero—numeris aſtrictam Orationem eſſe debere, carere verſibus*. *Ad. Brut. Orator.* ſ. 187.

In this Contemplation they found THE HEROIC FOOT, (which includes *the Spondee, the Dactyl,* and *the Anapæst)* to be majestic and grave, but yet *improper for Prose,* because, if employed too frequently, the Composition would appear *Epic.*   Ch. II.

ON the contrary, in THE IAMBIC they found *Levity;* it often made, tho' undesignedly, *a part of common discourse,* and could not, for that reason, but *want a suitable dignity* *.

WHAT Expedient then remained?—They recommended A FOOT, where *the former two were blended;* where *the Pomp of the Heroic,* and *the levity* of the *Iambic* were *mutually* to *correct,* and *temper* one another.

BUT as this appears to require explanation, we shall endeavour, if we can, to render it intelligible, saying something previously upon the nature of *Rhythm.*

RHYTHM differs from METRE, in as much as RHYTHM is *Proportion applied to any Motion whatever;* METRE is *Proportion, applied to the Motion of* WORDS SPOKEN. Thus, in the drumming of a March, or the dancing of a Hornpipe, there is *Rhythm,* tho' *no Metre;* in *Dryden's* celebrated Ode there is METRE as well as RHYTHM, because the Poet with the *Rhythm* has associated certain *Words.* And
hence

---

* See in the same Treatise of *Aristotle* what is said about these Feet, just after the Passage above cited. Τῶν δὲ ῥυθμῶν, ὁ μὲν ἡρῷος σεμνός, κ. τ. λ. All that follows is well worth reading.

Part II. hence it follows, that, tho' ALL METRE is RHYTHM, yet ALL RHYTHM is NOT METRE *.

THIS being admitted, we proceed and say, that the RHYTHM of *the Heroic Foot is one to one,* which conftitutes in Mufic what we call COMMON TIME; and in *mufical Vibration,* what we call THE UNISON.

The

---

* Διαφέρει δὲ μέτρον ῥυθμοῦ, ὅτι μὲν γὰρ τοῖς μέτροις ἡ συλλαβὴ, καὶ χωρὶς συλλαβῆς οὐκ ἂν γένοιτο μέτρον· ὁ δὲ ῥυθμὸς γίνεται μὲν καὶ ἐν συλλαβαῖς, γίνεται δὲ καὶ χωρὶς συλλαβῆς, καὶ γὰρ ἐν τῇ κρότῳ. Ὅταν μὲν γὰρ τὰς χαλκείας ἴδωμεν τὰς σφύρας καταφερομένας, ἅμα τῷ καὶ ῥυθμὸν ἀκούομεν—μέτρον δὲ οὐκ ἂν γένοιτο χωρὶς λέξεως ποιᾶς καὶ ποσῆς. METRE *differs from* RHYTHM, *becaufe with regard to Metre, the fubject matter is a fyllable,* and *without a fyllable* (that is a Sound articulate) *no Metre can exift.* But RHYTHM *exifts both* IN *and* WITHOUT *fyllables; for it may be perceived in mere* PULSATION OR STRIKING. '*Tis thus, when we fee Smiths hammering with their fledges, we hear at the fame time* (in their ftrokes) A CERTAIN RHYTHM,—*but as to* METRE, *there can be none, unlefs there be* AN ARTICULATE SOUND, *or* WORD, *having a peculiar Quality and Quantity,* (to diftinguifh it.) *Longini Fragm.* III. f. 5. p. 162. *Edit. Pearce,* qto.

METRUM *in verbis modo;* RHYTHMUS *etiam in corporis motu eft.* Quinctil. *Inft.* IX. 4. p. 598. *Edit. Capper.*

What thefe authors call RHYTHMUS, *Virgil* calls NUMERUS, or its plural NUMERI.

  —NUMEROS *memini, fi verba tenerem.* Bucol. IX. 45.

And, before that, fpeaking of the Fauns and wild Beafts *dancing,* he informs us—

  Tum vero in NUMERUM *Faunofq; ferafq; videres Ludere—*   Bucol. VI. 27.

So too, fpeaking of the *Cyclopes* at their Forge, he tells us,

  Illi inter fefe magnâ vi brachia tollunt IN NUMERUM——   Geor. IV. 174, 175.

Which fame verfes are *repeated* in the *eight Eneid.* So *Cicero*—NUMERUS *Latinè,* Græcè *Ῥυθμὸς*—Ad. *Brut.* Orat. f. 170.

No *Englifh Term* feems to exprefs RHYTHMUS better than the word, TIME; by which we denote *every* Species of *meafured Motion.* Thus we fay, there is TIME in *beating* a Drum, tho' but a *fingle* Sound; TIME in *Dancing,* and in Rowing, tho' no Sound at all, but what is quite *incidental.*

The RHYTHM *of the Iambic is One to Two,* which conftitutes in Mufic what we call TRIPLE TIME; and in *mufical Vibration,* what we call THE OCTAVE. *The* RHYTHM *next to thefe* is that of *Two to Three,* or elfe its equivalent, *Three to Two;* a *Rhythm* compounded of *the two former Times united;* and which conftitutes in mufical Vibration, what we call THE FIFTH.

'TWAS *here* then they difcovered THE FOOT they wanted; *that* FOOT, which, being neither the *Heroic,* nor the *Iambic,* was yet fo far connected with them, as to contain *virtually* within itfelf *the* RHYTHMS *of them both.*

THAT this is fact, is evident, from the following reafoning. The *Proportion of Two to Three* contains in *Two* the RHYTHM of the *Heroic* Foot; in *Three,* that of the *Iambic;* therefore, *in two and three united,* a Foot *compounded out of the two.*

NOW THE FOOT thus defcribed is no other than the PÆAN; *a* Foot conftituted either *by one long Syllable and three fhort,* and called *the Pæan a majori;* or elfe *by three fhort Syllables and one long,* and called *the Pæan a minori.* In either cafe, if we refolve *the long Syllable* into *two fhort,* we fhall find the Sum of the Syllables to be *Five;* that is, *Two to Three,* for the *firft* Pæan, *Three to Two* for the *fecond,* each being in what we call THE SESQUIALTER PROPORTION *.

THOSE

---

* The fum of this fpeculation is thus fhortly expreffed by Cicero. *Pes enim, qui adhibetur ad numeros, partitur in tria: ut neceffe fit partem pedis aut æqualem effe alteri parti; aut altero tanto, aut fefqui effe majorem. Ita fit æqualis, Dactylus; duplex, Iambus; fefqui, Pæon. Ad. Brut. Orat. f.* 189.

Ariftotle

THOSE, who aſk for examples, may find *the firſt Pæan* in the words ἐφάνισι, *Deſinite*; the ſecond, in the words μῖτᾰ ᾰ γῶ *Dŏmŭĕrānt.*

To the *Pæan* may be added THE CRETIC, a Foot of *one ſhort Syllable between two Long,* as in the words, ἰψῦμαῖ, quŏvĕ nūnc; a Foot *in power* evidently *equal to the Pæan,* becauſe reſolvable, like that, into *five* equal times.

WE dwell no longer here; perhaps we have already dwelt too long. 'Tis enough to obſerve, that, by a diſcreet uſe of theſe PÆANS, the antients obtained what they deſired, that is, they *enriched their Proſe,* without making it into *Verſe;* and, while vague and vulgar *Proſe* flowed *indefinitely* like a ſtream, theirs, like deſcending Drops, became capable of *being numbered* *.

IT may give Credit to theſe Speculations, trivial as they may appear, when 'tis known they have merited the attention of the ableſt Critics,

---

Ariſtotle reaſons upon the ſame Principles. Ἔτι δὲ τρίτος ὁ Παιὰν, καὶ ἐχόμενος τῶν εἰρημένων τρία γὰρ πρὸς δύο ἐστὶν ἐκείνων δὴ, ὁ μὲν ἓν πρὸς δύ' ὁ δὴ, δύο· ἔχεται δὲ τῶν λόγων τότων ὁ ἡμιόλιος, οὗτος δ' ἐστιν ὁ Παιὰν κ. τ. λ. Ariſt. Rhet. L. III. c. 8. p. 129, 130. *Edit. Sylb.*

Again, *Cicero,* after having held much the ſame doctrine, adds—*Probatur autem ab eodem illo* (ſcil. Ariſtotele) *maximè Pæan, qui eſt duplex; nam aut a longâ oritur, quàm tres breves conſequuntur, ut hæc verba, dēſĭnĭtĕ, Incĭpĭtĕ, cōmprĭmĭtĕ; aut a brevibus deinceps tribus, extremâ productâ atque longâ, ſicut illa ſunt, dŏmŭĕrānt, ſŏnĭpĕdĕs. De Orator.* III. 57, (183.) and in his *Orator. ad M. Brutum*—ſ. 205. and before, ſ. 191 to 197.

* NUMERUS *autem in Continuatione nullus eſt: Diſtinctio, et æqualium et ſæpe variorum intervallorum* Percuſſio, NUMERUM *conficit: quem in cadentibus guttis, quod intervallis diſtinguuntur, notare poſſumus; in omni præcipitante non poſſumus.* Cic. de Oratore, Lib. III. ſ. 186.

Critics, of *Ariſtotle* and *Demetrius Phalereus*, of *Cicero* and *Quinctilian* *.

Thε Productions ſtill remaining of this Golden Period ſeem (if I
may ſo ſay) to have been providentially preſerved, to humiliate modern Vanity, and check the growth of bad Taſte.

But this Claſſical Æra, tho' it laſted long, at length, terminated.
Many Cauſes, and chiefly the irruption and mixture of *Barbarians*,
contributed to the debaſing both of *Latin* and *Greek*. As *Diction*
was corrupted, ſo alſo was *Pronunciation*. *Accent* and *Quantity*,
which had been once *accurately* diſtinguiſhed, began now to be
blended. Nay more, *Accent* ſo far uſurped *Quantity's* place, as by a
ſort of Tyranny, to make ſhort ſyllables, long; and long ſyllables,
ſhort. Thus, in Poetry, as the accent fell upon Dε in *Dēus*, and upon
I in *ibi*, *the firſt* ſyllables of theſe two words were conſidered as *long*.
Again, where the Accent did *not* fall, as in the ultima's of *Regnŏ*, or
Saturnŏ, and even in ſuch ablatives as *Inſulā* or *Cretā*, there the
Poet aſſumed a Licence, if he pleaſed, to make them *ſhort*. In a
word, the whole doctrine of Pʀosoᴅʏ came to this—that, as an-
ciently *the Quantity of the Syllables* eſtabliſhed *the Rhythm of the
Verſe*,

* See *Ariſtotle* and *Cicero*, as quoted before, particularly the laſt in his *Orator*, ſ. 189
to the end; *Quinctilian*, L. IX. c. 4. *Demetrius Phalereus*, at the beginning of his
Tract *De Elocut.*

Cicero, in his *De Oratore*, introduces *Craſſus* uſing the ſame Arguments; thoſe, I
mean, which are grounded upon authority.

*Atque hæc quidem ab iis Philoſophis, quos tu maxime diligis, Catule, dicta ſunt: quod
eo ſæpius teſtificor, ut auctoribus laudandis ineptiarum crimen effugiam. De Oratore,
Lib. III. ſ. 187.*

 Verse, fo now *the Rhythm of the Verfe* eftablifhed *the Quantity of the Syllables.*

THERE was an ancient Poet, his name COMMODIANUS, who dealt much in this illicit Quantity, and is faid to have written (if that be poffible) in the fifth, nay fome affert, in the third Century. Take a fample of his Verfification.

> *Saturnufque fener, fi Dĕus, quando fenefcit ?*

And again,

> *Nec Divinus erat, fed Dĕum fefe dĭcebat.*

And again,

> *Jupiter hic natŭs ĭn ĭnfulă Cretă Săturno,*
> *Ut fuit ădultus, patrem de regnŏ privavit.*

And again,

> *Ille autem in Cretă regnavit, et ĭbi dĕfecit.*

I SHALL crown the whole with an admirable diftich, where (as I obferved not long ago) *the Rhythm* of the Verfe gives alone the Quantity, while the *Quantity* of the Syllables is wholly difregarded.

> *Tŏt rĕŭm crĭmĭnĭbŭs, părrĭcīdăm quŏque fŭtūrŭm,*
> *Ex auctŏrĭtātĕ vĕftră cŏntŭlĭfĭs ĭn āltŭm.*

Dr. *Davies*, at the end of his *Minutius Felix*, has thought it worth giving us an Edition of this wretched author, who, if he lived fo early as fuppofed, muft have been from among the dregs of the people, fince *Aufonius*, *Claudian*, *Sulpicius Severus*, and *Boethius*, who were all authors of the fame or a later period, wrote both in *Profe* and *Verfe* with Claffical Elegance.

WE

We have mentioned the Debasement of *Latin*, previously to that of *Greek*, because it was an Event, which happened much sooner. As early as the sixth Century, or the seventh at farthest, *Latin* ceased to be the common Language of *Rome*, whereas *Greek* was spoken with competent purity in *Constantinople*, even to the fifteenth Century, when that City was taken by the *Turks*.

Nor but that Corruption found its way also into *Greek* Poetry, when *Greek* began to degenerate, and *Accent*, as in *Latin*, to usurp dominion over *Quantity*.

'Twas then began the use of the *Versus Politici*[*], a species of Verses so called, because adapted to the *Vulgar*, and only fit for Vulgar Ears. 'Twas then the sublime *Hexameters* of *Homer* were debased into miserable *Trochaïcs*, not even legible as *Verses*, but by a suppression of *real* Quantity.

Take a Sample of these Productions, which, such as it is, will be easily understood, as it contains the Beginning of the First *Iliad* —

> Τὴν ὀργὴν ἄδε, κỳ λέγι,
> Ὦ θεά μȣ Καλλιόπη,
> Τὴ Πηλίδȣ Ἀχιλλέως,
> Πῶς ἐγένετ' ἐλευθερία,
> Καὶ πολλὰς λύπας ἐποίσε
> Εἰς τὰς Ἀχαίȣς δὴ πάντας,

Καὶ

---

[*] See Fabricii Biblioth. Græc. Vol. X. p. 253, 318, 319.

Καὶ πολλὰς ψυχὰς ἀνδρείας
Πῶς ἀπέςειλεν εἰς Ἅδην.

In reading the above Verses, we *must carefully regard* ACCENT, to which, and to which *alone* we must strictly adhere, and follow the same *Trochaïc Rhythm*, as in those well known Verses of *Dryden* —

> *Wár he súng is tóil and tróuble,*
> *Hónour bút an émpty búbble,* &c.

The *Accentual* Quantity in the Greek, as well as in the English, totally destroys the *Syllabic* — ἡ in ἆδι is made long; so also is λι in ἄλγι; α, in θεά; ο, in Καλλιόπῃ. Again μυ is short; so also is Πη in Πηλίδυ. In Ἀχιλλέως every Syllable is corrupted; the first and third, being short, are made long; the second and fourth, being long, are made short. We quote no farther, as all that follows is similar, and the whole exactly applicable to our *present* versification.

THIS disgraceful Form of *Homer* was printed by *Pinelli*, at *Venice*, in the year 1510, but the Work itself was probably some centuries older *.

BESIDES this anonymous Perverter of the *Iliad* and *Odyssey* (for he has gone thro' both) there are *Political Verses* of the same barbarous character by *Constantinus Manasses*, *John Tzetzes*, and others of that period.   AND

---

* A sort of Glossary is subjoined, whence, for curiosity, we select some very singular explanations, Πύλη, a *Gate*, is explained by Πόρτα—θύφυρα, those, *who keep Gates*, are called Πορτάροι, that is, PORTERS—κλίσιαι, TENTS, are called by the name of Τέντα—πύργος, a TOWER, by that of Τέρρα—and of σάλπιγξ we are informed, σημαίνει δὲ τὸν Τρομπετάρον, that it signifies in general A TRUMPETER.

And fo much for the *Verfe* of thefe times. Of their *Profe* (tho'
next in order) we fay nothing, it being lofs of time to dwell upon
authors, who being unable to imitate the Eloquence of their Predeceffors, could difcover no new Roads to Fame, but thro' Obfcurity
and Affectation. In this Clafs we range *the Hiftoriæ Auguftæ Scriptores, Marcianus Capella, Apuleius,* together with many others, whom
we may call *Authors of African Latinity.* Perhaps too we may add
fome of the *Byzantine Hiftorians.*

Before we quit Accentual Quantity, there is one thing we
muft not omit. Strange as it appears, there are traces of it extant,
even in *Claffical* Writers.

As *Dactyls* and *Anapæfts* were frequently intermixed with Iambics,
we find no lefs a writer, than the accurate Terence, make Syllables
fhort, which *by Pofition* were *long,* in order to form the Feet above-
mentioned. Take the following inftances among many others.

'Et Id grātum *fuiſſe advorſum te habeo gratiam.*
Andr. A. I. f. 1. v. 15.

Prŏptĕr hŏſpitaï *hujuſce conſuetudinem.*
Andr. A. II. f. vi. v. 8.

'Ego ĕxclūdor: *ille recipitur, quâ gratiâ?*
Eunuch. Act. I. f. ii. v. 79.

Among thefe Verfes, all beginning with Anapæfts, the fecond fyllable ID in the firft Verfe is made *fhort,* tho' followed by *three Confonants:* the firft Syllable propter in the fecond Verfe is made *fhort,*
tho' followed by *two Confonants:* and the third fyllable, 'ex in *ex-
cludor,

 cludor, in the third Verfe is made *fhort*, tho' followed by a *double Confonant, and two others* after it.

We are to obferve however that, while Licences were affumed by *the Dramatic Writers of the Comic Iambic*, and by TERENCE more than the reft; 'twas a practice unknown to the *Writers of Hexameter*. 'Tis to be obferved likewife, that thefe Licences were taken *at the beginning* of Verfes, and never *at the End*, where *a pure Iambic* was held indifpenfible. They were alfo *Licences ufually taken* with *Monofyllables, Diffyllables*, or *Prepofitions*; in general with Words *in common and daily ufe*, which in all Countries are pronounced with *rapidity*, and made fhort *in the very Speaking*. It has been fuggefted therefore with great probability, that TERENCE adopted fuch a Mode of Verfifying, becaufe it *more refembled* the common Dialogue of the *middle Life*, which no one ever imitated more happily than himfelf*.

We are now to proceed to the *modern Languages*, and to *our own* in particular, which, like the reft, has little of Harmony but what it derives from ACCENTUAL QUANTITY. And yet as this ACCENTUAL QUANTITY is wholly governed by *Ancient Rhythm*, to which, as far as poffible, *we accommodate Modern Words*, the Speculations are by no means detached from *Ancient Criticifm*, being wholly derived from *Principles*, which that Criticifm had *firft* eftablifhed.

---

* See the *valuable Tract* of the celebrated BENTLEY, prefixed to his *Terence*, under the title of *De Metris Terentianis* ΣΧΕΔΙΑΣΜΑ.

C H A P. III.

Quantity Verbal in English — a few Feet pure, and agreeable to Syllabic Quantity — instances — yet Accentual Quantity prevalent — instances — transition to Prose — English Pæans, instances of — Rhythm governs Quantity, where this last is Accentual.

IN the scrutiny which follows we shall confine ourselves to English, as no Language, *to us at least,* is equally familiar. And here, if we begin with quoting Poets, it must be remembered it is not purely for the sake of *Poetry,* but with a view to that *Harmony,* of which *our Prose is susceptible.*

A few pure Iambics of the *Syllabic* sort we have, tho' commonly blended with the *spurious* and *accentual.* Thus *Milton,*

 Fountains, and ye, that warble, as ye flow— P. L. V. 195.

And again, more completely in that fine Line of his—

 For Eloquence, the Soul; Song charms the Sense— P. L. II. 556.

In the first of these Verses the last Foot is (as it *always should be**) a pure Syllabic *Iambic;* in the second Verse every Foot is *such,* but the Fourth.

Besides

---

* Sup. p. 396.

BESIDES *Iambics*, our Language knows alfo *the Heroic* Foot. In the Verfe juft quoted,

> FOUNTAINS, *and ye, that warble as ye flow,*

the firft Foot is a SPONDEE: fo is the *fourth* Foot in that other Verfe,

> *For Eloquence, the Soul;* SONG CHARMS *the Senfe.*

This Foot feems to have been admitted among *the Englifh Iambics* precifely for the fame reafon as among the *Greek* and *Latin*; to infufe a certain *Stability*, which *Iambics* wanted, when alone—

> TARDIOR *ut paullo*, GRAVIORQUE *veniret ad aures,*
> SPONDEOS STABILES *in jura paterna recepit.* *Hor. Art. Poet.*

NOR do we want *that other Heroic Foot*, THE DACTYL, and that too accompanied (as ufual) with THE SPONDEE. Thus in the fecond *Pfalm* we read—

> *Why do the people* IMAGINE A VAIN THING?

And foon after—

> —*againft the Lord and* AGAINST HIS ANOINTED.

Where in both inftances we have the *Hexameter Cadence*, tho' perhaps it was cafual, and what the Tranflators never intended.

IT muft indeed be confeffed *this Metre* appears *not natural* to our Language, nor have its *Feet* a proper effect, but when mixt

with

with *Iambics*, to infuse that *Stability*, which we have lately mentioned *.

'Tis proper also to observe that, tho' metrical Feet in *English* have
a few *long* and *short* Syllables, even in their *genuine* character (that
I mean, which they derive from TRUE SYLLABIC QUANTITY) yet
is *their Quantity more often determined* BY ACCENT ALONE †, it being
enough to make a Syllable *long*, if it be ACCENTED; and short, if
it be UNACCENTED; whatever may be the *Position of* ANY *subsequent*
Consonants.

THUS in MILTON, we read,
    —— *on the secret top*
  Of Oreb didst INSPIRE——   P. L. I. 6. 7.

And again,
    *Hurl'd head*LONG, *flaming, from th' etherial sky.* P. L. I. 45.

IN these examples, the first Syllable of *Inspire* is *short* by *Accen-*
tual Quantity, tho' the *Position* of its Vowel is before *three Conso-*
nants; the last Syllable of *headlong*, and the last Syllable of *flaming*,
are *short*, even tho' *the consecutive Consonants* are in both cases *Four*.

SUCH

---

* Sup. p. 328.

The use of the *Heroic* and the *Iambic* is well explained by *Cicero* from *Aristotle*.

*Quod longe Aristoteli videtur secus, qui judicat Heroum Numerum grandiorem quam
desideret soluta oratio; Iambum autem nimis e vulgari sermone. Ita neque humilem, nec
abjectam orationem, nec nimis altam et exaggeratam probat; plenam tamen cum vult esse
gravitatis, ut eos, qui audiunt, ad majorem admirationem possit traducere.* Ad Brut,
Orat. f. 192.   † Sup. p. 321. 326.

    SUCH then in *English* being the force of ACCENTUAL QUANTITY,
we are now to confider thofe Feet, thro' which not *our Verfe*, but
OUR PROSE may be harmonized.

Now *thefe Feet* are no other than THE TWO PÆANS, already defcribed *, and their equivalent, THE CRETIC, which three may more
particularly be called the FEET FOR PROSE †.

IN *Profe-compofition* they may be called thofe Ingredients, which,
like Salt in a Banquet, ferve to give it a relifh.   Like Salt too, we
fhould fo employ them, that we may not feem to have miftaken the
Seafoning for the Food.— But more of this hereafter ‡.

As to *the Place of thefe* PÆANS, tho' they have their effect in
every part of a Sentence, yet have they a peculiar energy at its
Beginning, and its *End*.   The difference is, we are advifed *to begin
with the firft Pæan, and to conclude with the fecond*, that the Sentence
in each Extreme may be *audibly* markt §.   If the Sentence be
emphatical, and call for fuch attention, nothing can anfwer the
purpofe more effectually, than that CHARACTERISTIC LONG SYL-
                                                                                LABLE,

---

* Sup. p. 319, 320.

† *Sit igitur* [oratio] *(ut fupra dixi) permifta* et temperata numeris, nec *diffoluta*, nec
tota numerofa, PÆONE *maximè*, &c.   Ad Brut. Orat. f. 196—and foon before, f. 194.
PÆON *autem minimè eft aptus ad Verfum; quo* libentius eum recepit ORATIO.

‡ *Infr.* p. 341.

§ Vid. *Ariftot. Rhetor.* L. III. c. 8. p. 30.   *Edit. Sylb.*   Ἔστι δὲ Παιᾶνος δύο εἴδη, ἀντικείμενα
ἀλλήλοις· ὧν τὸ μὲν, κ. τ. λ.

LABLE, which in the *first* Pæan is always *inceptive*, in the *second* is always *conclusive*.

FOR want of better examples we venture to illustrate by the following, where we have markt the TWO PÆANS, together with their Equivalent THE CRETIC, and where we have not only markt *the Time* over each Syllable, but *separated each Foot* by a disjunctive stroke.

Beauty may be—lost, may be for—years outliv'd: but *Virtue remains the same, till Life itself—is at an end.*

Again—

Steep is the "A-scent by which we—mount to Fame;—nor is the Summit to be gain'd—but by Saga—city and toil. Fools are sure to lose their way, and Cowards sink beneath the difficulty: the wise and brave alone succeed; persist—in their attempt—and never yield—to the fatigue.

THE Reader in these examples will regard two things; one, that the *Strokes of Separation* mark *only the Feet,* and are not to be regarded *in the Reading;* another, that tho' he may meet perhaps a few instances agreeable to *ancient Prosody,* yet in *modern Rhythm* like this, be it *Prosaïc* or *Poetic,* he must expect to find it *governed* for the greater part BY ACCENT*.

AND

---

* Sup. p. 321. 326. 329.

   And so much for *Profaic Feet*, and *Numerous Profe*, which, upon the Principles eftablifhed by *ancient* Critics, we have aimed to ac-commodate to *our own Language*.

But we ftop not here, having a few more Speculations to fuggeft, which, appearing to arife from the Principles of the old *Critics*, are amply verified in our beft *Englifh* authors.   But more of this in the following Chapter.

C H A P. IV.

*Other Decorations of Prose besides Prosaïc Feet—*ALLITERATION*—*
SENTENCES*—*PERIODS*—Caution to avoid excess in consecutive*
Monosyllables—Objections, made and answered—Authorities alledged
—Advice about Reading.

BESIDES the Decoration of *Prosaïc Feet*, there are other Decorations, admissible into *English Composition*, such as ALLITERA-
TION, and SENTENCES, especially THE PERIOD.

FIRST therefore for the first; I mean ALLITERATION.

AMONG the Classics of old there is no finer illustration of this
Figure, than LUCRETIUS's Description of those blest abodes, where
his Gods, detached from *Providential* Cares, ever lived in the frui-
tion of *divine Serenity.*

> *Apparet Divum numen, sedesque* QUIETæ,
> QUAS *neque concutiunt venti, neque* NUBila NIMBis
> *Aspergunt,* NEQUE NIX *acri concreta pruinâ*
> CANa CADens *violat, semperque* INNubilus æther
> INtegit, et LARge diffuso LUmine ridet.   Lucret. III. 18.

THE sublime and accurate VIRGIL did not contemn *this Decora-*
tion, tho' he used it with such pure, unaffected *Simplicity,* that we
often

 often feel its Force, without contemplating the Cause. Take one Inftance out of infinite, with which his Works abound.

> *Avrora interea* MIfcris MORtalibus *ALMam*
>
> *Extulerat* LVcem, *referens opera atque* LAbores*.   Æn.* XI. v. 183.

To

---

* The following Account of this Figure is taken from *Pontanus*, one of thefe ingenious *Italians*, who flourifhed upon the revival of a purer Literature in *Europe*.

Ea igitur five figura, five ornatus, condimentum quafi quoddam numeris aff.rt, placet autem nominare ALLITERATIONEM, *quòd à Literarum allufione conflet. Fit itaque in verfu, quoties dictiones continuatæ, vel binæ, vel ternæ ab iifdem primis confonantibus, mutatis aliquando vocalibus, aut ab iifdem incipiunt* SYLLABIS, *aut ab* IISDEM *primis vocalibus. Delectat autem* ALLITERATIO *hæc mirificè in primis et ultimis locis facta, in mediis quoque, licet ibidem aures minùs fint intentæ. Ut,*

> " *Saxa fedens fuper arma* — Virg.
> " —*tales cafus Caffandra canebat.* ejufd.
> " *Infontem infando indicio.* — ejufd.
> " —*longè fale Saxa fonabant.* ejufd.
> " —*magno mifceri murmure pontum.* ejufd.
> " *Quæque lacus latè liquidos* — ejufd.

Fit interdum per continuationem infequentis verfus, ut in his Lucretianis.

> " —*adverfo flabra feruntur*
> " *Flumine.*—

Atqui ALLITERATIO *hæc ne Ciceroni quidem difplicuit in Oratione folutà, ut cum dixit in Bruto,* " *Nulla Res magis penetrat in animos, eofque* FINGIT, FORMAT, FLECTIT." *Et in fecundo de Oratore;* " *Quodque me* SOLLICITARE SUMME *folet.?" Quid quòd ne in jocis quidem illis tam lepidis neglecta eft à Plauto; ut cum garrientem apud herum induxit Panulum;* " *Ne tu oratorem hunc* PUGNIS PLECTAS *poftea." Atque hæc quidem* ALLITERATIO *quemadmodum tribus in iis fit vocibus, fit alibi etiam in duabus fimili modo. Ut,*

> " —*taciti ventura videbant.* Virg.
> " *Tamo tempus erit.*— ejufd.

JOHANNIS JOVIANI PONTANI *Actius*—*Dialogus.* Tom. II. p. 104. *Edit. Venetis, ap. Ald.* 1519.

To Virgil we may add the fuperior authority of Homer.

    Ἤτοι ὁ καππεδίον τὸ Ἀλήϊον οἶος Ἀλᾶτο,
    Ὃν θυμὸν κατέδων, πάτον Ἀνθρώπων Ἀλεείνων.   Il. Ζ. 201.

Hermogenes, the Rhetorician, when he quotes thefe Lines, quotes them as an example of the Figure here mentioned, but calls it by a *Greek* name, ΠΑΡΗΧΗΣΙΣ*.

Cicero has tranflated the above Verfes elegantly, and given us too Alliteration, tho' not under the fame letters.

    Qui mifer in campis errabat folus Aleïs,
    Ipfe fuum Cor edens, hominum vestigia vitans.   Cic.

Ariftotle knew this Figure, and called it ΠΑΡΟΜΟΙΩΣΙΣ, a name perhaps not fo précife as the other, becaufe it rather expreffes *Re-femblance in general*, than that, which arifes from *Sound in particular*. His example is — ΑΓΡΟΝ γὰρ ἔλαβεν, ΑΡΓΟΝ πὰρ αὐτῇ †.

The *Latin* Rhetoricians ftiled it Annominatio, and give us ex-amples of fimilar character ‡.

                                  But

---

* The Explanation of it, given by *Hermogenes*, exactly fuits his Inftance. Παρήχησίς ἐςι κάλλος ὀνόμαϲος ἐκ τοῦ, ὃ βαρέως γνῶσι ταὐτὰ ἐχόντων. Parechesis is Beauty in fimilar *Words*, which under a different Signification sound the fame. Ἑρμογ. περὶ Εὑρές. Τμ. δ. p. 193. Edit. Porti, 1570.

† Ariftot. Rhet. III. 9. p. 138. *Edit. Sylb.*

‡ Scrip. ad Herenn. L. IV. f. 29.

But the moſt ſingular Fact is, that ſo *early* in our own Hiſtory, as the reign of *Henry the Second*, this Decoration was eſteemed and cultivated both by the *Engliſh* and the *Welch*. So we are informed by *Giraldus Cambrenſis*, a contemporary Writer, who, having firſt given *the Welch* inſtance, ſubjoins *the Engliſh* in the following verſe —

GOD *is together* GAMMEN *and* WISEDÓME.

— that is, *God is at once both Joy and Wiſdom.*

He calls the Figure by the *Latin* Name ANNOMINATIO, and adds, " *that the two Nations were ſo attached to this verbal Ornament in* " *every high finiſhed Compoſition, that nothing was by them eſteemed* " *elegantly delivered, no Diction conſidered but as rude and ruſtic,* " *if it were not firſt amply refined with the poliſhing Art of this* " *Figure**.*"

'Tis perhaps from this National Taſte of ours that we derive many *Proverbial Similes*, which, if we except the Sound, ſeem to have no other merit — *Fine, as Five pence* — *Round, as a Robin* — &c.

Even SPENSER and SHAKSPEARE adopted the practice, but then it was in a manner ſuitable to ſuch Geniuſes.

SPENSER

---

* *Præ cunctis eutem Rhetoricis exornationibus* ANNOMINATIONE *magis utuntur, eáque precipue ſpecie, quæ primas dictionum litteras vel ſyllabas convenientiâ jungit. Adeo igitur hôc verborum ornatu duæ nationes (Angli ſcil. et Cambri) in omni ſermone exquiſito utuntur, ut nihil ab his eleganter dictum, nullum niſi rude et agreſte cenſetur eloquium, ſi non ſchematis hujus limâ plene fuerit expolitum. Girald. Cambrenſis Cambriæ Deſcriptio, p. 889. Edit. Foſ. Camdeni, 1603.*

Spenser says—

> For not to have been dipt in LETHE LAKE
> Could SAVE THE SON of THETIS from to die;
> But that BLIND BARD did him immortal make
> With Verses, DIPT in DEW of Castalie.

Shakspeare says—

> HAD my sweet HARRY HAD but HALF their numbers,
> This day might I, HANGING on HOTSPUR's neck,
> Have talked, &c.   Hen. IVth, Part 2d, Act 2d.

Milton followed them.

> For Eloquence, the SOUL; SONG charms the SENSE.
>   P. L. II. 556.

And again,

> BEHEMOTH, BIGGEST BORN of Earth, upheav'd
> His vastness—   P. L. VII. 471.

From Dryden we select one example out of many, for no one appears to have employed this Figure more frequently, or (like *Virgil*) with greater Simplicity and Strength.

> Better to HUNT in fields for HEALTH unbought,
> Than see the DOCTOR for a nauseous DRAUGHT.
> The Wise for cure on exercise DEPEND;
> God never MADE his Work for MAN to MEND.
>   Dryd. Fables.

Part II.   Pope sings in his *Dunciad*—

  'Twas chatt'ring, grinning, mouthing, jabb'ring all;
  And Noise, and Norton; Brangling, and Breval;
  Dennis, and Dissonance.—

Which Lines, tho' truly poetical and humorous, may be suspected by some to shew their Art *too conspicuously*, and too nearly to resemble that Verse of old *Ennius*—

  O! Tite, Tute, Tati, Tibi Tanta, Tyranne, Tulisti.

         Script. ad Herenn. L. IV. f. 18.

Gray begins a sublime Ode,

  Ruin *seize thee,* ruthless King, &c.

We might quote also Alliterations from *Prose Writers*, but those, we have alledged, we think sufficient.

Nor is Elegance only to be found in *single Words*, or in *single Feet*; it may be found, when we *put them together, in our peculiar mode* of putting them. 'Tis out of *Words and Feet thus compounded* that we form Sentences, and among *Sentences* none so striking, none so pleasing, as the Period. The reason is, that, while other Sentences are *indefinite*, and (like a Geometrical Right-line) may be *produced indefinitely*, the Period (like a Circular Line) is always *circumscribed*, returns, and terminates at a given point. In other words, while other Sentences, by the help of common Copulatives, have a sort of *boundless effusion;* the *constituent parts* of a Period*

                have

---

* Vid. Arist. Rhet. III. c. 9.   Demetr. Phal. de Elocut. f. 10, &c.

                The

Ch. IV.

have a fort of *refter* union, in which union the Sentence is fo far complete, as neither to require, nor even to admit *a farther* exten- fion. Readers find a pleafure in this *grateful Circuit*, which leads them fo agreeably to an acquifition of knowledge.

The Author, if he may be permitted, would refer by way of illuf- tration to the Beginnings of his Hermes, and his Philosophical Arrangements, where fome Attempts have been made in this *Periodical Stile*. He would refer alfo for much more illuftrious ex- amples, to the Opening of Cicero's Offices; to that of the capital Oration of Demosthenes concerning the Crown; and to that of the celebrated Panegyric, made (if he may be fo called) by *the father of Periods*, Isocrates.

Again—every *Compound Sentence* is compounded of *other Sen- tences more fimple*, which, compared to one another, have *a certain proportion of Length*. Now 'tis in general a good Rule, that among thefe *conftituent* Sentences the last (if poffible) fhould be *equal* to the first; or *if not equal*, then *rather longer* than fhorter*. The reafon is, that without a fpecial Caufe, abrupt *Conclufions are offenfive*, and the Reader, like a Traveller quietly purfuing his Journey, finds an unexpected precipice, where he is difagreeably ftopt.

To

The *compact combining* character *of the* Period is well illuftrated by *Demetrius* in the following Simile. Ταυτα γαρ τα μεν περιοδικα μαλα τοις λιθοις, τοις ανεχουσιν τας περφερεις ςεγας, και ουιχουσι—the *conftitutive Members of* the Period refemble thofe Stones, which *mutually fupport, and keep vaulted Roofs together.* § 13.

* —aut paria effe debent posteriora *fuperioribus*, extrema *primis*; aut, quod eft *etiam melius et jucundius*, longiora. *Cic. de Orat.* III. f. 196.

X x 2

To thefe Speculations concerning *Sentences*, we fubjoin a few others.

It has been called a fault in our Language, that it abounds in MONOSYLLABLES. As thefe, in too lengthened a fuite, difgrace a Compofition; *Lord Shaftefbury*, (who ftudied purity of Stile with great attention) limited their number to *nine*, and was careful, in his *Characterifticz*, to conform to his own Law. Even in *Latin* too many of them were condemned by *Quinctilian* *.

Above all, care fhould be had, that *a Sentence* END *not with a xrord of them*, thofe efpecially of the *vulgar*, *untunable* fort, fuch as, *to fet it up*, to *get by and by at it*, &c. for thefe difgrace a Sentence that may be otherwife laudable, and are like the Rabble at the clofe of fome pompous Cavalcade.

'Twas by thefe, and other arts of fimilar fort, that Authors in diftant ages have cultivated their STILE. Looking upon *Knowledge* (if I may be allowed the allufion) *to pafs into the Manfions of the Mind* THRO' LANGUAGE, they were careful (if I may purfue the metaphor) not to offend in THE VESTIBULE. They did not efteem it pardonable to defpife the *Public Ear*, when they faw the Love of Numbers fo univerfally diffufed †.

Non

---

* *Etiam* MONOSYLLABA, *fi plura funt, male continuabuntur: quia neceffe eft,* COMPOSITIO, *multis claufulis concifa,* SUBSULTET. Inft. Orat. IX. 4.

† *Nihil eft autem tam* COGNATUM MENTIBUS NOSTRIS, *quam* NUMERI *atque* VOCES; *quibus et excitantur, et incendimur, et lenimur, et languefcimus, et ad hilaritatem et ad triftitiam fæpe deducimur; quorum illa fumma vis,* &c. Cic. de Orat. III. f. 197.

Nor were they difcouraged, as if they thought their labour would be loft. In thefe *more refined,* but yet *popular* Arts, they knew the amazing difference between *the Power to execute,* and *the Power to judge;*—that to EXECUTE was the *joint* Effort of *Genius* and of *Habit;* a painful Acquifition, only attainable by the Few;—TO JUDGE, the fimple Effort of that *plain but common Senfe,* imparted by Providence in fome degree to every one[*].

But here methinks an Objector demands—" *And are Authors* " *then to compofe, and form their Treatifes by Rule?—Are they to* " *balance Periods?—To fcan Pæans and Cretics?—To affect Allitera-* " *tions?—To enumerate Monofyllables, &c.*"

If, in anfwer to this Objector, it fhould be faid, THEY OUGHT, the Permiffion fhould at leaft be *tempered* with much caution. Thefe Arts are to be fo *blended* with a pure but *common* Stile, that the Reader, as he proceeds, may *only feel* their *latent* force. If ever they become *glaring,* they degenerate into *Affectation;* an Extreme more difgufting, becaufe lefs natural, than even the vulgar language of an unpolifhed Clown. 'Tis in Writing, as in Acting——The beft Writers are like our late admired *Garrick.*—And how did that able Genius employ his Art?—Not by a vain *oftentation* of any *one* of its powers, but by a *latent ufe* of them *all* in fuch an exhibition of Nature, that, while we were prefent in a Theatre, and only beholding an Actor, we could not help thinking ourfelves in *Denmark* with HAMLET, or in *Bofworth* Field with RICHARD[†].   THERE

---

[*] *Mirabile eft, cum plurimum in Faciendo interfit inter doctum et rudem, quam non multum differat in Judicando.* Ibid. III. c. 197.

[†] *Ubicunque* ARS *oftentatur,* VERITAS *abeffe videtur.* Quinctil. Inftit. X. 3. p. 587. Edit. Capp.—*Quæ funt* ARTES ALTIORES, *plurumque* OCCULTANTUR, *ut Artes fint.*

Part II.   THERE is another Objection still—Thefe Speculations may be
called MINUTIÆ; things partaking at beſt more of *the elegant*, than
of *the ſolid*; and attended with difficulties, beyond the value of the
labour.

To anſwer this, it may be obſerved, that, when *Habit* is once
gained, nothing ſo eaſy as *Practice*. When the Ear is once habi-
tuated to theſe *Verbal Rhythms*, it forms them *ſpontaneouſly*, without
attention or labour. If we call for inſtances, what more eaſy to
every Smith, to every Carpenter, to every common mechanic, than
the ſeveral Energies of their proper Arts * ? How little do even *the
rigid* Laws of *Verſe* obſtruct a Genius truly Poetic? How little did
they cramp a *Milton*, a *Dryden*, or a *Pope*? *Cicero* writes that *Antipater the Sidonian* could pour forth Hexameters *extempore* † ; and
that, whenever he choſe to verſify, Words followed him of courſe.
We may add to *Antipater* the ancient *Rhapſodiſts* of the *Greeks*, and
the modern *Improviſatori* of the *Italians*. If this then be practicable
in *Verſe*, how much more ſo *in Proſe*? In *Proſe*, the Laws of which
ſo far differ from thoſe of Poetry, that we can at any time relax
                                                                them

---

ſint. Ejuſd. VIII. c. 3. p. 478. *Edit. Capper.*—DESINIT *Art eſſe, ſi* APPAREAT,
Ejuſd. IV. 2. p. 249.

* See *Dionyſ. Halicarn. de Struct. Orat.* ſ. 25. where this Argument is well enforced
by the *common well-known* HABIT OF READING, ſo difficult at firſt, yet gradually growing ſo familiar, that we perform it at laſt without deliberation, juſt as we ſee, or hear.

† Cic. de Oratore, L. III, 194. The ſame great writer in another place, ſpeaking
of the power of Habit, ſubjoins—*Id autem bonâ diſciplinâ exercitatis, qui et multa ſcrip-
ſerlat, et quæcunque etiam ſine ſcripto dicerent ſimilia ſcriptorum effecerint, non erit dif-
ficilimum. Ante enim circumſcribitur mente* SENTENTIA, *confeſtimque* VERBA *concurrunt*,
&c. Orator, ed. Brut. ſ. 200.

Ch. IV.

them as we find expedient? Nay more, where to relax them is not only expedient, but even *neceſſary*, becauſe tho' *Numerous Compoſition* may be a *Requiſite*, yet *regularly returning Rhythm* is a thing we ſhould avoid * ?

In every *whole*, whether natural or artificial, *the conſtituent Parts* well merit our regard, and in nothing more, than *in the facility of their co-incidence*. If we view a Landſkip, how pleaſing the Harmony between Hills and Woods, between Rivers and Lawns? If we ſelect from this Landſkip a Tree, how well does the Trunk correſpond with its Branches, and the whole of its Form with its beautiful Verdure? If we take an Animal, for example, a fine Horſe, what *a Union* in his Colour, his Figure, and his Motions? If one of human race, what *more pleaſingly congenial*, than when *Virtue* and *Genius* appear to animate *a graceful Figure?*

   —pulchro veniens e corpore virtus?

The charm increaſes, if to a graceful *Figure* we add a graceful *Elocution*. *Elocution* too is heightened ſtill, if it convey elegant *Sentiments*; and theſe again are heightened, if cloathed with graceful *Diction*, that is, with *Words*, which are pure, preciſe, and well arranged.

But this brings us *home* to the very *ſpot, whence we departed*. We are inſenſibly returned to *Numerous Compoſition*, and view in SPEECH

       however

---

* *Multum intereſt, utrum* NUMEROSA *fit (id eſt, ſimilis Numerorum) an planè è* NUMERIS, *conſtet Oratio. Alterum ſi fit, intolerabile vitium eſt: alterum niſi fit, diſſipata, et inculta, et fluens eſt Oratio. Ejuſd. ad Brut. ſ. 820.*

Part II. however referred, whether to the Body or the Mind, whether to the Organs of Pronunciation, or the Purity of Diction; whether to the Purity of Diction, or the Truth of Sentiment, how *perfectly natural the Co-incidence of every part.*

We must not then call these *verbal Decorations,* MINUTIÆ. They are essential to *the Beauty,* nay to *the Completion* of the *Whole.* Without them the Composition, tho' its *Sentiments* may be just, is like a Picture, with good *Drawing,* but with bad and defective Co-louring.

These we are assured were the Sentiments of CICERO, whom we must allow to have been a Master in his Art, and who has amply and accurately treated *verbal* Decoration and *numerous* Composition in no less than *two* Capital Treatises *, strengthening withal his own Authority with that of ARISTOTLE and THEOPHRASTUS; to whom, if more were wanting, we might add the names of DEMETRIUS PHALEREUS, DIONYSIUS of HALICARNASSUS, DIONYSIUS LONGINUS, and QUINCTILIAN.

HAVING presumed thus far to advise AUTHORS, I hope I may be pardoned for saying a word to READERS, and the more so, as the Subject has not often been touched.

WHOEVER reads a *perfect* or *finished Composition,* whatever be the Language, whatever the Subject, should read it, even if *alone,* both *audibly,* and *distinctly.* In

* His *Orator,* and his *De Oratore.*

In a Compofition of *this* Character not only *precife Words* are admitted, but Words *metaphorical* and *ornamental*. And farther—as every Sentence contains a latent Harmony, fo is that Harmony derived from the *Rhythm* of its conftituent Parts*.

A COMPOSITION then *like this*, fhould (as I faid before) be read both *diftinctly* and *audibly*; with due regard to Stops and Paufes; with occafional Elevations and Depreffions of the Voice, and whatever elfe conftitutes *juft* and *accurate*† PRONUNCIATION. He, who defpifing, or neglecting, or knowing nothing of all this, reads a Work of fuch character, as he would read a Seffions-paper, will not only mifs many beauties of *the Stile*, but will probably mifs (which is worfe) a large proportion of *the Senfe*.

SOMETHING ftill remains concerning the Doctrine of WHOLE and PARTS, and thofe Effentials of *Dramatic* Imitation, MANNERS, SENTIMENT, and THE FABLE. But thefe Inquiries properly form other Chapters.

---

* See before, from p. 327 to p. 340.

† *Vid. Scriptor. ad Herenn.* L. I. f. 3. L. III. f. 19. 20. 21. 22. 23. p. 4. 73. 74. 75. *Edit. Oxon.* 1718.

CHAP. V.

Concerning WHOLE *and* PARTS, *as essential to the constituting of a legitimate Work—the Theory illustrated from* THE GEORGICS OF VIRGIL, *and* THE MENEXENUS OF PLATO—*same Theory applied to smaller pieces—*TOTALITY, *essential to small Works, as well as great—Examples to illustrate—*ACCURACY, *another Essential—more so to smaller pieces, and why—Transition to* DRAMATIC SPECULATIONS.

Part II.

EVERY *legitimate* Work should be ONE, as much as a Vegetable, or an Animal; and, to be ONE like them, it should be a WHOLE, *consisting of* PARTS, and be in nothing *redundant*, in nothing *deficient.*—THE WHOLE *of an Animal,* or a Vegetable *consists of* PARTS, *which exist at once:* THE WHOLE *of an Oration, or a Poem, as it must be* either heard or perused, consists of Parts *not taken at once, but in a due and orderly Succession.*

The *Description of* SUCH A WHOLE is perfectly *simple,* but not, *for that Simplicity,* the less to be approved.

A WHOLE, we are informed, *should have a Beginning, Middle, and End*[*]*. If we doubt this, let us suppose a Composition to want them :—would not the very vulgar say, *it had neither head nor tail?*

NOR

---

[*] Ὅλον δέ ἐστι τὸ ἔχον ἀρχὴν καὶ μέσον καὶ τελευτήν. Arist. Poet. cap. 7. p. 231. Edit. Sylb.

Nor are the *Conſtitutive Parts*, tho' equally ſimple in their deſcription, for that reaſon leſs founded in truth. A Beginning is *that,*
which nothing neceſſarily precedes, but which ſomething naturally follows.
An End *is that, which nothing naturally follows, but which ſomething*
neceſſarily precedes. A Middle *is that, which ſomething precedes, to*
diſtinguiſh it from a Beginning; and which ſomething follows, to diſtin
guiſh it from an End *.

I might illuſtrate this from a Proposition in *Euclid. The ſtating*
of the thing to be proved, makes the Beginning; *the proving of*
it, makes the Middle; and the aſſerting of it to have been proved,
makes the Conclusion, or End: and thus is every ſuch *Propo*
ſition a complete and perfect *Whole.*

The ſame holds in Writings of a character totally different. Let
us take for an Example the moſt highly finiſhed Performance among
the *Romans,* and that in their moſt poliſhed period, I mean the
Georgics of Virgil.

> *Quid faciat lætas ſegetes, quo ſidere terram*
> *Vertere, Mæcenas, (ii) ulmiſque adjungere vites*
> *Conveniat; (iii) quæ cura boum, qui cultus habendo*
> *Sit pecori; (iv) apibus quanta experientia parcis,*
> *Hinc canere incipiam, &c.*   Virg. Georg. I.

In

---

* Ἀρχὴ δέ ἐστιν, ὃ αὐτὸ μὲν ἐξ ἀνάγκης μὴ μετ᾽ ἄλλο ἐστί· μετ᾽ ἐκεῖνο δ᾽ ἕτερον πέφυκεν εἶναι ἢ γίνεσθαι. Τελευτὴ δὲ τοὐναντίον, ὃ αὐτὸ μετ᾽ ἄλλο πέφυκεν εἶναι, ἢ ἐξ ἀνάγκης ἢ ὡς ἐπιτοπολύ, μετὰ δὲ τοῦτο ἄλλο οὐδέν. Μέσον δὲ καὶ αὐτὸ μετ᾽ ἄλλο, καὶ μετ᾽ ἐκεῖνο ἕτερον.—Ariſt. Poet. cap. 7. p. 231, 232. Edit. Sylb.

Part II. In these Lines, and so on (if we consult the Original) for forty-two Lines inclusive, we have THE BEGINNING; which *Beginning* includes two things, THE PLAN, and THE INVOCATION.

In the four first Verses we have THE PLAN, which *Plan gradually opens* and becomes the WHOLE WORK, as an Acorn, when developed, becomes a perfect Oak. After this comes THE INVOCATION, which extends to the last of the *forty-two Verses* above-mentioned. The two together give us the *true character of a* BEGINNING, which, as above described, *nothing can precede*, and which, 'tis necessary that *something should follow.*

THE remaining Part of the first Book, together with the three Books following, to Verse the 458th of Book the Fourth, make the MIDDLE, which also has its *true* character, that of *succeeding the Beginning*, where we expect *something farther*; and that of *preceding the End*, where we expect *nothing more.*

THE eight last Verses of the Poem make THE END, which, like *the Beginning, is short*, and which preserves its real character, by satisfying the Reader, that *all is complete*, and that *nothing is to follow*. The Performance is even *dated*. It finishes like an Epistle, giving us the *Place* and *Time* of writing; but then giving them in such a manner, as they ought to come from VIRGIL *.

BUT to open our thoughts into a farther Detail.

A

---

* See Vol. I. p. 155.

As *the Poem* from its very *Name* respects various MATTERS RE-LATIVE TO LAND, (GEORGICA) and which are either immediately or mediately connected with it: among the variety of these matters the Poem *begins* from the *lowest*, and thence *advances gradually* from *higher* to *higher*, till having reached the *highest*, it there properly *stops*.

The first Book begins from the *simple Culture of the* EARTH, and from its HUMBLEST PROGENY, Corn, Legumes, Flowers, &c. [*]

'TIS A NOBLER SPECIES OF VEGETABLES, which employs *the second* Book, where we are taught *the Culture* of *Trees*, and, among others, of that important pair, THE OLIVE and THE VINE [†]. Yet it must be remembered, that all this is nothing more than the culture of mere *Vegetable* and *Inanimate* Nature.

'TIS in *the third* Book that the Poet rises to Nature SENSITIVE and ANIMATED, when he gives us precepts about *Cattle, Horses, Sheep,* &c. [‡]

AT length, in *the fourth Book,* when matters draw to a Conclusion, then 'tis he treats his Subject in a MORAL and POLITICAL WAY.

He

---

[*] These are implied by *Virgil* in the *first* Line of his *first* Book, and in every other part of it, the *Episodes* and *Epilogue* excepted.

[†] This too is asserted at the *Beginning of his first* Book—*Ulmisque adjungere Vites*—and is the *intire subject* of the *second*, the same exceptions made as before.

[‡] This is *the third* subject mentioned in *the Proëme*, and fills (according to just order) the *intire third Book*, making the same exceptions, as before.

Part II. He no longer purfues the Culture of the *mere brute Nature*; he then defcribes, as he tells us,

  —Mores, et ftudia, et populos, et prælia, &c.

for fuch is the character of his Bees, thofe truly Social and Political Animals. 'Tis here he firft mentions *Arts*, and *Memory*, and *Laws*, and *Families*. 'Tis here (their great fagacity confidered) he fuppofes a portion imparted of a Sublimer Principle. 'Tis here that every thing *Vegetable* or merely *Brutal* feems forgotten, while all appears at leaft Human, and fometimes even Divine.

  Ilis quidam fignis, atque hæc exempla fecuti,
  Effe apibus partem Divinæ mentis, et hauftus
  Ætherios dixere: deum namque ire per omnes
  Terrafque tractufque maris, &c. Georg. IV. 219.

When the fubject will not permit him to proceed farther, he fuddenly conveys his Reader, by the Fable of Aristæus, among *Nymphs, Heroes, Demi-gods* and *Gods*, and thus leaves him in company, fuppofed more than mortal.

This is not only a fublime Conclusion to the *fourth Book*, but naturally leads to the Conclusion of the whole Work; for he does no more after this than *fhortly recapitulate*, and elegantly blend his recapitulating with a Compliment to *Auguftus*.

But even this is not all.

The dry, *didactic* character of the Georoics made it neceffary, they fhould be enlivened by Episodes and Digressions. It

           has

Ch. V

has been the Art of the Poet, that thefe *Epifodes* and *Digreffions* fhould be *homogeneous*; that is, fhould fo connect with the Subject, as to become (as it were) *Parts* of it. On thefe Principles every Book has for its END, what I call an *Epilogue*; for its BEGINNING, an *Invocation*; and, for its MIDDLE, the feveral *Precepts*, relative to its Subject, I mean *Hufbandry*. Having a *Beginning*, a *Middle*, and an *End*, EVERY PART ITSELF becomes A SMALLER WHOLE, tho' with refpect to the *general* Plan it is nothing more than A PART. Thus the *Human Arm* with a view to its Elbow, its Hand, its Fingers, &c. is as clearly A WHOLE, as it is fimply *but* A PART with a view to the *intire Body*.

THE SMALLER WHOLES of this divine Poem may merit fome attention; by thefe I mean *each particular Book*.

EACH Book has an INVOCATION. *The firft* invokes the Sun, the Moon, the various rural Deities, and laftly *Auguftus*; *the fecond* invokes *Bacchus*; *the third Pales* and *Apollo*; *the fourth*, his Patron *Mæcenas*. I do not dwell on thefe *Invocations*, much lefs on the Parts which follow, for this in fact would be writing a Comment upon the Poem. But the EPILOGUES, befides their own intrinfic beauty, are too much to our purpofe, to be paft in filence.

IN the arrangement of them the Poet feems to have purfued *fuch an Order*, as that *alternate Affections* fhould be *alternately excited*; and this he has done, well knowing the importance of that generally acknowledged Truth, *the Force derived to Contraries by their*

juxta-

Part II.   *juxta-position or succession* *.   *The first Book* ends with *those* PORTENTS
AND PRODIGIES, both upon Earth and in the Heavens, which pre-
ceded the Death of the Dictator *Cæsar*.   To these direful scenes the
Epilogue of *the second Book opposes* the TRANQUILITY AND FELI-
CITY OF THE RURAL LIFE, which (as he informs us) *Faction* and
civil Discord do not usually impair—

> *Non res Romanæ, periturague regna,*—

In the Ending of *the third Book* we read of a PESTILENCE, and of
Nature in devastation; in *the fourth*, of NATURE RESTORED, and, by
help of the Gods, *replenished*.

As this CONCLUDING EPILOGUE (I mean the Fable of *Aristæus*)
occupies the most important place, so is it decorated accordingly with
Language, *Events*, *Places*, and *Personages*.

No LANGUAGE was ever more polished and harmonious. The
descent of *Aristæus* to his mother, and of *Orpheus* to the shades, are
EVENTS; the watery Palace of the *Nereids*, the Cavern of *Proteus*,
and the Scene of the *Infernal Regions*, are PLACES; *Aristæus*, old
Proteus, *Orpheus*, *Eurydice*, *Cyllene* and her *Nymphs*, are PERSON-
AGES; all great, all striking, all sublime.

LET us view these Epilogues in the Poet's Order,
     I. CIVIL HORRORS.
     II. RURAL TRANQUILITY.
     III. NATURE LAID WASTE.
     IV. NATURE RESTORED.   Here,

---

* See before, p. 307, 308, &c.

Here, as we have said already, *different* Paffions are, by the *Subjects* being *alternate* *, *alternately* excited; and yet withal excited fo judicioufly, that, when the Poem concludes, and all is at an end, *the Reader leaves off with tranquility and Joy.*

From the Georgics of *Virgil* we proceed to the Menexenus of *Plato*; the firft being the moft finifhed Form of a *didactic Poem*, the latter, the moft confummate Model of a *Panegyrical Oration*.

The Menexenus is a *funeral* Oration in praife of thofe brave *Athenians*, who had fallen in battle by generoufly afferting the Caufe of their Country. Like the *Georgics*, and every other juft Compofition, this Oration has a Beginning, a Middle, and an End.

The Beginning is a folemn account of the deceafed having received *all the legitimate Rights of Burial*, and of the propriety of doing them honour not only by Deeps, but by Words; that is, not only by *funeral Ceremonies*, but by a Speech, to perpetuate the memory of their magnanimity, and to recommend it to their pofterity, as an object of imitation.

As the deceafed were brave and gallant men, we are fhewn *by what means* they came to poffefs their character, and *what noble exploits* they performed in confequence.

Hence

---

* See before, p. 351.

Part II.   Hence the Middle of the Oration contains firſt their *Origin*; next their *Education* and Form of Government; and laſt of all, the conſequence of ſuch an Origin and Education; their Heroic *Atchievements* from the earlieſt days to the time then preſent *.

The *middle Part* being thus complete, we come to the Conclusion, which is perhaps *the moſt ſublime piece of Oratory both for the Plan and Execution, which is extant of any age, or in any language.*

By an aweful *Proſopopœia*, the *Deceaſed* are called up to addreſs the *Living*; the *Fathers*, ſlain in battle, to exhort their living Children; the *Children*, ſlain in battle, to conſole their living Fathers; and this with every Idea of *manly* Conſolation, and with every generous incentive *to a contempt of Death*, and *a love of their Country*, that the powers of Nature, or of Art could ſuggeſt †.

'Tis here *this Oration concludes*, being (as we have ſhewn) a perfect Whole, executed with all the ſtrength of *a ſublime Language*, under the management of a great and *a ſublime Genius.*

If theſe Speculations appear *too dry*, they may be rendered more pleaſing, if *the Reader would peruſe the two Pieces criticized.* His labour, he might be aſſured, would not be loſt, as he would peruſe

two

---

* See Dr. *Bentham's* elegant Edition of this Oration, in his Λόγοι Ἐπιτάφιοι, printed at Oxford, 1746, from p. 81 to p. 40.

† See the ſame Edition from the words Ω Παῖδες, ἵνι μὲν ἐπι πάίρων ἀγαθὸν, p. 41, to the Concluſion of the Oration, p. 48.

two of *the finest pieces,* which the two *finest ages* of Antiquity produced.

WE cannot however quit *this Theory* concerning WHOLE and
PARTS, without obferving that it regards alike both *fmall* Works and
great; and that it defcends even to an *Effay,* to a Sonnet, to an
Ode. Thefe *minuter* efforts of Genius, unlefs they poffefs (if I may
be pardoned the expreffion) a certain character of TOTALITY, lofe
a capital pleafure derived from their UNION; from a *Union,* which,
collected in a few pertinent Ideas, combines them all happily, under
One amicable Form. Without this *Union,* the Production is no better
than a fort of *vague Effufion,* where Sentences follow Sentences, and
Stanzas follow Stanzas, with *no apparent reafon* why they fhould be
two rather than twenty, or twenty rather than two.

IF we want another argument for this MINUTER TOTALITY, we
may refer to *Nature,* which *Art* is faid *to imitate.* Not only *this
Univerfe* is one ftupendous Whole, but fuch alfo is *a Tree, a Shrub,
a Flower;* fuch thofe Beings, which, without the aid of glaffes, even
efcape our perception. And fo much for TOTALITY (I venture to
familiarize the term) that *common* and *effential Character* to every
legitimate Compofition.

THERE is *another* character left, which, tho' foreign to the prefent
purpofe, I venture to mention, and that is the character of ACCU-
RACY. Every Work ought to be as *accurate as poffible.* And yet,
tho' this apply to Works of *every* kind, there is a difference whether

the

Part II. the Work be *great* or *small.* In *greater* Works (such as Histories, Epic Poems, and the like) their *very Magnitude* excuses *incidental* defects, and their Authors, according to *Horace,* may be allowed to *slumber.* 'Tis otherwise in *smaller* Works, for the very reason, *that they are smaller.* Such, *thro' every part,* both in Sentiment and Diction, should be perspicuous, pure, simple and precise.

As Examples often illustrate better than Theory, the following short Piece is subjoined for perusal. The Reader may be assured, it comes not from the Author; and yet, tho' not his own, he cannot help feeling a *paternal* Solicitude for it; a wish for Indulgence to a Juvenile Genius, that never meant a private Essay for public Inspection.

Perdita to Florizel.

Argument.

Several Ladies in the Country having acted a Dramatic Pastoral, in which one of them under the name of Florizel, *a Shepherd, makes love to another under the name of* Perdita, *a Shepherdess; their acting being finished, and they returned to their proper characters, one of them addresses the other in the following lines.* —

  " No more shall we with trembling hear that Bell*,
  " Which shew'd Me, Perdita; Thee, Florizel.
  " No more thy brilliant eyes, with looks of love,
  " Shall in my bosom gentle pity move.

          " The

---

* The Play-bell.

" The curtain drops, and now we both remain,
" You free from mimic love, and I from pain.
" Yet grant one favour—tho' our Drama ends,
" Let the *feign'd* Lovers still be *real* Friends."

THE Author, in *his own* Works, as far as his Genius would affift, has endeavoured to give them a juft TOTALITY. He has endeavoured that each of them fhould exhibit a real *Beginning*, *Middle*, and *End*, and thefe *properly adapted* to the places, which they poffefs, and *incapable of Tranfpofition*, without Detriment or Confufion. He does not however venture upon a *Detail*, becaufe he does not think it worthy to follow *the Detail* of Productions, like *the Georgics*, or *the Menexenus*.

SO much therefore for the Speculation concerning WHOLE and PARTS, and fuch matters relative to it, as have incidentally arifen.

WE are now to fay fomething upon the Theory of SENTIMENT; and as SENTIMENT and MANNERS are intimately connected, and in a DRAMA both of them naturally rife out of the FABLE, it feems alfo proper to fay fomething upon DRAMATIC SPECULATION IN GENERAL, beginning, according to Order, firft from the firft.

CHAP. VI.

*Dramatic Speculations,—the constitutive Parts of every Drama
— Six in number—which of these belong to other Artists—which,
to the Poet—transition to those, which appertain to the Poet.*

Part II. THE Laws and Principles of *Dramatic* Poetry among the
Greeks, whether it was from the excellence of their *Pieces*,
or of their *Language*, or of both, were treated with attention even by
their *ablest Philosophers*.

We shall endeavour to give a sketch of their Ideas; and, if it shall
appear that we illustrate by Instances *chiefly Modern*, we have so done,
because we believe that it demonstrates the *Universality* of the Precepts.

A Dramatic Piece, or (in more common Language) a Play,
is, *the Detail or Exhibition of a certain Action*—not however an Action,
like one in *History*, which is supposed *actually* to have happened,
but, tho' taken from *History*, a Fiction or Imitation, in various
particulars derived from *Invention*. 'Tis by this that *Sophocles* and
Shakspeare differ from *Thucydides* and *Clarendon*. 'Tis Invention
makes them Poets, and not Metre, for had *Coke* or *Newton* written
in *Verse*, they could not for that reason have been called *Poets* *.

Again,

---

* Δῆλον δὲ ἐκ τούτων ὅτι τὸν ποιητὴν μᾶλλον τῶν μύθων εἶναι δεῖ ποιητὴν, ἢ τῶν μέτρων, ὅσῳ ποιητὴς κατὰ τὴν μίμησίν ἐστι· μιμεῖται δὲ τὰς πράξεις. 'Tis therefore evident hence, that a Poet or
Maker ought rather to be a Maker of Fables, than of Verses, in as much as he is a
Poet

AGAIN, A DRAMATIC PIECE, or PLAY is the Exhibition of an Action, *not simply related, as the* Eneid *or* Paradise Lost, but where the Parties concerned are made *to appear in person,* and PERSONALLY TO CONVERSE AND ACT THEIR OWN STORY. 'Tis by this that the *Samson Agonistes* differs from the *Paradise Lost,* tho' both of them Poems from the same sublime Author.

Now such DRAMATIC PIECE or PLAY, in order to make it pleasing (and surely, *to please* is an Essential to the Drama) must have A BEGINNING, MIDDLE, and END, that is, as far as possible, be a PERFECT WHOLE, *having Parts.* If it be defective here, it will be hardly comprehensible; and if hardly comprehensible, 'tis not possible that it should *please.*

BUT upon *Whole and Parts,* as we have spoken already *, we speak not *now.* At present we remark, that SUCH AN ACTION, *as here described,* makes in every *Play* what we call THE STORY, or (to use a Term more *technical*) THE FABLE; and that this STORY or FABLE is, and has been justly called the very SOUL OF THE DRAMA†, since from this it derives its very Existence.

WE proceed—THIS DRAMA then being an *Action,* and that *not rehearsed* like an *Epopee* or *History,* but *actually transacted* by certain

present

POET or MAKER *in virtue of his* IMITATION, *and as the Objects he imitates are human actions.* Arist. De Poet. cap. IX. p. 234. *Edit. Sylb.*

* Sup. Ch. V.

† Αρχὴ μὲν ἐν καὶ οἷον ΨΥΧΗ ΄Ο ΜΥΘΟΣ τῆς τραγῳδίας. *Arist.* Poet. C. VI. p. 231. *Edit. Sylb.*

Part II. *prefent living Agents,* it becomes neceſſary that *theſe Agents* ſhould *mutually converſe,* and that they ſhould have too *a certain Place,* where to hold their Converſation. Hence we perceive that in every Dramatic Piece, not only THE FABLE is a requiſite, but THE SCE-NERY, and THE STAGE, and more than theſe, a PROPER DICTION. Indeed the *Scenery* and *Stage* are not in the Poet's Department: they belong at beſt to the Painter, and after him to inferior Artiſts. The DICTION is the *Poet's,* and this indeed is important, ſince the Whole of his Performance is conveyed *thro' the Dialogue.*

BUT DICTION being admitted, we are ſtill to obſerve, that there are other things wanting, of no leſs importance. In the various tranſactions of *real* Life, every perſon does *not ſimply ſpeak,* but ſome way or other SPEAKS HIS MIND, and diſcovers by his behaviour certain TRACES OF CHARACTER. Now 'tis in theſe *almoſt inſeparable Accidents* to Human Conduct, that we perceive the riſe of SENTI-MENT and MANNERS. And hence it follows that as DRAMATIC FICTION copies real Life, not only DICTION is a neceſſary part of it, but MANNERS alſo, and SENTIMENT.

WE may ſubjoin one Part more, and that is MUSIC. The ancient Choruſſes between the Acts were probably *ſung,* and perhaps the reſt was delivered in *a ſpecies of Recitative.* Our modern Theatres have a Band of *Muſic, and* have *Muſic* often introduced, where there is no Opera. In this laſt (I mean the *Opera)* MUSIC ſeems to claim pre-cedence.

FROM

FROM thefe Speculations it appears, that *the Conftitutive Parts of the Drama are fix*, that is to fay, the FABLE, the MANNERS, the SENTIMENT, the DICTION, the SCENERY, and the MUSIC*.

BUT then, as out of thefe *fix* the *Scenery* and the *Mufic* appear to appertain to *other* Artifts, and the *Play* (as far as refpects the *Poet*) is *complete without them* ÷ it remains that its *four primary and capital Parts* are the FABLE, the MANNERS, the SENTIMENT, and the DICTION.

THESE by way of Sketch we fhall *fucceffively* confider, commencing from the FABLE, as *the firft* in dignity and rank.

---

* They are thus enumerated by *Ariftotle*—μῦθος, καὶ ἤθη, καὶ λέξις, καὶ διάνοια, καὶ ὄψις, καὶ μελοποιΐα. *De Poet.* C. VI. p. 230. *Edit. Sylb.*

The Doctrines of *Ariftotle* in this, and the following Chapters may be faid to contain in a manner *the whole Dramatic Art.*

C H A P. VII.

In the constitutive Parts of a Drama, the FABLE considered first—its different Species—which fit for Comedy; which, for Tragedy—Illustrations by Examples—REVOLUTIONS—DISCOVERIES—Tragic Passions—Jillo's Fatal Curiosity—compared with the Oedipus Tyrannus of Sophocles—Importance of Fables, both Tragic and Comic—how they differ—bad Fables, whence—other Dramatic Requisites, without the Fable, may be excellent—Fifth Acts, how characterised by some Dramatic Writers.

Part II.　IF we treat of DRAMATIC FABLES or STORIES, we must first inquire how many are their SPECIES; and these we endeavour to arrange, as follows.

ONE SPECIES is, when the *several Events flow in a similar Succession,* and calmly maintain that *equal* course, till the Succession stops, and *the Fable* is at an end. Such is the Story of a simple Peasant, who quietly dies in the Cottage where he was born, the same throughout his life, both in manners, and in rank.

THERE is A SECOND SPECIES of *Story* or *Fable, not simple,* but *complicated** ; a Species, where the *succeeding Events* differ widely
from

---

* Εἰσὶ δὲ τῶν μύθων οἱ μὲν ἁπλοῖ, οἱ δὲ πεπλεγμένοι· καὶ γὰρ αἱ πράξεις, ὧν μιμήσεις οἱ μῦθοί εἰσιν, ὑπάρχουσιν εὐθὺς οὖσαι τοιαῦται. λέγω δὲ κ. τ. λ. *Of* FABLES *some are* SIMPLE, *and some are* COMPLICATED; *for such are Human Actions, of which Fables are Imitations. By simple, I mean,* &c. *Arist. Poet.* cap. 10. p. 235. *Edit. Sylb.*

from *the preceding;* as for example, *the Story* of the well-known *Maſſinello,* who, in a few days, from a poor Fiſherman roſe to Sovereign Authority. Here the *Succeſſion* is *not equal* or *ſimilar,* becauſe we have A SUDDEN REVOLUTION from low to high, from mean to magnificent.

THERE IS ANOTHER COMPLICATED SPECIES, the reverſe of this laſt, where, THE REVOLUTION, tho' in extremes, is from high to low, from magnificent to mean. This may be illuſtrated by *the ſame Maſſinello,* who, after a ſhort taſte of Sovereignty, was ignominiouſly ſlain.

AND thus are all FABLES or STORIES either *ſimple* or *complicated;* and *the complicated* alſo of two ſubordinate ſorts; of which the one, beginning *from Bad,* ends *in Good;* the other, beginning *from Good,* ends *in Bad.*

IF we contemplate theſe various ſpecies, we ſhall find the *ſimple Story* leaſt adapted either to *Comedy* or *Tragedy.* It wants thoſe *ſtriking Revolutions,* thoſe *unexpected Diſcoveries* *, ſo eſſential to engage, and to detain a Spectator,

'Tis

---

* Theſe REVOLUTIONS and DISCOVERIES are called in *Greek* Περιπέτειαι and Ἀναγνωρισμοι. They are thus defined. Ἐςὶ ἡ Περιπέτεια μὲν ἡ εἰς τὸ ἐναντίον τῶν πραττομένων μεταβολὴ καθάπερ εἴρηται, καὶ τοῦτο δὲ—μετὰ τὸ εἰκὸς, ἢ ἀναγκαῖον. *A* REVOLUTION *is, as has been already ſaid, a Change into the reverſe of what is doing, and that either according to Probability, or from Neceſſity.* Ariſt. Poet. c. 11. p. 233. Edit. Sylb. Again—Ἀναγνώρισις δ᾽ ἐςὶν, ὥσπερ καὶ τοὔνομα σημαίνει, ἐξ ἀγνοίας εἰς γνῶσιν μεταβολὴ, ἢ εἰς φιλίαν ἢ ἔχθραν τῶν πρὸς εὐτυχίαν ἢ δυςυχίαν ὡρισμένων. *A* DISCOVERY *is, as the name implies, a Change from Ignorance to Knowledge, a Knowledge leading either to Friendſhip or Enmity between thoſe, who [in the courſe of the Drama] are deſtined to Felicity or Infelicity.* Ariſt. Poet. ut ſupra.

3 A 2

Part II.   'Tis not ſo with COMPLICATED STORIES. Here every ſudden
REVOLUTION, every DISCOVERY has a charm, and the *unexpected
events* never fail to *intereſt*.

IT muſt be remarked however of *theſe complicated* Stories, that,
where the REVOLUTION is *from Bad to Good*, as in the firſt ſubordinate Sort, they are more natural to COMEDY * than to *Tragedy*,
becauſe Comedies, however *Perplext* and *Turbid* may be their Beginning, generally produce at laſt (as well the ancient as the modern)
a Reconciliation of Parties, and a Wedding in conſequence. Not
only TERENCE, but every modern, may furniſh us with examples.

ON the contrary, when the REVOLUTION, as in the *ſecond* ſort,
is *from Good to Bad*, (that is, *from Happy to Unhappy*, from *Prof-
perous to Adverſe*) here we diſcover the *true Fable*, or *Story*, proper
for TRAGEDY. Common ſenſe leads us to call, even in *real life*,
ſuch Events, TRAGICAL. When *Henry the fourth of France*, the
triumphant Sovereign of a great people, was unexpectedly murdered by a wretched Fanatic, we cannot help ſaying, *'twas a TRA-
GICAL STORY*.

BUT to come to the TRAGIC DRAMA itſelf.

We

---

* The *Stagirite* having approved the practice, that *Tragedy ſhould end with Infelicity*,
and told us that the Introduction of *Felicity* was a ſort of Complement paid by the Poet
to the wiſhes of the Spectators, adds upon the ſubject of a HAPPY ENDING—ἔστι δὲ οὐχ αὕτη
ἀπὸ Τραγῳδίας ἡδονή, ἀλλὰ μᾶλλον τῆς Κωμῳδίας οἰκεία· ἐκεῖ γὰρ οἳ ἂν ἔχθιστοι ὦσιν ἐν τῷ μύθῳ, οἷον Ὀρέστης
καὶ Αἴγισθος, φίλοι γενόμενοι ἐπὶ τελευτῆς ἐξέρχονται, καὶ ἀποθνῄσκει οὐδεὶς ὑπ' οὐδενός. This is not a
Pleaſure ariſing from TRAGEDY, but is rather peculiar to COMEDY. For there, if the
characters are moſt hoſtile; (as much ſo, as Oreſtes and Ægiſthus were;) they become
Friends at laſt, when they quit the Stage, nor does any one die by the means of any other.
Ariſt. Poet. c. 13. p. 938. *Edit. Sylb.*

We see this kind of REVOLUTION sublimely illustrated in the Ch. VII *Oedipus of Sophocles*, where *Oedipus*, after having flattered himself in vain, that his *Suspicions* would be relieved by his *Inquiries*, is at last *by those very Inquiries* [*] plunged into the deepest woe, from finding it confirmed and put beyond doubt, that he had murdered *his own Father*, and was *then married to his own Mother*.

We see the force also of such a REVOLUTION in *Milton's Sampson Agonistes.* When his Father had specious hopes to redeem him from Captivity, these hopes are at once blasted by *his unexpected destruction* [†].

OTHELLO commences with a prospect of *Conjugal Felicity*; LEAR [‡] with that of *Repose*, by *retiring from Royalty.* DIFFERENT REVOLUTIONS (arising from Jealousy, Ingratitude, and other culpable affections) change both of these pleasing prospects into the deepest distress, and with this distress each of the Tragedies concludes.

NOR is it a small heightening to these REVOLUTIONS, if they are attended, as in the *Oedipus*, with A DISCOVERY [§], that is, if the

Parties

---

[*] See the same Poetics of Aristotle, in the beginning of Chap. 11th.——Περι β τ Ὀδίπ κ. τ. λ. p. 235. *Edit. Sylb.*

[†] See *Samson Agonistes*, v. 1452, &c.

[‡] This Example refers to the *real Lear of Shakspeare*, not the *spurious* one, commonly acted under his name, where the imaginary Mender seems to have paid the same Compliment to his audience, as was paid to other audiences two thousand years ago, and *is* justly censured. See Note, in the preceding page.

[§] See the preceding page.

Part II. Parties *who suffer*, and those *who cause* their sufferings, are *discovered* to be connected, for example, to, be Husband and Wife, Brother and Sister, Parents and a Child, &c. &c.

If a man in *real Life* happen to kill another, it certainly heightens the Misfortune, even tho' *an Event of mere Chance*, if he *discover* that person to be his Father or his Son.

'Tis easy to perceive, if these Events are *Tragic* (and can we for a moment doubt them to be such?) that Pity and Terror are *the true Tragic Passions* * ; that they truly bear that *Name*, and are necessarily diffused thro' every *Fable truly Tragic*.

Now, whether our ingenious Countryman, Lillo, in that capital Play of his, the Fatal Curiosity, learnt this Doctrine from others, or was guided by pure Genius, void of Critical Literature; 'tis certain that in *this Tragedy* (whatever was the cause) we find the model of a Perfect Fable, under *all* the Characters here described.

"A long-

---

* It has been observed that, if persons of *consummate Virtue and Probity* are made unfortunate, it does not move our *Pity*, for we are *shocked*; if Persons *notoriously infamous* are *unfortunate*, it may move our *Humanity*, but hardly then our *Pity*. It remains that Pity, and we may add Fear, are naturally excited by *middle* characters, those who are no way distinguished by their *extraordinary Virtue*, nor who bring their misfortunes upon them so much by *Improbity*, as by *Error*.

As we think the sufferings of such persons *rather hard*, they move our Pity; as we think them *like ourselves*, they move our Fear.

This will explain the following expressions—ΕΛΕΟΣ μὲν, περὶ τὸν ἀνάξιον ΦΟΒΟΣ δὲ, περὶ τὸν ὅμοιον. *Arist. Poet. c. 13, p. 237. Edit. Sylb.*

Ch. VII

" A long-loſt Son, returning home unexpectedly, finds his Parents
" alive, but periſhing with indigence.

" THE young man, whom from his long abſence his Parents
" never expected, diſcovers himſelf firſt to an amiable friend, his
" long-loved *Charlotte;* and with her concerts the manner how to
" diſcover himſelf to his Parents.

" 'TIS agreed he ſhould go to their Houſe, and there remain *un-*
" *known*, till *Charlotte* ſhould arrive, and make the happy Diſcovery.

" HE goes thither accordingly, and having by a Letter of *Char-*
" *lotte's* been admitted, converſes, tho' unknown, both with Father
" and Mother, and beholds their miſery with filial Affection—com-
" plains at length he was fatigued, (which in fact he really was)
" and begs he may be admitted for a while to repoſe. Retiring
" he delivers a Caſket to his Mother, and tells her 'tis a depoſit, ſhe
" muſt guard, till he awakes."

" CURIOSITY tempts her to open the Caſket, where ſhe is dazzled
" with the ſplendor of innumerable Jewels. Objects *ſo alluring*
" ſuggeſt *bad* Ideas, and *Poverty* ſoon gives to thoſe Ideas *a ſanction.*
" Black as they are, ſhe communicates them to her huſband, who,
" at firſt reluctant, is at length perſuaded, and for the ſake of the
" Jewels ſtabs the ſtranger, while he ſleeps.

" THE fatal murder is *perpetrating*, or at leaſt but *barely perpe-*
" *trated,* when *Charlotte* arrives, *full of Joy* to inform them, that the
" ſtranger within their walls was *their long-loſt Son.*"

WHAT

 WHAT a DISCOVERY? What a REVOLUTION? How irrefifti-
bly are the *Tragic* Paffions of *Terror* and *Pity* excited *.

'TIS no fmall Praife to this *affecting Fable*, that it fo much refembles that of the Play juft mentioned, the *Oedipus Tyrannus.* In both
Tragedies that, which *apparently* leads to *Joy*, leads in its completion to
Mifery; both Tragedies concur in the *horror* of their DISCOVERIES;
and both in thofe great outlines of a truly TRAGIC REVOLUTION,
where (according to the nervous fentiment of *Lillo* himfelf) we fee

    ——— *the two extremes of Life,*
    The higheft Happinefs, and deepeft Woe,
    With all the fharp and bitter Aggravations
    Of fuch a vaft tranfition ———

A FARTHER concurrence may be added, which is, that each Piece
begins and proceeds in *a train of Events*, which *with perfect probability* lead to its Conclufion, without the help of Machines, Deities,
Prodigies, Spectres, or any thing elfe, incomprehenfible, or incredible †.

WE may fay too, in both Pieces there exifts TOTALITY, that is
to fay, they have a *Beginning*, a *Middle*, and an *End* ‡.

WE mention this *again*, tho' we have mentioned it already, becaufe
we think we cannot enough enforce fo abfolutely effential a Re-
                                quifite;

---

* See p. 364, &c.

† It is true that in one Play mention is made of an *Oracle*; in the other, of a *Dream*;
but neither of them affects the Cataftrophe; which in both Plays arifes from Incidents
perfectly natural.

‡ See before, Ch. V.

quifite; a Requifite, defcending in *Poetry* from the mighty *Epopee* Ch VII
down to the minute *Epigram*; and never to be difpenfed with, but
in Seffions Papers, Controverfial Pamphlets, and thofe pafling Productions, which, like certain infects of which we read, live and die
within the day *.

And now, having given in the above inftances this Defcription of
the Tragic Fable, we may be enabled to perceive its amazing
efficacy. It does not, like *a fine Sentiment*, or *a beautiful Simile*,
give an *occafional* or *local* Grace; it is never out of fight; it adorns
every Part, and paffes through the whole.

'Twas from thefe reafonings that the great *Father of Criticifm*,
fpeaking of the Tragic Fable, calls it the very Soul of Tragedy †.

. Nor is this affertion lefs true of the Comic Fable, which has
too, like *the Tragic*, its Revolutions, and its Discoveries; its
Praife from natural Order, and from a just Totality.

The difference between them *only lies* in the *Perfons* and the
Cataftrophe, in as much as (contrary to the ufual practice of *Tragedy*)
the Comic Persons are moftly either of *Middle* or *Lower* Life, and
the Catastrophe for the greater part from *Bad* to *Good*, or (to
talk lefs in extremes) from *turbid* to *tranquil* ‡.

On

---

* *Vid. Ariftot. Animal. Hiftor. L. 5. p. 143. Edit. Sylb.*
† See before, p. 359.   ‡ See p. 364.

  On Fables, Comic as well as Tragic, we may alike remark;
that, when *good*, like *many other fine things*, they are *difficult*. And
hence perhaps the Cause, why *in this respect* so many *Dramas* are defective; and why their *Story or Fable* is commonly no more, than either *a jumble of Events* hard to comprehend, or *a Tale taken from
some wretched Novel*, which has little foundation either in Nature or
Probability.

Even in the Plays we most admire, we shall seldom find our Admiration to arise from the Fable: 'tis either from the Sentiment,
as in *Measure for Measure*; or from the purity of the Diction, as
in *Cato*; or from the Characters and Manners, as in *Lear*,
Othello, *Falstaff*, *Benedict* and *Beatrice*, *Ben the Sailor*, *Sir Peter* and
Lady Teazle, with the other Persons of that pleasing Drama, *the School
for Scandal*.

To these merits, which are great, we may add others far inferior,
such as the *Scenery*; such, as in Tragedy, the *Spectacle* of Pomps
and Processions; in Comedy, the amusing *Bustle* of Surprizes and
Squabbles; all of which have their effect, and keep our Attention
alive.

But here, alas! commences the Grievance. After Sentiment,
Diction, Characters and Manners; after the elegance of Scenes;
after Pomps and Processions, Squabbles and Surprizes; when, these
being over, *the whole draws to a conclusion*—'tis then unfortunately
comes the *Failure*. At that critical moment, of all the most interesting (by that *critical moment* I mean the Catastrophe), 'tis then the
                                                                    poor

poor Spectator is led into a Labyrinth, where both himself and the Poet are often lost together.

In *Tragedy* this Knot, like the *Gordian* Knot, is frequently solved *by the sword.* The principal Parties are *slain;* and, these being dispatched, the Play *ends of course.*

In *Comedy* the Expedient is little better. The *old Gentleman* of the Drama, after having fretted, and stormed thro' *the first four* Acts, towards the Conclusion of *the fifth* is unaccountably *appeased.* At the same time *the dissipated Coquette,* and *the dissolute fine Gentleman,* whose Vices cannot be *occasional,* but must clearly be *habitual,* are in the space of half a Scene *miraculously reformed,* and grow at once as completely good, as if they had *never* been otherwise.

'Twas from a sense of this concluding Jumble, this unnatural huddling of Events, that a witty Friend of mine, who was himself a Dramatic Writer, used pleasantly, tho' perhaps rather freely, *to damn the man, who invented fifth Acts**.

AND

---

* So said the celebrated HENRY FIELDING, who was a respectable person both by Education and Birth, having been *bred at Eton School and Leyden,* and being lineally *descended from an Earl of Denbigh.*

His JOSEPH ANDREWS and TOM JONES may be called *Master-pieces* in the COMIC PROPER, which none since have equalled, tho' multitudes have imitated; and which he was peculiarly qualified to write in the manner he did, both from his *Life,* his *Learning,* and his *Genius.*

** Had his *Life* been *less irregular* (for irregular it was, and spent in a promiscuous intercourse with persons of *all ranks*) his *Picture of Human kind* had neither been so *various,* nor so *natural.*

Had

 AND so much for *the Nature* or *Character* of THE DRAMATIC FABLE.

WE are now to inquire concerning MANNERS and SENTIMENT, and first for the Theory of MANNERS.

Had he poffeft lefs of *Literature,* he could not have infufed fuch a fpirit of *Claffical Elegance.*

Had his *Genius* been lefs fertile in *Wit and Humour,* he could not have maintained that *uninterrupted Pleafantry,* which never fuffers his Reader to feel fatigue.

CHAP. VIII.

Concerning DRAMATIC MANNERS—*what constitutes them*—*Manners of Othello, Macbeth, Hamlet*—*those of the last questioned, and* WHY—*Consistency required*—*yet sometimes blameable, and* WHY—*Genuine Manners in Shakspeare*—*in Lillo*—*Manners, morally bad, poetically good.*

" WHEN the *principal* Persons of any *Drama* preserve such
" a *consistency of Conduct*, (it matters not whether that
" Conduct be virtuous, or vicious) that, after they have appeared
" for a Scene or two, *we conjecture* WHAT THEY WILL DO HERE-
" AFTER, *from* WHAT THEY HAVE DONE ALREADY, such Persons
" in *Poetry* may be said to have MANNERS, for by this, and *this*
" *only*, are POETIC MANNERS constituted *."

To explain this assertion, by recurring to instances—As soon as
we have seen the violent *Love* and weak *Credulity* of OTHELLO, the

fatal

---

* "Ἔτι δὲ ΗΘΟΣ μὲν τὸ τοιοῦτον, ὃ δηλοῖ τὴν προαίρεσιν ὁποία τις ἐστίν, ἐν οἷς οὐκ ἔστι δῆλον, ἢ προαιρεῖται, ἢ φεύγει ὁ λέγων. MANNERS or CHARACTER *is that which discovers*, WHAT THE DETER-
MINATION [of a Speaker] *will be, in matters, where it is* NOT YET MANIFEST, *whether
he chuses to do a thing, or to avoid it.* Arist. Poet. c. 6. p. 231. *Edit. Sylb.*

It was from our being unable, in the Persons of some Dramas, *to conjecture what they
will determine,* that the above author immediately adds—διόπερ οὐκ ἔχουσι ἦθος ἔνια τῶν λόγων—
for which reason some of the Dramatic Dialogues have no MANNERS *at all.*

And this well explains another account of MANNERS given in the same Book—Τὰ δὲ
ΗΘΗ, καθ᾽ ἃ τοιούς τινας εἶναι φαμὲν τοὺς πράττοντας.—MANNERS *are those qualities, thro' which
we say the actors are men of such, or such a character.* ibid.

Bossu, in his *Traité du Poeme Epique,* has given a fine and copious Commentary on
this part of *Aristotle's Poetics.* See his Work, Liv. IV. chap. 4, 5, &c.

Part II. *fatal Jealoufy,* in which they terminate, is no more than what we may *conjecture.* When we have marked the *attention* paid by MACBETH to *the Witches,* to the perfuafions of *his Wife,* and to the flattering dictates of *his own Ambition,* we fufpect *fomething atrocious;* nor are we furprifed, that, in the Event, he murders *Duncan,* and then *Banquo.* Had he changed his conduct, and been only wicked by halves, his MANNERS would not have been as they now are, *poetically good.*

IF the leading Perfon in a Drama, for example HAMLET, appear to have been *treated moft injurioufly,* we naturally infer that he will meditate *Revenge;* and fhould that Revenge prove fatal to thofe who had injured him, 'tis no more than was *probable,* when we confider the Provocation.

BUT fhould *the fame Hamlet* by chance kill an *innocent old Man,* an old Man, from whom he had *never received Offence;* and with whofe *Daughter* he *was actually in love;*—what fhould we expect then? Should we not look for *Compaffion,* I might add, even for *Compunction?* Should we not be fhockt, if, inftead of this, he were to prove *quite infenfible*—or (what is even worfe) were he *to be brutally jocofe?*

HERE the MANNERS are *blameable,* becaufe they are *inconfiftent;* we fhould *never conjecture from* HAMLET any thing *fo unfeelingly cruel.*

NOR are *Manners* only to be blamed for being thus *inconfiftent.* CONSISTENCY itfelf is blameable, if it exhibit *Human* Beings com
pletely

pletely abandoned; *completely* void of Virtue; prepared, like King *Richard*, at their very *birth*, for mifchief. 'Twas of fuch models that a jocofe Critic once faid, they might make *good Devils*, but they could never make *good Men:* not (fays he) that they want *Confiftency*, but 'tis of a *fupernatural* fort, which *Human* Nature never knew.

       Quodcumque oftendis mihi fic, incredulus odi.   Hor.

THOSE, who wifh to fee Manners in a more genuine Form, may go to the characters already alledged in the preceding chapter *; where, from our *previous* acquaintance with the feveral parties, we can hardly fail, as incidents arife, to *conjecture* † their *future* Behaviour.

WE may find alfo Manners of this fort in the *Fatal Curiofity*. Old *Wilmot* and his Wife difcover *Affection* for one another; nor is it confined here—they difcover it for their abfent Son; for his beloved *Charlotte*; and for their faithful fervant *Randal*. Yet, at the fame time, from the memory of 'paft Affluence, the preffure of prefent Indigence, the fatal want of Refources, and the cold ingratitude of Friends, they fhew to all others (the few above excepted) a gloomy, proud, unfeeling *Mifanthropy*.

IN this ftate of mind, and with thefe manners an Opportunity offers, *by murdering an unknown Stranger*, to gain them immenfe Treafure, and place them above want. As the Meafure was at once both

---

* See p. 372.   † See p. 373.

Part II. both tempting and eafy, was it not natural that *fuch a Wife* fhould perfuade, and that *fuch a Hufband* fhould be perfuaded?—We may *conjecture* from their paft behaviour what part they would prefer, and that part, tho' *morally* wicked, is yet *poetically* good, becaufe *here* all we require, is *a fuitable Confiftence* *.

We are far from juftifying Affaffins. Yet Affaffins, if truly drawn, are not *Monfters,* but *Human Beings*; and, as fuch, being chequered with *Good* and with *Evil,* may by their *Good* move our *Pity,* tho' their *Evil* caufe *Abhorrence.*

But this in the prefent cafe is not all. The innocent parties, made miferable, exhibit a diftrefs, which comes home; a diftrefs, which, as mortals, it is impoffible we fhould not feel.

     Sunt lacrymæ rerum, et mentem mortalia tangunt †.   Virg. Æn.

---

* See p. 375.

† It was intended to illuftrate, by large Quotations from different parts of this affecting Tragedy, what is afferted in various parts of thefe Inquiries. But the intention was laid afide, (at leaft in greater part) by reflecting that the Tragedy was eafily to be procured, being modern, and having paft thro' feveral Editions, one particularly fo late, as in the year 1775, when it was printed with *Lillo's* other Dramatic Pieces.

If any one read this Tragedy, the author of thefe Inquiries has a requeft or two to make, for which he hopes a candid Reader will forgive him—one is, not to cavil at minute Inaccuracies, but look to the fuperior merit of *the whole taken together*—another is, totally to expunge thofe *wretched Rhimes,* which conclude many of the Scenes; and which 'tis probable are not from *Lillo,* but from fome other hand, willing to conform to an abfurd Fafhion, *then* practifed, but now laid afide, the Fafhion (I mean) of a *Rhiming Conclufion.*

CHAP. IX.

Concerning Dramatic Sentiment—*what constitutes it—Connected
with* Manners, *and how—Concerning* Sentiment, Gnomologic, *or* Preceptive—*its Description—Sometimes has a Reason
annexed to it—Sometimes laudable, sometimes blameable—whom it
most becomes to utter it, and why—Bossu—Transition to* Diction.

FROM Manners we pass to Sentiment; a Word, which tho'
sometimes confined to mere *Gnomology*, or *moral Precept*, was
often used by the *Greeks* in *a more comprehensive* Meaning, *including
every thing*, for *which men employ Language*; for proving and solving;
for raising and calming the Passions; for exaggerating and depre-
ciating; for Commands, Monitions, Prayers, Narratives, Interroga-
tions, Answers, &c. &c. In short, Sentiment *in this Sense* means
little less, than *the universal Subjects of our* Discourse *.

It

---

* There are two species of Sentiment successively here described, both called in
English either a Sentiment or a Sentence; and in *Latin*, Sententia. The *Greeks*
were more exact, and to the *different Species* assigned *different Names*, calling the one
Διάνοια, the other Γνώμη.

Of Γνώμη we shall speak hereafter; of Διάνοια their descriptions are as follows. Ἔστι δὲ
κατὰ τὴν διάνοιαν ταῦτα, ὅσα ὑπὸ τοῦ λόγου δεῖ παρασκευασθῆναι· μέρη δὲ τούτων, τό τε ἀποδεικνύναι, καὶ τὸ
λύειν, καὶ τὰ πάθη παρασκευάζειν, οἷον ἔλεον, ἢ φόβον, ἢ ὀργὴν, καὶ ὅσα τοιαῦτα, καὶ ἔτι μέγεθος καὶ
σμικρότητα. All those things belong to Sentiment (or Διάνοια) that are to be performed
thro' the help of Discourse: now the various branches of these things, are, to prove, and
to solve, to excite Passions (such as Pity, Fear, Anger, and the like) and, besides this, to
magnify, and to diminish. Arist. Poet. c. 19. p. 245. Edit. Sylb.

We

 It was under this meaning the word was originally applied to the
Drama, and this appears not only from Authority, but from Fact:
for what can conduce more effectually than Discourse, to establish
with precision *Dramatic* Manners and Characters?

To refer to a Play already mentioned, *the Fatal Curiosity*—When
old Wilmot discharges his faithful Servant from pure affection, that he
might not starve him, how strongly are his Manners delineated by
his Sentiments? The following are among his Monitions—

> *Shun my example; treasure up my precepts;*
> *The world's before thee;* Be a Knave and Prosper.

The *young man*, shockt at such advice from a Master, whose Virtues he had been accustomed so long to venerate, ventures modestly
to ask him,

> *Where are your* former Principles?

The old Man's Reply is a fine Picture of *Human Frailty;* a striking and yet a natural blending of *Friendship* and *Misanthropy;* of
particular Friendship, of *general* Misanthropy.

> *No Matter* (says he) *for Principles;*
> *Suppose I have* renounc'd 'em; *I have passions,*

And.

---

* We have here chosen the fullest Description of Διάνοια; but in the same work there
are others more concise, which yet express the same meaning. In the sixth chapter
we are told it is—τὸ λέγειν δύνασθαι τὰ ἐνόντα καὶ τὰ ἁρμόττοντα—*to be able to say* (that is, to
express justly) *such things as necessarily belong to a subject, or properly suit it.* And
again soon after—Διάνοια δ', ἐν οἷς ἀποδεικνύουσί τι, ὡς ἔστιν, ἢ ὡς οὐκ ἔστιν, ἢ καθόλου τι ἀποφαίνονται—
Διάνοια *or Sentiment exists, where men demonstrate any thing either to be, or not to be; or
thro' which they assert any thing general or universal.* Ibid. p. 231.

And LOVE THEE *still; therefore would have thee think,*
THE WORLD *is all a* SCENE OF DEEP DECEIT,
And he, WHO DEALS WITH MANKIND ON THE SQUARE,
Is HIS OWN BUBBLE, *and undoes* HIMSELF.

HE departs with these expressions, but leaves the young man far from being convinced.

THE suspicious gloom of *Age*, and the open simplicity of *Youth*, give the strongest *Contrast* to THE MANNERS of each, and *all this from the* SENTIMENTS *alone*; *Sentiments*, which, tho' *opposite*, are still perfectly just, as being perfectly suited to their *different* characters.

'TIS to this *comprehensive* Meaning of SENTIMENT that we may in a manner refer the Substance of these Inquiries; for SUCH SENTIMENT is every thing, either written or spoken.

SOMETHING however, must be said upon that other, and *more limited* SPECIES of it, which I call THE GNOMOLOGIC, or PRECEPTIVE; a species, not indeed peculiar to the Drama, but, when properly used, one of its capital ornaments.

THE following Description of it is taken from Antiquity. A GNOMOLOGIC SENTIMENT or Precept is an *Assertion* or *Proposition* — not however *all Assertions*, as that, *Pericles was an able Statesman*; *Homer a great Poet*, for these assertions are *Particular*, and *such a Sentiment must be* General — nor yet is it *every* assertion, tho' *General*; as that *The Angles of every Triangle are equal to two right Angles* — but it is

an

 an *Assertion, which, tho' general, is only relative to Human Conduct, and to such Objects, as in moral action we either seek or avoid* [*].

Among the Assertions of this sort we produce the following — the Precept, which forbids *unseasonable Curiosity* —

> *Seek not to know, what must not be reveal'd.*

Or that, which forbids *unrelenting Anger* —

> *Within thee cherish not immortal Ire.*

We remark too, that these *Sentiments* acquire additional strength, if we *subjoin the Reason.*

For example —

> *Seek not to know, what must not be reveal'd;*
> Joys only flow, where FATE is MOST CONCEAL'D.

Or again,

> *Within thee cherish not* IMMORTAL *Ire,*
> *When* THOU THYSELF *art* MORTAL — [†].

It

---

[*] We now come to the second species of Sentiment, called in Greek ΓΝΩΜΗ, and which *Aristotle* describes much in the same manner as we have done in the Text. Ἔτι δὲ ΓΝΩΜΗ ἀπόφανσις, [...] *Arist. Rhetor.* L. II. c. 21. p. 96. *Edit. Sylb.* So too the *Scriptor ad Herennium,* L. IV. c. 24. SENTENTIA *est Oratio sumpta de vitâ, quæ aut quid sit, aut quid esse oporteat in vitâ, breviter ostendit, hoc modo — Liber is est existimandus, qui nulli turpitudini servit.*

[†] The first of these *Sentiments* is taken from *Dryden,* the second is quoted by *Aristotle,* in his *Rhetoric,* L. II. c. 22. p. 97. *Edit. Sylb.*

Ἀθάνατα μὴ φρόνει, θνητὸς ὤν.

In some instances the *Reason* and *Sentiment* are so blended, as to be
in a manner inseparable. Thus *Shakspeare* —

> ——— *He, who filches from me my good name,*
> *Robs me of that, which not enriches Him,*
> *But makes Me poor indeed* —

There are too Sentiments of bad moral, and evil tendency —

> *If* SACRED RIGHT *should ever be infring'd,*
> *It should be done for* EMPIRE *and* DOMINION:
> *In* OTHER *things* PURE CONSCIENCE BE THY GUIDE *.

And again,

> ——— *the Man's a Fool,*
> *Who, having* SLAIN *the Father,* SPARES *the Son* †.

These Ideas are *only fit* for Tyrants, Usurpers, and other profligate Men; nor ought they to appear in a *Drama*, but to shew *such*
Characters.

On

On this the Philosopher well observes, that if the Monition had been no more, than that
we should not cherish our Anger for ever, it had been a SENTENCE or MORAL PRECEPT;
but, when the words θνητὸς ὤν, being *Mortal*, are added, the Poet then gives us *the*
Reason, τὸ διὰ τί λέγω. *Rhet. ut sup.* The Latin Rhetorician says the same. *Sed illud*
quoque probandum est genus SENTENTIÆ, *quod confirmatur* SUBJECTIONE RATIONIS,
hoc modo: omnes bene vivendi rationes in Virtute sunt collocandæ, PROPTEREA QUOD
sola Virtus in suâ potestate est. Scriptor. ad Heren. L. IV. f. 24.

  * *Vid. Cic. de Officiis,* L. III. c. 21. who thus translates *Euripides* —

> *Nam si violandum est Jus, regnandi gratiâ*
> *Violandum est? aliis rebus virtutem colas.*

  † Νήπιος, ὃς, πατέρα κτείνας, παῖδας καταλίπῃ. *Arist. Rhet.* L. I. c. 16. L. III. c. 22. p. 98.
Edit. Sylb.

Part II.   On *Gnomologic Sentiments* in general it has been observed that, tho' they decorate, they should not be *frequent*, for then the Drama becomes affected and declamatory *.

It has been said too, they come most naturally from *aged persons*, because *Age* may be supposed to have taught them *Experience*. It must however be an *Experience*, suitable to their *characters*; an Old General should not talk upon *Law*, nor an Old Lawyer upon *War* †.

We are now to proceed to DICTION.

---

* So the same *Latin Rhetorician*, above quoted—SENTENTIAS interponi RARO convenit, ut rei actores, non vivendi praeceptores esse videamur. Scriptor. ad Herenn. Lib. IV. f. 23.

† [Greek] It becomes HIM to be Sententious, who is ADVANCED IN YEARS, and that upon *subjects*, IN WHICH HE HAS EXPERIENCE. *Aristot. Rhet. ut supra*, p. 97. *Edit. Sylb.* See also the ingenious *Bossu*, in his *Traité du Poeme Epique*, Liv. VI. chap. 4. 5. who is, as usual, copious, and clear.

CHAP. X.

Concerning DICTION *— the vulgar — the affected — the elegant — this last, much indebted to the* METAPHOR *— Praise of the* METAPHOR *— its Description; and, when good, its Character; the best and most excellent, what — not turgid — nor enigmatic — nor base — nor ridiculous — Instances — Metaphors by constant use sometimes become common Words —* PUNS *—* Rupilius REX *—* OTTIE *—* ENIGMAS *— Cupping — The God* TERMINUS *— Ovid's Fasti —*

AS every *Sentiment* must be exprest by *Words;* the Theory of SENTIMENT naturally leads to that of DICTION. Indeed the *Connection* between them is so intimate, that the same *Sentiment,* where the *Diction differs,* is as different in *appearance,* as the same person, drest like a Peasant, or drest like a Gentleman. And hence we see, how much Diction merits a serious Attention.

But this perhaps will be better understood by an Example. Take then the following — *Don't let a lucky Hit slip; if you do, be-like you mayn't any more get at it.* The *Sentiment* (we must confess) is exprest clearly, but the DICTION surely is rather *vulgar* and *low.* Take it another way — *Opportune Moments are few and fleeting; seize them with avidity, or your Progression will be impeded.* Here the DICTION, tho' *not low,* is *rather obscure.* The *Words* are *unusual, pedantic,* and *affected.* — But what says SHAKSPEARE? —

(3)

There

Ch. X.

There is a TIDE *in the affairs of men,*
Which, taken at the flood, leads on to fortune;
Omitted, all the Voyage of their life
Is bound in shallows ————

Here the DICTION is *Elegant,* without being *vulgar* or *affected;* the Words, tho' *common,* being taken under a *Metaphor,* are so far estranged by this *metaphorical use,* that they acquire thro' the change a competent dignity, and yet, *without becoming vulgar,* remain intelligible and *clear;*

KNOWING therefore the stress laid by the ancient Critics on THE METAPHOR, and viewing its admirable effects in *the decorating of Diction,* we think it may merit a farther regard.

THERE is not perhaps any *Figure of Speech* so pleasing, as THE METAPHOR. 'Tis at times the Language of *every Individual,* but above all is peculiar to *the Man of Genius* [*]. His *Sagacity* discerns

not

---

[*] —τὸ δὲ μέγιστον μεταφορικὸν εἶναι· μόνον γὰρ τοῦτο ἔτι παρ ἄλλου ἐπι λαβεῖν, εὐφυΐας τε σημεῖόν ἐστι τὸ γὰρ εὖ μεταφέρειν, τὸ ὅμοιον θεωρεῖν ἐστι—*the greatest thing of all is to be powerful in Metaphor; for this alone cannot be acquired from another, but is a mark of original Genius: for to metaphorize well, is, to* DISCERN *in* DIFFERENT *objects that which is* SIMILAR. Arist. Poet. c. 22. p. 250. *Edit. Sylb.*

Δεῖ δὲ μεταφέρειν—ἀπὸ οἰκείων καὶ μὴ φανερῶν, οἷον καὶ ἐν φιλοσοφίᾳ τὸ ὅμοιον καὶ ἐν πολὺ διέχουσι θεωρεῖν, εὐστόχου—*We ought to metaphorize, that is,* TO DERIVE METAPHORS, *from Terms, which are proper and yet not obvious; since even in* PHILOSOPHY *to discern* THE SIMILAR *in things widely* DISTANT, *is the part of one, who* CONJECTURES HAPPILY. *Arist.* Rhetor. L. III. c. 11. p. 187. *Edit. Sylb.*

That METAPHOR is an effort of *Genius,* and *cannot be taught,* is here again asserted in the Words of *the first* Quotation.—καὶ λαβεῖν ἐστι ἕτερον ἄλλου (scil. Μεταφορὰς) παρ ἄλλου Rhetor. L. III. c. 2. p. 140. *Edit. Sylb.*

not only *common Analogies*, but thofe others *more remote, which efcape Ch. X.
the Vulgar*, and which, tho' they feldom invent, they feldom fail to
recognife, when they hear them from perfons, more ingenious than
themfelves.

It has been ingenioufly obferved, that the METAPHOR took its
rife from the *Poverty* of Language. Men, not finding upon every
occafion *Words ready made* for their ideas, were compelled to have
recourfe to *Words Analogous*, and transfer them from their *original*
meaning to the meaning *then* required. But tho' *the Metaphor
began in Poverty*, it did not *end* there. When *the Analogy was juft*
(and this often happened) there was fomething *peculiarly pleafing* in
what was both *new*, and yet *familiar*; fo that *the Metaphor* was then
cultivated, not out of *Neceffity*, but for *Ornament*. 'Tis thus that
Cloaths were firft affumed to defend us againft the Cold, but came
afterwards to be worn for Diftinction, and Decoration.

It muft be obferved, there is a force in the *united* words, NEW
and FAMILIAR. What is NEW, but *not Familiar*, is often *unintelli-
gible*: what is FAMILIAR, but *not New*, is no better than *Common
place*. 'Tis in the union of the two, that *the Obfcure* and the *Vulgar*
are happily removed, and 'tis in *this union*, that we view the *character of a juft Metaphor*.

But after we have fo praifed the METAPHOR, 'tis fit at length
we fhould explain *what it is*, and this we fhall attempt as well by a
Defcription, as by Examples.

Part II.

"A Metaphor is the transferring of a word from its *usual*
"*Meaning* to an *Analogous Meaning*, and then the employing it,
"*agreeably to such Transfer* [*]." For example: the usual meaning
of Evening is *the Conclusion of the Day*. But Age too is a *Conclusion*; the Conclusion of *human Life*. Now there being an Analogy *in all Conclusions*, we arrange in order *the two* we have alledged,
and say, that, *As* Evening *is to the* Day, *so is* Age *to* Human
Life. Hence, by an easy permutation, (which furnishes at once
two Metaphors) we say *alternately, that* Evening *is the* Age of
the Day; *and that* Age *is the* Evening of Life †.

There are other *Metaphors* equally pleasing, but which we only
mention, as their *Analogy* cannot be mistaken. 'Tis thus that old
Men have been called Stubble; and the Stage or Theatre,
the Mirror of human Life ‡.

In

---

[*] Μεταφορὰ δ' ἐστὶν ὀνόματος ἀλλοτρίου ἐπιφορά, κ. τ. λ. *Arist. Poet.* cap. 21. p. 247. *Edit.
Sylb.*

† —ὁμοίως ἔχει ἑσπέρα πρὸς ἡμέραν, καὶ γῆρας πρὸς βίον· ἐρεῖ τοίνυν τὴν ἑσπέραν γῆρας ἡμέρας, καὶ
τὸ γῆρας ἑσπέραν βίου. *Aristot. Poet.* c. 21. p. 248. *Edit. Sylb.*

‡ The Stagirite having told us what a natural pleasure we derive from Information,
and having told us that, in the subject of Words, Exotic words want that pleasure,
from being obscure, and *Common words from being too well known*, adds immediately—
ἡ δὲ Μεταφορὰ ποιεῖ τοῦτο μάλιστα· ὅταν γὰρ εἴπῃ τὸ γῆρας καλάμην, ἐποίησε μάθησιν καὶ γνῶσιν διὰ τοῦ
γένους, ἄμφω γὰρ ἀπηνθηκότα—*But the* Metaphor *does this most effectually, for when Homer*
(in metaphor) *said that* Age *was* Stubble, *he conveyed to us Information and Knowledge thro' a common Genus* (thro' the Genus of Time) *as both old Men, and Stubble, have
past the Flower of their existence.*

The words in *Homer* are,

Ἀλλ' ἔμπης καλάμην γέ σ' ὀΐομαι εἰσορόωντα
Γινώσκειν— *Odyss.* Ξ. v. 214. 215.

Sed

In Language of this sort there is a *double* Satisfaction: it is strikingly *clear*; and yet *raised*, tho' clear, above the low and *vulgar* Idiom. 'Tis a Praise too of such Metaphors, to be *quickly comprehended*. The Similitude and the thing illustrated are commonly dispatched *in a single Word*, and comprehended by an immediate, and instantaneous Intuition.

Thus a Person of wit, being dangerously ill, was told by his Friends, two more Physicians were called in. *So many! says he—do they fire then in Platoons?—*

These instances may assist us to discover, what Metaphors may be called *the best*.

They

Sed tamen stipulam saltem te arbitror intuentem
Cognoscere—

In which Verse we cannot help remarking an Elegance of the Poet.

Ulysses, for his protection, had been metamorphosed by *Minerva* into the Figure of an old Man. Yet even then the Hero did not chuse to lose his dignity. By his discourse he informs *Eumæus* (who did not know him) that altho' he was *old*, he was still *respectable—I imagine (says he) that even now you may know* the Stubble *by the look*. As much to suggest, that, tho' he had compared himself to Stubble, it was neverthelefs to that *better sort*, left after the reaping of the *best* Corn.

See the Note upon this Verse by my learned Friend, the late Mr. *Samuel Clarke*, in his *Greek* Edition of the *Odyssey*, and *Klotzlus* upon *Tyrtæus*, p. 26.

As *to the next Metaphor*, 'tis an Idea not unknown to *Shakspeare*, who, speaking of *Acting* or *Playing*, says with energy,

> *That its End, both at first, and now, was, and is,*
> To hold as 'twere the Mirror up to Nature. *Hamlet.*

According to *Aristotle*, the *Odyssey* of *Homer* was elegantly called by *Alcidamas*,—καλὸν ἀνθρωπίνου βίου κατόπτρον—a beautiful Mirror of Human Life. Rhet. L. III. c. 3, p. 124. *Edit. Sylb.*

3 D2

THEY ought not, in an *elegant* and *polite* Stile (the Stile, of which we are fpeaking) to be derived from Meanings too *fublime*; for then the *Diction* would be *turgid* and *bombaft*. Such was the Language of that Poet, who, defcribing the Footmen's Flambeaux at the end of an Opera, fung or faid,

> *Now blaz'd* A THOUSAND FLAMING SUNS, *and bade*
> *Grim Night retire*——

NOR ought a METAPHOR to be *far-fetched*, for then it becomes an *Enigma*. 'Twas thus a Gentleman once puzzled his Country Friend, in telling him by way of Compliment, that *He was become a perfect* CENTAUR. His honeft Friend knew nothing of *Centaurs*, but being fond of Riding, was hardly ever off his Horfe.

ANOTHER Extreme remains, *the reverfe* of the too *fublime*, and that is, *the transferring* from Subjects too contemptible. Such was the cafe of that Poet quoted by *Horace*, who, to defcribe Winter, wrote——

> *Jupiter hybernas cand nive* CONSPUIT *Alpes* [*]. .
>
> *O'er the cold Alps Jove* SPITS *his hoary fnow.*

NOR was that modern Poet more fortunate, whom *Dryden* quotes, and who, trying his Genius upon the fame fubject, fuppofed Winter——

> To PERRIWIG *with fnow the* BALD-PATE *Woods.*

WITH the fame clafs of Wits we may arrange that pleafant fellow, who fpeaking of an old Lady, whom he had affronted, gave us in

one

---

[*] Hor. L. II. Sat. 5.

one short Sentence no less than *three* choice *Metaphors*. *I perceive*
(said he) *her Back is up:—I must curry Favour—or the Fat will be in
the fire.*

Nor can we omit that *the same* Word, when *transferred to different*
Subjects, produces Metaphors very *different,* as to *Propriety,* or *Im-
propriety.*

'Tis with *Propriety* that we *transfer* the word, To Embrace, from
Human Beings to things purely *Ideal.* The *Metaphor* appears just,
when we say, *To Embrace a Proposition; To Embrace an Offer; To
Embrace an Opportunity.* Its Application perhaps was not quite so
elegant when the old Steward wrote to his Lord, upon the Subject of
his Farm, that *" if he met any* Oxen, *he would not fail* To Embrace
" them*."

If then we are to avoid *the Turgid, the Enigmatic,* and *the Base* or
Ridiculous, no other *Metaphors* are left, but such as may be described
by Negatives; such as are neither turgid, nor enigmatic, nor base
and ridiculous.

Such is the character of many Metaphors already alledged,
among others that of Shakspeare's, where *Tides are transferred to*
speedy

---

* The Species of Metaphors, here condemned, are thus enumerated,—εἰσὶ γὰρ καὶ
Μεταφοραὶ ἀπρεπεῖς, αἱ μὲν διὰ τὸ γελοῖον—αἱ δὲ διὰ τὸ σεμνὸν ἄγαν καὶ τραγικὸν ἀσαφεῖς δὲ, ἂν πόῤῥωθεν,
κ. τ. λ.—For Metaphors *are unbecoming, some from being* Ridiculous, *and others,
from being* too Solemn *and* Tragical: *there are likewise the* Obscure, *if they are
fetched from too great a distance.* Arist. Rhet. L. III. c. 3. p. 124. Edit. Sylb. See
Cic. de Oratore, L. III. p. 155, &c.

 speedy and determined Conduct. Nor does his* WOOLSEY *with less propriety moralize upon his Fall in the following beautiful Metaphor, taken from Vegetable Nature.*

 This is the state of Man; to day he PUTS FORTH
 THE TENDER LEAVES *of Hope; to-morrow* BLOSSOMS,
 And bears his BLUSHING HONOURS THICK *upon him:*
 The third day comes A FROST, A KILLING FROST,
 And — nips his root —

IN *such Metaphors* (besides their intrinsic elegance) we may say the Reader is flattered; I mean flattered by being left to discover something *for himself.*

THERE is one Observation, which will at the same time shew both *the extent* of this Figure, and *how natural* it is to all Men.

THERE are METAPHORS *so obvious,* and of course *so naturalized,* that ceasing to be *Metaphors,* they are become (as it were) THE PROPER WORDS. 'Tis after this manner we say, *a sharp fellow;* a *great Orator; the Foot* of a Mountain; *the Eye* of a Needle; *the Bed* of a River; to *ruminate, to ponder, to edify,* &c. &c.

THESE we by no means reject, and yet *the Metaphors we require* we wish to be *something more,* that is, to be formed under the respectable conditions here established.

           WE

---

* Sup. p. 383.—Vol. I. p. 171.

We observe too, that a singular Use may be made of *Metaphors*, either *to exalt*, or *to depreciate*, according to the *Sources*, from which we derive them.   In ancient Story, *Orestes* was by some called *the Murtherer of his Mother;* by others, *the Avenger of his Father.* The Reasons will appear by referring to the Fact. The Poet *Simonides* was offered money to celebrate certain Mules, that had won a race. The sum being pitiful, he said with disdain, he should not write upon Demi-Asses.—A more competent Sum was offered,—he then began,

> *Hail* DAUGHTERS OF THE GENEROUS HORSE,
> *That skims, like Wind, along the Course* [*].

There are times, when, in order *to exalt*, we may call *Beggars, Petitioners;* and *Pick-pockets, Collectors;* other times, when in order *to depreciate,* we may call *Petitioners, Beggars;* and *Collectors, Pick-pockets.*—But enough of this.

We say no more of *Metaphors,* but that 'tis a general Caution with regard to every Species, NOT TO MIX THEM, and that more particularly, if taken from Subjects, which are *Contrary.*

Such was the Case of that Orator, who once asserted in his Oration, that—" *If Cold Water were thrown upon a certain Measure, it* " *would kindle a Flame, that would obscure the Lustre,* &c. &c."

                                        A WORD

---

[*] For these two facts, concerning *Orestes,* and *Simonides,* see *Arist. Rhet.* L. III. c. 2. p. 122. *Edit. Sylb.* The different appellations of *Orestes* were, ὁ Μητροφόντης, and ὁ Πατρὸς ἀμύντωρ—*Simonides* called the *Mules* ἡμίονοι at first; and then began—

Χαίρετ' ἀελλοπόδων θύγατρες ἵππων—

A word remains upon Enigmas and Puns. It shall indeed be short, because, tho' they resemble the *Metaphor*, it is as Brass and Copper resemble Gold.

A Pun seldom regards Meaning, being chiefly confined to Sound.

Horace gives a sad sample of this *spurious* Wit, where (as *Dryden* humorously translates it) he makes *Persius* the Buffoon exhort the Patriot *Brutus* to kill Mr. King, that is, Rupilius Rex, because *Brutus*, when he slew *Cæsar*, had been accustomed to King-killing.

  Hunc Regem *occide; operum hoc mihi crede tuorum est* *.

We have a worse attempt in *Homer*, where *Ulysses* makes *Poly-pheme* believe his name was ΟΥΤΙΣ, and where the dull *Cyclops*, after he had lost his Eye, upon being asked by his Brethren who had done him so much mischief, replies 'twas done by ΟΥΤΙΣ, that is, by Nobody †.

Enigmas are of a more complicated nature, being involved either in *Pun*, or *Metaphor*, or sometimes in both.

  Ἄνδρ' ἴδον πυρὶ χαλκὸν ἐπ' ἀνέρι κολλήσαντα.

  I saw a man, who, unprovok'd with Ire,
  Stuck Brass upon another's back by Fire ‡.

This

---

* *Horat. Sat. Lib.* I. VII.   † *Homer, Odyss.* I. v. 366—408, &c.

‡ *Arist. Rhet.* L. III. c. 2. p. 121. *Edit. Sylb.*

This Enigma is ingenious, and means the *operation of Cupping*, performed in ancient days by a machine of *Brass*.

In such Fancies, contrary to the Principles of good *Metaphor*, and good Writing, a *Perplexity* is caused, *not by Accident*, but *by Design*, and *the Pleasure* lies in the being able *to resolve it*.

Aulus Gellius has preserved a LATIN ENIGMA, which he also calls a *Sirpus* or *Sirpos*, a strange thing, far below the *Greek*, and debased with all the quibble of a more barbarous age.

> *Semel minusne, an bis minus, (non sat scio)*
> *An utrumque eorum (ut quondam audivi dicier)*
> *Jovi ipsi regi noluit concedere* * ?

This, being sifted, leaves in *English* the following small quantity of Meaning:

Was it ONCE MINUS, *or* TWICE MINUS (*I am not enough informed), or was it not rather* THE TWO TAKEN TOGETHER, (*as I have heard it said formerly) that would not give way to Jove himself, the sovereign?*

THE TWO TAKEN TOGETHER, (that is, ONCE MINUS and TWICE MINUS) make, when so taken, THRICE MINUS; and THRICE MINUS in Latin is TER MINUS, which, taken as a *single* word, is TERMINUS, *the God of Boundaries*.

HERE

---

* Aul. Gell. XII. 6.

 Here the *Riddle,* or *Conceit,* appears. The Pagan Legend says, that, when in honour of *Jove* the Capitol was founded, the other Gods confented to retire, but the God TERMINUS refuſed.

THE Story is elegantly related in the *Faſti* of *Ovid,* III. 667.

> *Quid, noɣa cum fierent Capitolia? nempe Deorûm*
> *Cunɛla Jovi ceſſit turba, locumque dedit.*
> TERMINUS (*ut celeres memorant*) *conɣentus in æde*
> RESTITIT, *et magno cum Jove templa tenet.*

THE moral of the Fable is juſt and ingenious; *that Boundaries are facred, and never ſhould be moved.*

THE Poet himſelf ſubjoins the reaſon with his uſual addreſs.

> TERMINE, *poſt illud Levitas tibi libera non eſt;*
> *Quâ poſitus fueris in ſtatione,* MANE.
> *Nec Tu vicino quicquam concede roganti,*
> *Ne videare hominem præpoſuiſſe Jovi.*

AND, ſo much for the ſubject of *Puns* and *Enigmas,* to which, like other things of bad Taſte, *no Age* or *Country* can give a Sanction.

MUCH ſtill remains upon the ſubject of DICTION, but, as much has been ſaid already[a], we here conclude.

---

[a] See Chapters II. III. IV.

CHAP. XI.

RANK or PRECEDENCE *of the constitutive Parts of the Drama—*
Remarks and Cautions both for Judging, and Composing.

THE *four constitutive Parts* of Dramatic Poetry, which properly
belong to *the Poet* [*], have appeared to be THE FABLE, THE
MANNERS, THE SENTIMENT, and THE DICTION, and something
has been suggested to explain the nature of each.

SHOULD we be asked, to which we attribute *the first* Place, we
think it due to THE FABLE [†].

IF THE FABLE be an *Action*, having a necessary reference to some
End; it is evident that *the Manners* and *the Sentiment* are for the
sake of that *End*; the *End* does not exist, for the sake of the *Man-*
ners and the *Sentiment* [‡].   AGAIN,

---

[*] Sup. p. 361.

[†] Ἀρχὴ μὲν οὖν, καὶ οἷον ψυχὴ ὁ Μῦθος τῆς Τραγῳδίας—THE FABLE *therefore is* THE PRIN-
CIPLE, *and (as it were)* THE SOUL *of Tragedy.*—And not long before, after the consti-
tuent *Parts of the Drama* have been enumerated, we read—μέγιστον δὲ τούτων ἐστὶν ἡ τῶν
πραγμάτων σύστασις.—*But* THE GREATEST *and the most important of all these is* THE COM-
BINING OF THE INCIDENTS, *that is to say,* THE FABLE. Arist. Poet. cap. 6. p. 231.
Edit. Sylb.

[‡] Οὐκ οὖν ὅπως τὰ ἤθη μιμήσωνται, πράττουσιν, ἀλλὰ τὰ ἤθη συμπεριλαμβάνουσι διὰ τὰς πράξεις.—
The Persons of the Drama do not act, that they may exhibit Manners; but they include
Manners, on account of the Incidents in the Fable. Arist. Poet. c. 6. p. 230. Edit.
Sylb.

3 E 2

AGAIN, the finest *unconnected* Samples either of *Manners* or of *Sentiment* cannot *of themselves* make a *Drama*, without a *Fable*. But, without either of these, *any Fable* will make a *Drama*, and have pretensions, (such as they are) to be called *a Play*[*].

A THIRD *superiority*, is, that the most *affecting* and *capital Parts* of every *Drama* arise out of its FABLE; by these I mean every unexpected DISCOVERY of unknown Personages, and every unexpected REVOLUTION[†] from one condition to another. The *Revolutions* and *Discoveries* in the *Oedipus*, and the *Fatal Curiosity* have been mentioned already. We add to these the striking *Revolution* in the *Samson Agonistes*, where, while every thing appears tending to Samson's *Release*, a horrible Crash announces his *Destruction*[‡].

THESE

---

[*] *The Stagirite* often illustrates his *Poetic* Ideas from *Painting*, an Art at that time cultivated by the ablest Artists, *Zeuxis*, *Polygnotus*, and others. In the present case, he compares the DRAMATIC MANNERS to COLOURING; the DRAMATIC FABLE to DRAWING; and ingeniously remarks—Εἰ γάρ τις ἐναλείψειε τοῖς καλλίστοις φαρμάκοις χύδην, ἐκ ἂν ὁμοίως εὐφράνειεν, καὶ λευκογραφήσας εἰκόνα—*If any one were to make a* CONFUSED DAUBING *with* THE MOST BEAUTIFUL COLOURS, *he would not give so much delight, as if he were* TO SKETCH A FIGURE IN CHALK ALONE. Arist. Poct. c. 6. p. 231. *Edit. Sylb.*

—Ἔτι ἐὰν τις ἐφεξῆς θῇ ῥήσεις ἠθικὰς, καὶ λέξεις, καὶ διανοίας, εὖ πεποιημένας, ὁ ποιήσει ὃ ἦν τῆς τραγῳδίας ἔργον, ἀλλὰ πολὺ μᾶλλον ἡ καταδεεστέροις τούτοις κεχρημένη τραγῳδία, ἔχουσα δὲ μῦθον καὶ σύστασιν πραγμάτων—*Were any one to arrange in order the best formed* EXPRESSIONS RELATIVE TO CHARACTER, *as well as the best* DICTION, *and* SENTIMENTS, *he would not attain what is the Business of a Tragedy; but much more would that Tragedy attain it, which, having these requisites in a very inferior degree, had at the same time a just* FABLE, *and Combination of Incidents.* Arist. Poct. c. 6. p. 230. *Edit. Sylb.*

[†] A REVOLUTION, Περιπέτεια) A DISCOVERY, Ἀναγνώρισις. See before what is said about these two, from p. 363 to 365.

[‡] *Samf. Agon.* v. 1587, and v. 1458 to v. 1507.

These *Dramatic* Incidents are properly *Tragic*—but there are others of *similar* character, not wanting even to *Comedy*.—To refer to a *modern* Drama—what DISCOVERY more pleafing than that, where, in *the Drummer of Addifon*, the worthy loft Mafter is *difcovered* in the fuppofed Conjurer? or, to refer ftill to the fame Drama, what REVOLUTION more pleafing, than where, in confequence of this *Difcovery*, the Houfe of Diforder and Mourning changes into a Houfe of Order and Joy? Now thefe *interefting* Incidents, as well *Comic* as *Tragic*, arife neither from *Manners*, nor from *Sentiment*, but purely from THE FABLE.

IT is alfo a plaufible Argument for the *Fable's Superiority*, that, from its fuperior difficulty, *more Poets* have excelled in *drawing Manners* and *Sentiment*, than there have in the forming of *perfect Fables* *.

BUT, altho' we give a fuperiority to *the Fable*, yet the other conftitutive *Parts*, even fuppofing *the Fable bad*, have ftill an important value; fo important indeed, that thro' them, and them alone, many Dramas have merited Admiration.

AND here next to the *Fable* we arrange the MANNERS. The *Manners*, if well formed, give us *famples of Human Nature*, and feem in Poetry as much to excel *Sentiment*, as *the Drawing* in Painting to excel *the Colouring*.

THE

---

* —δι ἐγχειρῶντες ποιεῖν, πρότερον δύνανται τῇ λέξει καὶ τοῖς ἤθεσιν ἀκριβοῦν, ἢ τὰ πράγματα συνίςαςθαι, οἷον καὶ οἱ πρῶτοι ποιηταὶ σχεδὸν ἅπαντες. *Thofe, who attempt to write Dramatically, are firft able to be accurate in* THE DICTION *and* THE MANNERS, *before they are able to* COMBINE INCIDENTS *[and form a Fable] which was indeed the cafe of almoft all the firft Poets.* Arift. Poet. c. 6. p. 210. *Edit. Sylb.*

THE third Place after *the Manners* belongs to THE SENTIMENT, and that *before the Diction*, however they may be united, it being evident that Men *speak*, because they think; they *seldom think*, because they speak.

AFTER this, the fourth and last Place falls to THE DICTION.

HAVING settled *the Rank* of these several *Constitutive* Parts, a few cursory Remarks remain to be suggested.

ONE is this—that if *all* these Parts are *really* essential, *no Drama* can be *absolutely complete*, which in any one of them is *deficient*.

ANOTHER Remark is, that tho' a Drama be not absolutely complete in *every* Part, yet *from the excellence of one or two* Parts *it may still merit Praise* *. 'Tis thus in Painting, there are Pictures admired for *Colouring*, which fail in the Drawing; and others for *Drawing*, which fail in the Colouring.

THE

---

* This is a Case expressly decided by that able Critic, *Horace*, as to the MANNERS and the SENTIMENT.

    —SPECIOSA LOCIS, MORATAQUE RECTE,
    FABULA NULLIUS VENERIS, *sine pondere et arte,*
    Valdius oblectat populum, meliusque moratur,
    Quam versus inopes rerum, nugaque canoræ.   Art. Poet. *v.* 320, &c.

Which may be thus paraphrased—

" A FABLE (or Dramatic Story) OF NO BEAUTY, *without dignity or contrivance, if it excel in* SENTIMENT, *and have its* CHARACTERS *well drawn, will please an audience much more than a trifling Piece barren of Incidents, and only to be admired for the Harmony of its Numbers.*" See p. 404.

THE next Remark is in fact a Caution; a Caution not to miftake *one Conftitutive Part* for *another*, and ftill, much more, not to miftake it for *the Whole*. We are never to forget the *effential differences* between FABLE, MANNERS, SENTIMENT, and DICTION.

IF, without attending to thefe, we prefume to admire, we act, as if in Painting we admired a *Rembrant* for *Grace*, becaufe we had been told, that he was capital in *Colouring*.

THIS Caution indeed applies not only to *Arts*, but to *Philofophy*. For here if men fancy, that a Genius for *Science*, by having excelled *in a fingle part* of it, is fuperlative *in all* parts; they infenfibly make fuch a Genius their Idol, and their Admiration foon degenerates into a fpecies of Idolatry,

Decipit exemplar, vitiis imitabile ---   Hor.

'TIS to be hoped that our ftudies are at prefent more liberal, and that we are rather adding to that Structure, which our forefathers have begun, than tamely leaving it to remain, as if nothing farther were wanting.

OUR Drama among other things is furely capable of Improvement. Events from OUR OWN HISTORY (and none can be more interefting) are at hand to furnifh FABLES, having *all the Dramatic Requifites*. Indeed fhould any of them be wanting, INVENTION may provide a Remedy, for here we know Poets have unbounded Privilege *.   IN

---

* Infra, 404.

In the mean time the subjects, by being *domestic*, would be as interesting *to Us*, as those of *Ajax* or *Orestes* were of old to *the Greeks*. Nor is it a doubt, that our Drama, were it thus rationally cultivated, might be made the School of Virtue even in a dissipated age.

And now, having shewn such a regard for *Dramatic Poetry*, and recommended so many different RULES, as *essential to its Perfection*; it may not perhaps be improper *to say something in their Defence*, and, when that is finished, to conclude this Part of our Inquiries.

CHAP. XII.

Rules defended — do not cramp GENIUS, but guide it — flattering Doctrine that GENIUS will suffice — fallacious, and why — farther defence of RULES — No GENIUS ever acted without them; nor ever a Time, when RULES did not exist — Connection between RULES and GENIUS — their reciprocal aid — End of THE SECOND PART — Preparation for THE THIRD.

HAVING mentioned RULES, and indeed our whole Theory having been little more than RULES DEVELOPED, we cannot but remark upon a common opinion, which seems to have arisen either from Prejudice, or Mistake.

" *Do not* RULES, say they, *cramp* GENIUS? *Do they not abridge* " *it of certain Privileges?*"

'Tis answered, if the obeying of RULES were to induce a Tyranny like this; to defend them would be absurd, and against the liberty of Genius. But the truth is, RULES, supposing them *good*, like good Government, *take away no Privileges.* They do no more, than save Genius from Error, by shewing it, that *a Right to err is no Privilege at all.*

'Tis surely no Privilege to violate in Grammar the *Rules of Syntax;* in Poetry, those of *Metre;* in Music, those of *Harmony;* in Logic, thofe of *Syllogifm*; in Painting, thofe of *Perfpective*; in Dramatic Poetry, thofe of *probable Imitation*.

If we enlarge on one of thefe *Inflances*, we fhall illuftrate the reft.

The *probable Imitation* juft now mentioned, like that of every other kind, is, when *the Imitation refembles the thing imitated in as many circumflances as poffible*; fo that *the more* of thofe Circumftances are *combined, the more probable* the Refemblance.

'Tis thus in Imitation by Painting tho' Refemblance is more complete, when to the *Out-line* we add *Light and Shade*; and more complete ftill, when to *Light and Shade* we add *the Colours*.

The real Place of every *Drama* is a *Stage*, that is, a fpace of a few Fathoms deep, and a few Fathoms broad. Its real Time is *the Time it takes in acting, a limited Duration*, feldom exceeding a few hours.

Now *Imagination*, by the help of *Scenes*, can enlarge *this Stage* into a Dwelling, a Palace, a City, &c. and it is a decent Regard to this, which conftitutes Probable Place.

Again, the *ufual Intervals* between the Acts, and even the *Attention paid by the Mind* to an interefting Story, can enlarge without violence *a few Hours* into *a Day or two*; and 'tis in a

decent

decent regard to this, we may perceive the Rise of PROBABLE Ch. XII
TIME *.

Now *'tis evident* that THE ABOVE PROBABILITIES, if they belong
to the *Fable*, cannot but affect us, because they are both of them
Requisites, which heighten the *Refemblance*, and because RESEM-
BLANCE is fo univerfally an ESSENTIAL to IMITATION.

IF this Doctrine want confirming, we may prove it *by the contrary*,
I mean by a fuppofition of SUCH *Time* and SUCH *Place*, as are both
of them *improbable*.

FOR example, as to TIME, we may fuppofe a Play, where Lady
Defmond in *the first Act* shall dance at the Court of *Richard the
Third*, and be alive *in the last Act* during the reign of *James the
First* †.

As to PLACE, we may fuppofe a Tragedy, where *Motefuma* shall
appear at *Mexico* in *the first Act*; shall be carried to *Madrid* in *the
third*; and be brought back again *in the fifth*, to die at *Mexico*.

'TIS

---

* What this implies, we are told in the following paffage—ὅτι μάλιστα πειρᾶται ὑπὸ μίαν
περίοδον ἡλίου εἶναι, ἢ μικρὸν ἐξαλλάττειν. *Tragedy aims as far as poffible to come within a fingle
Revolution of the Sun* (that is, A NATURAL DAY) *or but a little to exceed.* Arift. Poet.
c. 5. p. 229. Edit. Sylb.

† *Ariftotle* fpeaking upon the *indefinite duration* of the *Epopee*, which is fometimes
extended to *years*, adds—κατὰ τὸ πρῶτον καὶ ἐν ταῖς τραγῳδίαις τοῦτο ἐποίουν.—*at first* THEY
DID THE SAME IN TRAGEDIES, *that is, their duration, like that of the Epopee, was
alike undefined, till a better tafte made them more correct.* Arift. Poet. c. 5. p. 229.
Edit. Sylb.

3 F 2

'Tis true indeed, did such Plays exist, and were *their other Dramatic Requisites good*; these *Improbabilities* might be endured, and the Plays be *still* admired. *Fine Manners* and *Sentiment*, we have already said *, may support a wretched *Fable*, as a beautiful Face may make us forget a bad Figure. But *no Authority* for that reason can justify Absurdities, or make them *not to be so*, by being fortunately associated.

Nor is it enough to say, that *by this apparent Austerity many a good Play would have been spoilt* †. The Answer is obvious—*chuse another, and a fitter Subject*. Subjects are *infinite*. Consult the inexhaustible Treasures of HISTORY; or if these fail, the more Inexhaustible Fund of INVENTION ‡. Nay more—if you are distrest, bring *History* and *Invention* TOGETHER, and let the Richness of the *last* embellish the Poverty of the *former*. *Poets*, tho' bound by the Laws of *Common Sense*, are not bound to the Rigours of *Historical Fact*.

It must be confest, 'tis a flattering Doctrine, to tell a young Beginner, *that he has nothing more to do, than to trust his own* GENIUS, *and to condemn all* RULES, *as the Tyranny of Pedants*. The painful
Toils

---

* See p. 398. in the Note.

† *Aristotle*, speaking about introducing any thing irrational into the Drama, adds— ὅτι δὲ λόγον, ὅτι ἀπόλοιτο ἂν ὁ Μύθος, γελοῖον· ἐξ ἀρχῆς γὰρ ὁ δεῖ συνίστασθαι τοιούτους—*that is to say (by this restriction) the Fable would have been destroyed, is ridiculous; for they ought not, from the very beginning, to form Fables upon such a Plan.* Arist. Poet. c. 24. p. 253. Edit. Sylb.

‡ Sup. p. 399. 400.

Toils of *Accuracy* by this expedient are eluded, for GENIUSES (like Ch. XII. *Milton's Harps**) are fuppofed to be *ever tuned*.

BUT the misfortune is, that Genius is fomething rare, nor can he, who poffeffes it, even then, *by neglecting Rules*, produce what is accurate. Thofe on the contrary, who, tho' they *want Genius*, think *Rules* worthy their attention, if they cannot become good *Authors*, may ftill make tolerable *Critics*; may be able to fhew the difference between the Creeping and the Simple; the Pert and the Pleafing; the Turgid and the Sublime; in fhort, to fharpen, like the Whetftone, that Genius in others, which Nature in her frugality has not given to themfelves.

INDEED I have never known, during a life of many years, and fome finall attention paid to Letters, and Literary men, that GENIUS *in any Art had been ever crampt by* RULES. On the contrary, I have feen *great Geniufes* miferably err by *transgreffing* them, and, like vigorous Travellers, who lofe their way, only wander the wider on account of their own ftrength.

AND yet 'tis fomewhat fingular in *Literary Compofitions*, and perhaps *more fo in* '*Poetry* than elfewhere, that many things have been done *in the beft and pureft tafte, long before* RULES *were efta-blifhed, and fyftematized in form*. This we are certain was true with refpect to HOMER, SOPHOCLES, EURIPIDES, and other GREEKS. In *modern* times it appears as true of our admired SHAKSPEARE;
for

---

* *Par. Loft*, Book III. v. 365, 366.

 for who can believe that *Shakspeare* ſtudied Rules, or was ever verſed in *Critical Syſtems?*

A *ſpecious* Objection then occurs. " *If theſe great Writers were* " *ſo excellent* before *Rules* were eſtabliſhed, or at leaſt were known " to them, *what had they to direct their Genius, when* RULES *(to them* " *at leaſt)* DID NOT EXIST?"

To this Queſtion 'tis hoped the Anſwer will not be deemed too hardy, ſhould we aſſert, that THERE NEVER WAS A TIME, WHEN RULES DID NOT EXIST; that they *always* made *a Part* of that IMMUTABLE TRUTH, the natural object of every *penetrating Genius;* and that, if at that *early Greek Period,* Syſtems of *Rules* were not eſtabliſhed, THOSE GREAT and SUBLIME AUTHORS WERE A RULE TO THEMSELVES.. They may be ſaid indeed to have excelled, not by *Art,* but by NATURE; yet by a *Nature,* which gave birth to the perfection of ART.

THE Caſe is nearly the ſame with reſpect to our SHAKSPEARE. There is hardly any thing we applaud, among his *innumerable beau-* *ties, which will not be found ſtrictly conformable to the* RULES *of ſound* *and ancient Criticiſm.*

THAT this is true with reſpect to his CHARACTERS and his SEN-TIMENT, is evident hence, that, in explaining *theſe Rules,* we have ſo often recurred to him for Illuſtrations *.

BESIDES

---

* See before, p. 310. 336. 341. 365. 370. 374. 384. 389. 390.

Besides Quotations *already alledged*, we subjoin the following as to Character. Ch. XII.

When Falstaff and *his suite* are so *ignominiously routed*, and the scuffle is by *Falstaff* so *humorously exaggerated*; what can be more natural than *such a Narrative* to *such a Character*, distinguished for his Humour, and withal for his want of Veracity and Courage*?

The Sagacity of *common Poets* might not perhaps have suggested so good a Narrative, but it certainly would have suggested something of the kind, and 'tis in this we view the *Essence of Dramatic Character*, *which is, when we conjecture what any one* will *do or say, from what he* has *done or said* already†.

If we pass from Characters (that is to say Manners) to Sentiment, we have already given Instances‡, and yet we shall still give another.

When *Rosincrosse* and *Guilderstern* wait upon *Hamlet*, he offers them a Recorder or Pipe, and desires them *to play*—they reply, *they cannot*—He repeats his Request—they answer, *they have never learnt*—He assures them nothing was so easy—they *still* decline.— 'Tis *then* he tells them with disdain, *There is much Music in this little Organ, and yet you cannot make it speak*—*Do you think I am easier to be plaid on, than a Pipe?* Hamlet, Act III.

This

---

* See Hen. IV. Part 2d.   † See before, p. 373, &c.

‡ See before, p. 377, &c.

Part II.   This I call an elegant Sample of SENTIMENT, taken under its
*comprehensive Sense**. But we stop not here—We consider it as a
complete instance of SOCRATIC REASONING, tho' 'tis probable *the
Author* knew nothing, how SOCRATES used *to argue.*

To explain—XENOPHON makes SOCRATES reason as follows with
an ambitious youth, by name *Euthydemus.*

'Tis strange (says he) that those who desire to play upon the Harp,
" *or upon the Flute, or to ride the managed Horse, should not think*
" *themselves worth notice, without having practised under the best Maf-*
" *ters—while there are those, who aspire to the governing of a* STATE,
" *and can think themselves completely qualified, tho' it be without prepa-*
" *ration or labour.*" Xenoph. Mem. IV. c. 2. f. 6.

ARISTOTLE's Illustration is similar in his reasoning against *Men,*
CHOSEN BY LOT *for Magistrates.* *'Tis* (says he) *as if Wrestlers were
to be appointed* BY LOT, *and not those* THAT ARE ABLE *to wrestle : or,
as if from among Sailors we were to chuse a Pilot* BY LOT, *and that
the Man so* ELECTED *were to navigate, and not the Man* WHO KNEW
the business. Rhetor. L. II. c. 20. p. 94. *Edit. Sylb.*

NOTHING can be more ingenious than this *Mode of Reasoning.*
The Premises are *obvious* and *undeniable;* the Conclusion *cogent* and
yet *unexpected.* It is a species of that Argumentation, called in Dia-
lectic Ἐπαγωγή, or INDUCTION.

ARISTOTLE

ARISTOTLE in his *Rhetoric* (as above quoted) calls such Reasonings τὰ Σωκρατικὰ, THE SOCRATICS; in the beginning of his *Poetics*, he calls them the Σωκρατικοὶ λόγοι, THE SOCRATIC DISCOURSES; and HORACE, in his Art of *Poetry*, calls them the SOCRATICÆ CHARTÆ *.

IF TRUTH *be always the same*, no wonder *Geniuses should co-incide*, and that too in *Philosophy* as well as in *Criticism*.

WE venture to add, returning *to* RULES, that if there be any things in *Shakspeare* OBJECTIONABLE (and who is hardy enough to deny it?) THE VERY OBJECTIONS, as well as THE BEAUTIES, *are to be tried* BY THE SAME RULES, as the same Plummet alike shews, both what is *out of* the Perpendicular, and *in* it; the same Ruler alike proves, both what is *crooked*, and what is *strait*.

WE cannot admit, that *Geniuses*, tho' *prior to Systems*, were *prior also to* Rules, because RULES from the beginning *existed in their own Minds*, and were a part of that *immutable Truth*, which is eternal and every where †. *Aristotle* we know did not form *Homer, Sophocles,*

and

---

* See a most admirable instance of this INDUCTION, quoted by CICERO from THE SOCRATIC ÆSCHINES. *Cic. de Invent.* Lib. I. C. 51.

† The Author thinks it superfluous, *to panegyrize* TRUTH; yet in favour of SOUND AND RATIONAL RULES (which must be *founded in Truth*, or they are good for nothing) he ventures to quote the *Stagirite* himself. Ἀλλὰ μὴν οὐδὲ οὐκ ἐνδέχεται ἐναντίαν εἶναι ἔτι δόξαν, ἐπ' ἀληθινῶν—*It is not possible for* A TRUE OPINION, *or* A TRUE CONTRADICTORY PROPOSITION *to be* CONTRARY TO ANOTHER TRUE ONE. *Aristot De Interpret.* c. 19. p. 78. *Edit. Sylb.*

Th'a

 and *Euripides*; 'twas *Homer*, *Sophocles*, and *Euripides*, that formed *Aristotle*.

AND this surely should teach us to pay attention to RULES, in as much as THEY and GENIUS are so *reciprocally* connected, that 'tis GENIUS, which discovers *Rules*; and then RULES, which govern *Genius*.

'TIS by this *amicable concurrence*, and by *this alone*, that every Work of Art justly merits Admiration, and is rendered as highly perfect, as by human Power it can be made*.

BUT we have now (if such language may be allowed) travelled over a vast and mighty Plain; or (as *Virgil* better expresses it)—
—*immensum spatio confecimus æquor.*

'TIS not however improbable that some intrepid spirit may demand again†, *What avail these subtleties?*—*Without so much trouble, I can be full enough pleased.*—I KNOW WHAT I LIKE.—We answer, *And so does the Carrion-crow, that feeds upon a Carcase.* The difficulty

---

This may be thus illustrated. *If it be* TRUE, *that* THE TIME *and* PLACE *of every Drama should be circumscribed,* THE CONTRARY CANNOT BE TRUE, *that its Time and Place need not to be circumscribed.* See p. 351.

* This is fairly stated, and decided by *Horace.*
         Natura fieret laudabile carmen, an Arte,
         Quæsitum est. Ego nec studium sine divite venâ,
         Nec rude quid prosit video ingenium; alterius sic
         Altera poscit opem res, et conjurat amicè. Art. Poet. v. 408, &c.

† See p. 341.

culty lies not in knowing WHAT *we like;* but in knowing HOW *to* Ch. XII.
like, and WHAT IS WORTH LIKING. Till thefe Ends are obtained,
we may admire *Durfey* before *Milton;* a fmoaking Boor of *Hem-
fkirk,* before an Apoftle of *Raphael.*

Now as to the knowing, HOW TO LIKE, and then WHAT IS WORTH
LIKING, the firft of thefe, being the Object of *Critical* Difquifition,
has been attempted to be fhewn thro' the courfe of *thefe Inquiries.*

As to the fecond, WHAT IS WORTH OUR LIKING, this is beft
known by ftudying *the beft* Authors, beginning from the GREEKS;
then paffing to the LATINS; nor on any account excluding thofe,
who have excelled among the MODERNS.

AND here, if, while we perufe fome Author of high rank, we perceive we don't inftantly relifh him, let us not be difheartened — let us
even FEIGN a *Relifh, till we find a Relifh come.* A *morfel* perhaps
pleafes us — Let us cherifh it — *Another Morfel,* ftrikes us — let us
cherifh this alfo. — Let us thus proceed, and fteadily perfevere, till
we find we can relifh, *not Morfels,* but *Wholes;* and feel that, what
began *in* FICTION, terminates *in* REALITY. The Film being in this
manner removed, we fhall difcover *Beauties,* which we never imagined; and contemn for *Puerilities,* what we once *foolifhly* admired.

ONE thing however in this procefs is indifpenfibly required: we
are *on no account* to expect that FINE THINGS SHOULD DESCEND
TO US; OUR TASTE, if poffible, MUST BE MADE ASCEND TO THEM.

                    THIS

 This is the Labour, this the Work; there is *Pleasure* in the Success, and *Praise* even in the Attempt.

This Speculation applies not to Literature only; it applies to Music, to Painting, and, as they are all *congenial*, to all the *liberal* Arts. We should in each of them endeavour to investigate WHAT IS BEST, and there (if I may so express myself) *there* to fix our abode.

By only seeking and perusing what is *truly* excellent, and by contemplating always *this* and *this alone*, the Mind insensibly becomes *accustomed* to it, and finds that *in this alone* it can acquiesce with content. It happens indeed *here*, as in a subject far more important, I mean in a *moral* and a *virtuous* Conduct. IF WE CHUSE THE BEST LIFE, USE WILL MAKE IT PLEASANT*.

And thus having gone thro' the Sketch we promised, (for our concise manner cannot be called any thing more) we here finish THE SECOND PART of these Inquiries, and, according to our original Plan, proceed to THE THIRD PART, THE TASTE AND LITERATURE OF THE MIDDLE AGE.

---

* Ἑλοῦ βίον ἄριστον, ἡδὺν δὲ αὐτὸν ἡ συνήθεια ποιήσει. *Plutarch. Moral.* p. 602. *Edit. Wolfii.*

END OF THE SECOND PART.

PHILOLOGICAL

INQUIRIES.

PART THE THIRD.

PHILOLOGICAL INQUIRIES.

PART THE THIRD.

CHAPTER I.

Design of the whole—Limits and Extent of THE MIDDLE AGE—THREE CLASSES *of* MEN, *during that interval, conspicuous;* THE BYZANTINE GREEKS; THE SARACENS *or* ARABIANS; *and the* LATINS *or* FRANKS, *Inhabitants of Western Europe—Each Class in the following Chapters considered apart.*

WHEN THE MAGNITUDE OF THE ROMAN EMPIRE grew *enormous,* and there were *two* Imperial Cities, ROME and CONSTANTINOPLE, then that happened, which was natural; out of *one Empire* it became *two,* distinguished by the different names of the WESTERN, and the EASTERN.

THE

Part III. THE WESTERN EMPIRE foon funk. So early as in the *fifth* Century*, ROME, once the Miftrefs of Nations, beheld herfelf at the feet of a *Gothic* Sovereign. THE EASTERN EMPIRE lafted many Centuries longer, and, tho' often impaired by *external* Enemies, and weakened as often by *internal* Factions, yet ftill it retained traces of its *ancient* Splendor, refembling in the language of *Virgil* fome fair, but faded flower,

Cui neque fulgor adhuc, necdum fua forma receffit.   VIRG.

AT length, after various plunges and various efcapes, it was totally annihilated in the *fifteenth* Century by the victorious arms of *Mahomet the Great*†.

THE INTERVAL BETWEEN THE FALL OF THESE TWO EMPIRES (the *Weftern* or *Latin* in the *fifth* Century, the *Eaftern* or *Grecian*

in

---

* About the year of Chrift 475, *Auguftulus* was compelled to abdicate the *Weftern Empire* by *Odoacer*, King of the *Heruli*. As *Auguftulus* was the laft *Roman*, who poffeft the Imperial Dignity at *Rome*, and as the Dominion both of *Rome* and *Italy* foon after paft into the hands of *Theodoric the Goth*, it has been juftly faid, that *then* terminated *the Roman Empire in the Weft*.

During thefe wretched times, ROME had been facked not long before by *Alaric*, as it was a fecond time (about the middle of the fixth Century) by *Totila*; after which events the *Roman* Name and Authority were fo far funk, that early in the feventh Century they ceafed *to fpeak Latin*, even in *Rome* itfelf. See Blair's Chronology.

† See the various Hiftories of the *Turkifh* Empire. *The unfortunate Greeks, at this period, when, to refift fuch an Enemy as the Turks, they fhould have been firmly combined, were never fo miferably diftracted. An union with the Church of Rome* was at the time projected. The *Greeks*, who favoured it, imputed their Calamities to their *Not-uniting*; thofe, who oppofed it, to their *Uniting*. Between the two Factions all was loft, and *Conftantinople* taken in the year 1453.

in the *fifteenth*) making a space of near a thousand years, *constitutes* what we call THE MIDDLE AGE.

DOMINION past during this interval into the hands of rude, illiterate men; men, who conquered more by *multitude*, than by *military skill*; and who, having little or no taste either for Sciences or Arts, naturally despised those things, from which they had reaped no advantage.

THIS was the age of Monkery and Legends; of *Leonine Verses* [*], (that is of *bad Latin put into rhime*;) of *Projects to decide Truth* by Plough-shares and Battoons [†]; of *Crusades* to conquer Infidels, and

extirpate

---

[*] See below, Chap. XI.

[†] This alludes to the two methods of TRIAL, much practised in those dark times, the Trial by ORDEAL, and that by DUEL.

Heated Plough-shares were often employed in Trials by ORDEAL, and 'tis remarkable that express mention is made of this absurd method of *Purgation by Fire*, even in the *Antigone of Sophocles.* The Messenger there says, in order to justify himself and his Companions—

> Ἥμεν δ᾽ ἕτοιμοι καὶ μύδρας αἴρειν χεροῖν,
> Καὶ πῦρ διέρπειν, καὶ θεοὺς ὁρκωμοτεῖν,
> Τὸ μήτε δρᾶσαι, μήτε, κ. τ. λ.

> *Ready we were with both our hands* TO LIFT
> THE GLOWING MASS; *or slowly* CROSS THE FIRE,
> *And by the Gods to swear, we neither did*
> *The Deed, nor knew, &c.*   Antig. v. 270.

This carries up the Practice to the time of *Eteocles* and *Polynices*, before the *Trojan War.*

Perhaps the Poet, by the incidental mention of so strange a Custom, intended to characterise the manners of a *ruder* age; an age, widely different from *his own*, which was an Age of Science and Philosophical Disquisition.

Part III. extirpate Heretics; of Princes *depofed*, not as *Crœfus* was by *Cyrus*,
but

As to *Trials by* BATTLE, they were either before *the Earl Marſhal*, or *the Judges of Weſtminſter Hall*. If before the Earl Marſhal, they were upon accuſations of Treaſon or other capital Crimes, and the Parties were uſually of high and noble rank. If before the Judges of Weſtminſter Hall, the Cauſe was often of inferior ſort, as well as the Parties litigating.

Hence the Combats differed in their Ends. That before the Earl Marſhal was *Victory*, often attended with *ſlaughter*; that before the Judges was *Victory alone*, with no ſuch conſequence.

The Weapons too differed, as well as the Ends. The Weapons before *the Earl Marſhal* were a long Sword, a ſhort Sword, and a Dagger: that before *the Judges* was a *Battoon* above mentioned, called in barbarous Latin *Druncus*, but in words more intelligible *Fuſtis tres*.

So late as the reign of *Queen Elizabeth* an inſtance occurs of this Trial being inſiſted upon. But that wiſe Princeſs, tho' ſhe permitted the previous forms, I mean that of the Liſts being incloſed, of the Judges taking their ſeats there, of the Champions making their appearance, &c. (*Forms*, which perhaps could not *legally* be prevented) had too much ſenſe to permit ſo fooliſh a deciſion. She compelled the Parties to a compromiſe, by the Plaintiff's taking an equivalent in money for his claim, and making in conſequence a voluntary default.

Wyvil, Biſhop of Saliſbury, in the reign of *Edward the Third*, recurred to *Trial by* BATTLE in a diſpute with the Earl of Saliſbury, and ordered public Prayers thro' his Dioceſe for the ſucceſs of his Champion, till the matter, by the King's authority, was compromiſed.

But notwithſtanding this Biſhop's Conduct, 'twas A PRACTICE which THE CHURCH *diſapproved*, and wiſely, as well as humanely endeavoured to prevent. TRUCULENTUM MOREM *in omni ævo acriter inſectarunt* THEOLOGI, *præ aliis Agobardus, et plurimo Canone* IPSA ECCLESIA. See *Spelman*, under the words *Campus, Campſtus*, and *Campio*.

I muſt not omit that there is a complete Hiſtory of ſuch a *Duel*, recorded by *Walſingham*, in the reign of *Richard the Second*, between *Aneſtee* a Knight, and *Karryngton* an Eſquire. *Karryngton* was accuſed by the other of Treaſon, for ſelling a Caſtle to the *French*, and, being defeated in the Combat, died the next day raving mad. *Walſingham's* Narrative is curious and exact, but their Weapons differed from thoſe above mentioned, for they firſt fought with *Lances*, then with *Swords*, and laſtly with *Daggers*, *Walſing. Hiſtor.* p. 637.

but by one, who had no Armies, and who did not even wear a sword *.

DIFFERENT Portions of this *Age* have been distinguished by different descriptions; such as *Sæculum Monotheleticum, Sæculum Eiconoclasticum, Sæculum Obscurum, Sæculum Ferreum, Sæculum Hildibrandinum,* &c. strange names it must be confest, some more obvious, others less so, yet none tending to furnish us with any high, or promising Ideas †.

AND yet we must acknowledge for the honour of *Humanity,* and of its GREAT and DIVINE AUTHOR, who *never forsakes it,* that some sparks of *Intellect* were *at all times* visible, thro' the whole of this dark and dreary Period. 'Tis *here* we must look for the TASTE and LITERATURE OF THE TIMES.

THE few, who were *enlightened,* when Arts and Sciences were thus *obscured,* may be said to have *happily maintained the Continuity*

of

---

* Such was Pope *Innocent the third,* who, besides his Crusades to extirpate Heretics by Armies *not his own,* excommunicated *Philip,* King of France; *Alphonso,* King of Leon; *Raimond,* Earl of Toulouse; and *John,* King of England.

Nor is this wonderful, when we view *in his own Language* the Opinion he had of his own Station and Authority.

I am placed (says he) IN THE MIDDLE, *between* GOD *and* MAN, ON THIS SIDE *God, but* BEYOND *Man; nay I am greater than* MAN, *as I can judge of all Men, but can be judged by no one. Sum enim inter* DEUM *et* HOMINEM MEDIUS *constitutus, ultra Deum sed ultra Hominem; imò major Homine, qui de omnibus judicem, a nemine vero judicari possim.* Innocen. III. *Serm.* 2. *in Historiâ Transubstantiationis Joannis Cosin.* Episcop. Dunelm. Lond. 1675. See also *all the Church Histories of this Period.*

† Those, who would be farther informed concerning these *Sæcula,* may, among other authors, consult two very learned ones, CAVE in his *Historia Literaria,* and MOSHEIM in his *Ecclesiastical History.*

3 II 2

Part III. *of Knowledge;* to have been (if I may use the expression) like the *Twilight* of a Summer's Night; that auspicious Gleam between the setting and the rising Sun, which, tho' it cannot retain the Lustre of the Day, helps at least to save us from the *Totality* of Darkness.

A cursory Disquisition, illustrated by a few select Instances, will constitute the Subject of the present Essay; and these Instances we shall bring from among THREE CLASSES OF MEN, who had each a large share in the transactions of those times; from THE BYZANTINE GREEKS, from THE ARABIANS or SARACENS, and from *the Inhabitants of Western Europe,* at that time called THE LATINS. We shall give Precedence, as we think they merit it, to the GREEKS OF CONSTANTINOPLE, altho' it is not always easy to preserve an *exact* Chronology, because in each of these three Classes many eminent men were contemporary.

CHAP. II.

Concerning the first Class, THE BYZANTINE GREEKS—SIMPLICIUS —AMMONIUS—PHILOPONUS,—*Fate of the fine Library at Alexandria.*

SIMPLICIUS and AMMONIUS were *Greek* Authors, who flourished at ATHENS during the sixth Century; for *Athens,* long after her Trophies at *Marathon,* long after her *political Sovereignty* was no more, still maintained her Empire in *Philosophy* and the *fine Arts* *.

Philosophy indeed, when these Authors wrote, was sinking apace. The *Stoic System,* and even the *Stoic Writings* were the greater part of them lost †. Other Sects had shared the same fate. None subsisted but *the Platonic,* and *the Peripatetic;* which, being both derived from a common source (that is to say, *the Pythagorean)* were at this period *blended,* and commonly cultivated by the *same* Persons.

SIMPLICIUS and AMMONIUS, being bred in this School, and well initiated in its Principles, found no reason, from their education, to make Systems *for themselves;* a practice, referable *sometimes* to real Genius, but *more often* to not knowing, *what others have invented before.*

CONSCIOUS

---

* See below, Chap. III. † See Vol. I. p. 144.

Part III.   CONSCIOUS therefore they could not excel their great Predeceffors,
they thought, like many others, that the *Commenting* of their Works
was doing mankind the moft effential Service.

'TWAS this, which gave rife, long before *their* time, to that Tribe
of COMMENTATORS, who, in the perfon of *Andronicus the Rhodian*,
began under *Auguftus*, and who continued, for ages after, in an
orderly fucceffion.

SIMPLICIUS wrote a variety of Comments upon different parts
of *Ariftotle*, but his *Comment upon the Phyfics* is peculiarly valuable,
as it is filled with quotations from *Anaxagoras, Democritus, Parme-
nides*, and *other* Philofophers, who flourifhed fo early, as before the
time of *Ariftotle*, and whofe fragments many of them are not to be
found elfewhere.

As this *Compilation* muft have been the refult of *extenfive Reading*,
we may juftly diftinguifh him by the title of a *learned* Commentator *.

AMMONIUS wrote *Comments* on the firft and fecond Tracts of *Ariftotle's Logic*, as likewife upon the *Introductory Difcourfe* of the Philofopher *Porphyry*. His *manner* of writing is orderly; his ftile *clear*
and *copious*; copious in its better fenfe, by leaving nothing unex-
plained, not copious by perplexing us with tirefome Tautology.

To

---

* For a fuller and more accurate account of SIMPLICIUS, fee *Fabricii Biblioth. Grae.*
Tom. VIII. p. 620, &c.

To thofe, who wifh for a tafte of this Literature, I know no Author, who better merits perufal. The Preface to his *Comment on Porphyry* is a curious account of *Philofophy* under its many and different *Definitions*, every one of which he explains with perfpicuity, and precifion. The Preface to his *Comment on the Predicaments* gives us an ingenious *Plan of Critical Scrutiny;* in other words furnifhes us with *a fuite of leading Queries*, by which, before we read a Book, we may learn *what it is*, and judge, when analyzed, if it be a *legitimate* Compofition *.

When things change by uninterrupted *Continuity*, as (to ufe an idea already fuggefted) the fplendor of the Day to the darknefs of the Night, 'tis hard to decide precifely, where the one concludes, and the other commences. By parity of reafoning 'tis difficult to determine, *to what age* we fhall *adjudge* the two Philofophers juft mentioned; whether to the Commencement of a *bafer* age, or rather (if we regard their merit) to the Conclufion of a *purer*. If we arrange them with the Conclufion, 'tis, as *Brutus* and *Caffius* were called *the laft of the Romans* †.

We can have lefs doubt about the difciple of *Ammonius*, John the Grammarian, called Philoponus from his love of labour. 'Twas his misfortune to live during the time of *Mahomet*, and to fee *Alexandria* taken by the Arms of one of his immediate Succeffors. What paft there on this occafion with regard to *the Library*, tho' recorded

---

* See *Fabr. Biblioth. Græc.* T. IV. p. 161.

† See *Tacit. Annal.* IV. 34.

Part III. corded in modern Books, is too curious to be omitted here. I tranflate it from the accurate version of *Abulpharagius's History,* made by
that able Orientalift, *Pococke.*

" When *Alexandria* was taken by the *Mahometans,* Amrus, their
" Commander, found there Philoponus, whofe converfation highly
" pleafed him, as *Amrus* was a lover of Letters, and *Philoponus* a
" learned Man.   On a certain day *Philoponus* faid to him : *You have
" vifited all the Repofitories or Public Warehoufes in Alexandria, and
" you have fealed up things of every fort, that are found there. As to
" thofe things, that may be ufeful to you, I prefume to fay nothing ; but
" as to things of no fervice to You, fome of them perhaps may be more
" fuitable to* Me. *Amrus* faid to him : *And what is it you want ?*
" *The Philofophical Books* (replied he) *preferved in the Royal Libra-
" ries. This,* fays Amrus, *is a requeft, upon which I cannot decide :
" You defire a thing, where I can iffue no orders, till I have leave from
" Omar, the Commander of the Faithful.* Letters were accordingly
" written to *Omar,* informing him of what *Philoponus* had faid, and
" an Anfwer was returned by Omar to the following purport. —
" *As to the Books, of which you have made mention, if there be contained
" in them, what accords with the Book of God* (meaning the Alco-
" ran) *there is without them, in the Book of God, all that is fufficient.
" But if there be any thing in them repugnant to that Book, we in no
" refpect want them. Order them therefore to be all deftroyed.* Am-
" rus upon this ordered them to be difperfed thro' the Baths of *Alex-
" andria,* and to be there burnt in making the Baths warm. After
" this manner, in the fpace of fix months, they were all confumed."

THE

Ch. II.

The Historian, having related the Story, adds from his own feelings, HEAR WHAT WAS DONE, AND WONDER*.

Thus ended this noble Library; and thus began, if it did not begin sooner, *the Age of Barbarity and Ignorance.*

---

* Vid. *Abulpharagii Dynastiar.* p. 114. *Oxon.* 1663.

THE Reader will *here* observe, that in the many Quotations, which we shall hereafter make from *Abulpharagius,* we shall *always* quote from the same Edition; that is, from the *Latin Version* of the learned *Pocock,* subjoined to the *original Arabic.*

C H A P. III.

Digreſſion to a ſhort Hiſtorical Account of ATHENS, *from the time of her Perſian Triumphs, to that of her becoming ſubject to the Turks — Sketch, during this long interval, of her Political and Literary State; of her Philoſophers; of her Gymnaſia; of her good and bad Fortune, &c. &c. — Manners of the preſent Inhabitants — Olives and Honey.*

Part III.   HAVING mentioned ATHENS, I hope that celebrated City will juſtify a Digreſſion, and the more ſo, as that Digreſſion will terminate in Events, which belong to *the very Age,* of which we are now writing. But 'tis expedient to deduce matters from a much earlier period,

WHEN the *Athenians* had delivered themſelves from the tyranny of PISISTRATUS, and after this had defeated the vaſt Efforts of the *Perſians,* and that againſt two ſucceſſive Invaders, DARIUS and XERXES, they may be conſidered as at the ſummit of their *national* Glory. For more than half a century afterwards they maintained, without controul, *the Sovereignty of Greece* *,

As their *Taſte* was naturally good, *Arts* of every kind ſoon roſe among them, and flouriſhed. Valour had given them Reputation; Reputation

* For theſe *Hiſtorical Facts* conſult the *ancient* and *modern Authors* of *Grecian Hiſtory.*

Reputation gave them an Afcendant; and that Afcendant produced a Security, which left their minds at eafe, and gave them leifure to cultivate every thing liberal, or elegant *.

'TWAS then that PERICLES adorned the City with Temples, Theatres, and other beautiful public Buildings. PHIDIAS, the great Sculptor, was employed as his Architect, who, when he had erected Edifices, adorned them himfelf, and added *Statues* and Baffo-relievo's, the admiration of every beholder †. 'Twas then that POLYGNOTUS and MYRO painted; that SOPHOCLES and EURI‑ PIDES wrote; and not long after, that they faw *the divine* SO‑ CRATES.

HUMAN affairs are by nature prone to change, and ftates as well as individuals are born to decay. Jealoufy and Ambition infen‑ fibly fomented wars, and Succefs in thefe wars, as in others, was often various. The *military* ftrength of the ATHENIANS was firft impaired by the LACEDÆMONIANS; after that, it was again humi‑ liated,

---

* 'Twas in a fimilar period of *Triumph*, after a formidable Adverfary had been crufhed, that *the Romans* began to cultivate a more refined and polifhed Literature.

——*poſt Punica bella* QUIETUS, *quærere cœpit*,
Quid Sophocles, et Thefpis, et Æfchylus utile ferrent.

Horat. Ep. II. L. II. v. 162.

See the Note from a Greek MS. in my Firft Volume, p. 195, where the Progrefs of Arts and Sciences, from their Dawn to their Meridian, is elegantly and philofophically exhibited.

† See *Plutarch's* Life of *Pericles*, p. 350, 351, 352, 353, 354. in the Quarto Greek Edition of *Bryan*, Vol. I. and *Stuart's Antiquities of Athens.*

Part III. liated, under Epaminondas, by the *Thebans;* and laſt of all it was wholly cruſhed by *the Macedonian,* Philip *.

But tho' their *political* Sovereignty was loſt, yet, happily for Mankind, their *Love* of Literature and Arts did not ſink along with it.

Just at the cloſe of their *Golden Days of Empire* flouriſhed Xenophon and Plato, the diſciples of Socrates, and from *Plato* deſcended that Race of Philoſophers, called *the old Academy* †.

Aristotle, who was *Plato's* diſciple, may be ſaid, not to have invented *a new* Philoſophy, but rather to have tempered the ſublime, and rapturous myſteries of his maſter with Method, *Order,* and a ſtricter Mode of reaſoning ‡.

Zeno, who was himſelf alſo educated in the principles of *Platoniſm,* only differed from *Plato* in the *comparative* Eſtimate of things, allowing nothing to be *intrinſically good but* Virtue, nothing *intrinſically bad but* Vice, and conſidering all other things to be *in themſelves indifferent* §.

He

---

* See, as before, the ſeveral Hiſtories of *Greece.*

† See *Cic. de Fin.* L. V. and *Academ.* L. I. ſ. 5. p. 21.   *Edit. Daviſii.*

‡ See *Hermes,* p. 440.

§ See *Cicer. de Fin.* L. III. ſ. 7. 8. 16.—the beginning of the *Enchiridion of Epictetus,* Τῶν ὄντων τὰ μὲν ἐφ' ἡμῖν, κ. τ. λ.   *Diogen. Laert. in vitâ Zenon.* L. VII. ſ. 102.

He too and *Ariſtotle* accurately cultivated *Logic*, but in *different* ways; for *Ariſtotle* chiefly dwelt upon the *ſimple* Syllogiſm; *Zeno* upon that which is derived out of it, the *Compound* or *Hypothetic*. Both too, as well as other *Philoſophers*, cultivated *Rhetoric* along with *Logic*; holding a knowledge in *both* to be requiſite for thoſe, who think of addreſſing mankind with all the efficacy of *Perſuaſion*. ZENO elegantly illuſtrated the force of theſe *two* powers by a Simile, taken from the Hand: the *cloſe* power of *Logic* he compared to the *Fiſt*, or *Hand compreſſ*; the *diffuſe* power of *Rhetoric*, to the *Palm*, or *Hand open* *.

I ſhall mention but *two* Sects more, *the New Academy*, and *the Epicurean*.

THE *New Academy*, ſo called from *the Old Academy*, (the name given to the School of *Plato*) was founded by ARCESILAS, and ably maintained by CARNEADES. From a miſtaken imitation of the great parent of *Philoſophy*, *Socrates*, (particularly as he appears

in

---

* ZENO quidem ille, a quo diſciplina Stoicorum eſt, MANU demonſtrare ſolebat, quid inter has artes [Dialecticam ſcil. et Eloquentiam] intereſſet. Nam, cum compreſſerat digitos, PUGNUMque fecerat, DIALECTICAM aiebat ejuſmodi eſſe; cum autem diduxerat, et manum dilataverat, PALMÆ illius ſimilem ELOQUENTIAM eſſe dicebat. *Cicer. Orator.* ſ. 113.

Both *Peripatetics* and *Stoics* wrote Tracts of *Rhetoric* as well as *Logic*. The RHE-TORIC of *Ariſtotle* is perhaps one of the moſt valuable Remains of Antiquity, and deſervedly worth ſtudying, be it for *Speculation* or *Practice*.

As for the Rhetoric of the *Stoics*, there is extant, among the *Latin* Rhetoricians, publiſhed in a thin *Quarto* by *Plantin* at *Paris*, an. 1599, a Tract by *Sulpitius Victor*, called *Inſtitutiones Oratoriæ*, wherein he has this Expreſſion at the beginning—ZENONIS pracepta maximè perſecutus. See p. 240—alſo p. 247, 264, of the ſaid Treatiſe.

Part III. in the Dialogues of *Plato)* because *Socrates* doubted *some* things, therefore *Arcesilas* and *Carneades* doubted *all* *.

EPICURUS drew from another source; DEMOCRITUS had taught him *Atoms* and *a Void:* by the *fortuitous concourse of Atoms* he fancied he could *form a World,* while by a *feigned* Veneration he complimented away his GODS, and totally denied their *Providential Care,* left the *Trouble* of it should impair their *uninterrupted* State of Bliss. VIRTUE he recommended, tho' *not* for the sake of *Virtue,* but *Pleasure;* PLEASURE, according to him, being *our chief* and *sovereign Good.* It must be confest however, that, tho' his Principles were *erroneous* and even *bad,* never was a Man more *temperate* and *humane;* never was a Man more beloved by his Friends, or more cordially attached to them in affectionate esteem †.

WE have already mentioned the alliance between *Philosophy* and *Rhetoric.* This cannot be thought wonderful, if *Rhetoric* be the Art, by which men are *persuaded,* and if *Men* cannot be persuaded, without a knowledge of *Human Nature;* for what, but PHILOSOPHY, can procure us *this knowledge?*

'TWAS for this reason the ablest *Greek Philosophers* not only taught (as we hinted before) but wrote also Treatises upon *Rhetoric.* They had

---

* Vid. Cic. Acadcm. L. I. f. 13. p. 48. Edit. Dav. *Itaque Arcesilas negabat esse quicquam,* &c,

† See *Diogen. Laert.* L. X. f. 9, &c. where an ample Detail is given of *Epicurus,* his Friends, his last Will, and his Death, all tending to establish his *Amiable Character,* however *erroneous* and *blameable* his *Doctrines.*

had a farther inducement, and that was the *intrinſic beauty of their Language*, as it was then ſpoken among the learned and polite. They would have been aſhamed to have delivered *Philoſophy*, as it has been too often delivered ſince, in Compoſitions as clumſy, as the common Dialect of the mere Vulgar.

THE ſame *Love of Elegance*, which made them attend to their STILE, made them attend even to the PLACES, where their Philoſophy was taught.

Plato delivered his Lectures in a Place ſhaded with Groves, on the Banks of the River *Iliſſus*; and which, as it once belonged to a perſon called *Academus*, was called, after his name, THE ACADEMY [*]. *Ariſtotle* choſe another ſpot of a *ſimilar* character, where there were *Trees* and *Shade*; a ſpot called THE LYCÆUM [†]. *Zeno* taught in a PORTICO or COLONADE, diſtinguiſhed from other buildings of that ſort (of which *the Athenians* had many) by the name of the VARIEGATED PORTICO, the Walls being decorated with *various Paintings* of *Polygnotus* and *Myro*, two capital Maſters of that tranſcendent Period [‡]. *Epicurus* addreſſed his hearers in thoſe well known

---

[*] Vid. *Diog. Laert. Lib.* III. ſ. 7. *Potter's Arch. Græc.* Vol. I. p. 40.

[†] See *Potter's Arch. Græc.* Vol. I. p. 40.

[‡] Of theſe two Artiſts it appears that *Myro* was *paid*, and that *Polygnotus* painted *gratis*, for which generoſity he had the teſtimony of public Honours. *Plin. N. Hiſt.* L. XXXV. cap. 9. ſect. 35.

We learn from Hiſtory that the Pictures, which adorned this *Portico*, were four; two on *the back part* of it (open to the Colonnade) and a Picture at each end, upon *the right* and *left*.

We

Part III. known *Gardens*, called after his own name, THE GARDENS OF EPICURUS.

Some of thefe *Places* gave names to the *Doctrines*, which were taught there. *Plato's* PHILOSOPHY took its name of ACADEMIC from *the Academy* †; that of *Zeno* was called THE STOIC, from a *Greek* word, fignifying *a Portico* ‡.

THE Syftem indeed of *Ariftotle* was not denominated from the Place, but was called PERIPATETIC, from the manner in which he taught; *from his walking about*, at the time, *when he dif- ferted.*

We learn alfo the Subjects; on one of the fides a Picture of the *Athenian* and *Lacedæmonian* Armies et *Oenoe* (an *Argive* City) facing each other, and ready to engage; on the back Ground, or middle part of the Portico, the Battle between the *Athenians* under *Thefeus*, and *the Amazons*: next to that, on the fame middle, the *Grecian Chiefs*, after the taking of *Troy*, deliberating upon the Violence offered by *Ajax* to *Caffandra*, *Ajax* himfelf being prefent, together with *Caffandra* and other Captive *Trojan* women: laftly, on the other fide of the Portico oppofite to the firft, the triumphant Victory at *Marathon*, the Barbarians puſhed into the Morafs, or demoliſhed, while they endeavoured to efcape to their ſhips; Miltiades and the Greek Leaders being to be known by their Portraits.

As the Portico was large, and the Pictures were only four, thefe we may fuppofe muſt have been large likewife, for 'tis probable they occupied the whole fpace. *Vid. Paufan. Attic. Lib.* 1. c. 15. p. 30. *Edit. Lipf.* 1696.

From the painting of this *Portico* to the time of *Honorius*, when it was defaced, ſtript, and its pictures deftroyed *, was an Interval of about eight hundred years.

It may merit Inquiry among the curious, *upon what fort of Surface*, and *with what fort of Colours*, Pictures were painted, *that could Indure fo long*.

† See the Note, next after the following.

‡ Στοὰ, Στωϊκοὶ.

* Synef. Epif. 135.

ferted *. The Term, Epicurean Philosophy, needs no Explanation.

Open Air, Shade, Water, and pleafant Walks feem above all things to favour that *Exercife*, the beft fuited to *Contemplation*, I mean *gentle walking without inducing fatigue*. The many agreeable Walks in and about Oxford may teach my own Countrymen the truth of this affertion, and beft explain how *Horace* lived, while a ftudent at Athens, employed (as he tells us)

—*inter* silvas Academi *quærere verum*.

These *Places of Public Inftitution* were called among the *Greeks* by the name of Gymnasia, in which, whatever that word might have originally meant, were taught all thofe *Exercifes*, and all thofe *Arts*, which tended to cultivate not only the Body, but the Mind. As *Man* was a Being confifting of *both*, the *Greeks* could not confider that Education as complete, in which *both* were not regarded, and *both* properly formed. Hence their *Gymnafia*, with reference to this *double* End, were adorned with *two Statues*, thofe of Mercury and of Hercules, the *corporeal* Accomplifhments being patronized (as they fuppofed) by *the God of Strength*, the *mental* Accomplifhments by the *God of Ingenuity* †.

'Tis

---

* *Qui erant cum Ariftotele*, Peripatetici *dicti funt, quia difputabant* inambulantes *in Lyceo; illi autem, qui Platonis inftituto in* Academia, *quod eft alterum gymnafium, cœtus erant et fermones habere foliti*, a loci vocabulo nomen *habuerunt.* Cic. Academ. L. I. c. 4. p. 21, *Edit. Davif.*

† Vid. *Athen. Deipnof.* L. XIII. p. 561. Edit. Lugduni, 1657, Fol. Sometimes the two Gods were made into *one* Statue. Such compound Statues were called Ἑρμηρακλαι. See *Cic. ad Atticum*, L. I. Epift. X.

Part III.   'Tis to be feared, that many Places, *now called Academics*, fcarce deferve the name upon this *extenfive* Plan, if the Profeffors teach no more, than how to dance, fence, and ride upon horfes.

'Twas for the Cultivation of *every liberal Accomplifhment* that Athens was celebrated (as we have faid) during many Centuries, long after her *Political* Influence was loft, and at an end.

When Alexander the Great died, *many Tyrants*, like many *Hydras*, immediately fprung up. Athens then, tho' fhe ftill maintained the form of her *ancient* Government, was perpetually checked and humiliated by their infolence. Antipater deftroyed her *Orators*, and fhe was *facked* by Demetrius*. At length fhe became fubject to the all-powerful Romans, and found the cruel Sylla her fevereft Enemy.

His Face (which perhaps indicated his Manners) was of a purple red, intermixed with white. This circumftance could not efcape *the witty Athenians*: they defcribed him in a verfe, and ridiculoufly faid,

Sylla's *face is a Mulberry, fprinkled with meal*†.

                                                    The

---

*-See the Writers (antient and modern) of *Grecian* Hiftory.

† The original Verfe is a Trochaïc.

Συνάμιχεν τοῦ ὁ Σύλλας, ἀνθίτη πεπασμένον.

Plutarch. in vit. Syllæ, T. III. p. 44. *Ed. Bryan*, Quarto.

For his devaftations of the Groves in the *Academy* and *Lyceum*, his demolition of their fine Buildings, and above all, his cruel muffacre of the Inhabitants, when he took the City, fee pages 61, 63, 64, 65 of the fame Work, in the fame Edition.

THE Devaſtations and Carnage, which he cauſed ſoon after, gave them too much reaſon to repent their *Sarcaſm*.

THE civil War between CÆSAR and POMPEY ſoon followed, and their *natural Love of Liberty* made them ſide with *Pompey*. Here again they were unfortunate, for *Cæſar* conquered. But CÆSAR did not treat them like *Sylla*. With that Clemency, which made ſo amiable a part of his character, he diſmiſſed them by a fine alluſion to their illuſtrious Anceſtors, ſaying, *that he ſpared the Living for the ſake of the Dead*[*].

ANOTHER ſtorm followed ſoon after this, the wars of BRUTUS and CASSIUS with AUGUSTUS and ANTONY. Their Partiality for *Liberty* did not here forſake them: they took part in the conteſt with the two *patriot Romans*, and erected their Statues near their own ancient Deliverers, *Harmodius* and *Ariſtogiton*, who had ſlain *Hipparchus*. But they were ſtill unhappy, for their Enemies triumphed.

THEY made their peace however with AUGUSTUS, and having met afterwards with different treatment under different Emperors, ſometimes favourable, ſometimes harſh, and never more ſevere than under VESPASIAN, their Oppreſſions were at length relieved by the virtuous NERVA and TRAJAN[†].

MANKIND

---

[*] Vid. *Meurſium de Fortunâ Athenarum, in Gronov. Theſaur. Antiquitat. Græcar.* T. V, p. 1745, 1746.

[†] See the ſame Tract, in the ſame Volume of Gronovius's Collection, 1746, 1747.

 MANKIND during the interval, which began from NERVA, and which extended to the death of that beſt of Emperors, MARCUS ANTONINUS, felt a refpite from thoſe evils, which they had ſo ſeverely felt before, and which they felt ſo ſeverely revived under COMMODUS, and his wretched fucceſſors.

ATHENS, during the above golden period, enjoyed more than all others the general felicity, for ſhe found in ADRIAN ſo generous a *Benefaſtor*, that her citizens could hardly help eſteeming him a *ſecond Founder*. He reſtored their old Privileges; gave them new; repaired their ancient Buildings, and added others of his own. MARCUS ANTONINUS, altho' he did not do ſo much, ſtill continued to ſhew them his benevolent attention *.

IF from this period we turn our eyes back, we ſhall find, for Centuries before, that ATHENS was the *place of Education*, not only for *Greeks*, but for *Romans*. 'Twas hither, that HORACE was ſent by his father; 'twas here that CICERO put his ſon MARCUS under CRATIPPUS, one of the ableſt Philoſophers then belonging to that City †.

THE Sects of Philoſophers, which we have already deſcribed, were ſtill exiſting, when St. PAUL came thither. We cannot enough admire the ſuperior Eloquence of that Apoſtle, in his manner of
addreſſing

---

* See the ſame Author, in the ſame Volume, p. 1748, 1749.

† See *Horat. Epiſt.* II. L. II. v. 43, and the beginning of *Cicero's Offices*, addreſt to his Son—*Quamquam, Marce Fili,* &c.

addreffing fo intelligent an Audience. We cannot enough admire Ch. III.
the fublimity of his Exordium; the propriety of his mentioning *an
Altar*, which he had found there; and his Quotation from ARATUS,
one of their well-known Poets *.

NOR was *Athens* only celebrated for the Refidence of Philofophers, and the Inflitution of Youth: Men of rank and fortune
found pleafure in a *retreat*, which contributed fo much to their
liberal Enjoyment.

THE friend and correfpondent of *Cicero*, T. POMPONIUS, from
his long attachment to this City and Country, had attained fuch a
perfection in its Arts and Language, that he acquired to himfelf
the additional name of ATTICUS. This great Man may be faid
to have lived during times of the worft and crueleft factions. His
youth was fpent under *Sylla* and *Marius*; the middle of his life
during all the fanguinary fcenes that followed; and, when he was
old, he faw the profcriptions of *Antony* and *Octavius*. Yet tho'
Cicero and a multitude more of the beft men perifhed, he had the
good fortune to furvive every danger. Nor did he feek a fafety
for himfelf alone; his Virtue fo recommended him to the Leaders
of every fide, that he was able to fave not himfelf alone, but the
lives and fortunes of many of his friends†.

WHEN

---

* ACTS, Ch. xvii. v. 22, &c.

† The Life of this extraordinary man is finely and fully written by *Cornelius Nepos*,
a Life well worthy of perufal. See alfo the large and valuable Collection of *Confiden-
tial Letters*, addreft to him by *Cicero*.

Part III. WHEN we look to this amiable character, we may well suppose, that it was not merely for amusement that he chose to live at *Athens*; but rather that, by residing there, he might so far realize Philosophy, as to employ it for the conduct of Life, and not merely for Ostentation.

ANOTHER person, during a better period, (that I mean between *Nerva* and *Marcus Antoninus)* was equally celebrated for his affection to this City. By this person I mean HERODES ATTICUS, who acquired the *last* name from the same reasons, for which it had formerly been given to *Pomponius* * . "

WE have remarked already, that Vicissitudes befal both Men and Cities, and changes too often happen from prosperous to adverse. Such was the state of ATHENS under the successors of *Alexander*, and so on from *Sylla* down to the time of *Augustus*. It shared the same hard fate with the *Roman* Empire in general upon the accession of *Commodus*.

AT length, after a certain period, the Barbarians of the North began to pour into the South. *Rome* was taken by ALARIC, and *Athens* was besieged by the same. Yet here we are informed (at least we learn so from History) that it was miraculously saved by *Minerva* and *Achilles*. The Goddess it seems and the Hero both of them appeared, compelling the Invader to raise the siege †.

'TWAS

---

* See *Fabric. Bibl. Græc.* T. IV. p. 371, and *Suidas*, under the word *Herodes*.

† See *Zosimi Histor.* L. V. c. 5 and 6, p. 511, &c. *Edit. Gr. Lat.* 8vo. 1679. where the whole story is related at length.

'Twas thus we are told, that, many years before, *Castor* and *Pollux* had fought for the *Romans* *; and that, many centuries afterwards, *St. George*, at *Iconium*, difcomfited the *Saracens* †—nay, fo late as in the fixteenth century, a gallant *Spaniard*, *Peter de Paz*, was feen to affift his countrymen, *fome months after his deceafe*, when they made an affault at the fiege of *Antwerp* ‡.

Instead of giving my own Sentiments upon thefe events, I chufe to give thofe of an abler man upon *a fimilar* fubject. After having related fome fingular ftories of equal probability, *Lord Bacon* concludes with the following obfervation—

My Judgment (fays he) *is, that they* (he means the ftories) *ought all to be defpifed, and ought to ferve but for winter-talk by the fire-fide.*
　　　　　　　　　　　　　　　　　　　　　　　　Tho'

---

* See *Florus* L. 1, 2. L. II. 12.—*Juftin*. Lib. XX. 3.

† *Fuller's Holy War*, p. 27. *Matt. Paris*, p. 43. According to this laft Author there were three that fought, *St. George*, *St. Demetrius*, and *St. Mercury*.

‡ The following Extract is taken from the *Difquifitiones Magicæ* of *Martin Del-Rio*, printed at *Mentz*, an. 1617. *cum gratia et privilegio Cæfar. Majeft.* together with the approbation of *Oliverius Manareus*, *Vice-Provincial of the Belgic Jefuits*, and *Gulielmus Fabricius*, ftiled *Apoftolicus et Regius Librorum Cenfor;* and attefted alfo by the evidence *multorum gravium militum*, QUI VIDISSE SE SANCTE JURABANT.

The befieged it feems and their Allies, *the Dutch* and *English*, were upon the point of forcing a Poft (Aggerem) poffeft by the *Spaniards*, who befieged the City.—*Del-Rio's* words after this are—*Tum a regiis militibus* (Hifpanis fcil.) *primo paucioribus* CONSPECTIS PROPE AGGEREM PETRUS DE PAZ, *Hifpanus Tribunus, vir et militarib. et pietatis ornamentis laudatiffimus, qui, jam* MENSIBUS ALIQUOT ANTE DEFUNCTUS, *vifus his armatus,* UT SOLEBAT, *legionem præcedere, et fuis quondam militibus,* MANU ADVOCATIS, *fequerentur ut fe* IMPLEXERE. *Indicant primi fecundis; fic tertiis; fic fequentibus;* VIDENT OMNES IDEM, *mirantur, animifque refumptis* NOTUM SEQUUNTUR DUCEM, &c. *Difquifit. Mag.* p. 262.

Part III. *Tho' when I ſay deſpiſed, I mean it as for Belief; for otherwiſe the ſpreading or publiſhing of them is in no ſort to be deſpiſed, for they have done much miſchief *.*

SYNESIUS, who lived in the fifth Century, viſited *Athens*, and gives in his Epiſtles an account of his viſit. Its luſtre appears at that time to have been greatly diminiſhed. Among other things he informs us, that the celebrated Portico or Colonade, the *Greek* name of which gave name to the Sect of Stoics, had by an oppreſſive Proconſul been deſpoiled of its fine Pictures; and that, on this devaſtation, it had been forſaken by thoſe Philoſophers †.

IN the thirteenth Century, when the *Grecian Empire* was cruelly oppreſſed by the *Cruſaders*, and all things in confuſion, *Athens* was beſieged by one *Segurus Leo*, who was unable to take it; and, after that, by a *Marquis of Montſerrat*, to whom it ſurrendered ‡.

ITS fortune after this was various; and it was ſometimes under the *Venetians*, ſometimes under the *Catalonians*, till *Mahomet the Great* made himſelf Maſter of *Conſtantinople*. This fatal cataſtrophe (which happened near two thouſand years after the time of *Piſiſtratus*) brought ATHENS and with it all GREECE into the hands

of

---

* *Eſſays* and Counſels by *Ld. Verulam*, No. XXXV.

† See *Syneſii Epiſt.* 135. In *Gronovius's Collection*, T. V. (as before) p. 1751, and of this work, p. 431.

‡ See *Gronovius's Collection* (as before) p. 1751, 1752, 1753, 1754.

of the *Turks*, under whofe defpotic yoke it has continued ever fince.

The City from this time has been occafionally vifited, and De-fcriptions of it publifhed by different Travellers. Wheeler was there along with Spon in the time of our *Charles the Second*, and both of them have publifhed curious and valuable Narratives. Others, as well natives of this Ifland, as foreigners, have been there fince, and fome have given (as Monfr. *Le Roy)* fpecious publications of what we are *to fuppofe* they faw. None however have equalled the Truth, the Accuracy, and Elegance of Mr. Stuart, who, after having refided there between three and four years, has given us fuch Plans, and Elevations of the *capital Buildings* now ftanding, together with learned Comments to elucidate every part, that he feems, as far as was poffible for the power of *Defcription*, to have reftored the City to its *ancient* Splendor.

He has not only given us the greater Outlines and their Meafures, but feparate Meafures and Drawings of the *minuter* Decorations; fo that a *Britifh* Artift may (if he pleafe) follow Phidias, and build in *Britain*, as *Phidias* did at Athens *.

Spon, fpeaking of *Attica*, fays that the Road near Athens was pleafing, and the very Peafants polifhed. Speaking of the *Athenians* in general, he fays of them—*ils ont une politeffe d'efprit na-*
turelle,

---

* This moft curious and valuable Book was publifhed at London, in the year 1762.

 *turelle, & beaucoup d'addreſſe dans toutes les affaires, qu'ils entre-
prenent *.

WHEELER, who was *Spon's* fellow-traveller, ſays as follows, when
he and his Company approached ATHENS—*We began now to think
ourſelves in a* MORE CIVILIZED COUNTRY, *than we had yet paſt : for
not a Shepherd, that we met, but bid us* WELCOME, AND WISHED US
a good journey—p. 335, ſpeaking of the ATHENIANS, he adds—*This
muſt with great truth be ſaid of them, their bad fortune hath not been
able to take from them, what* THEY HAVE BY NATURE, *that is, much*
SUBTLETY *or* WIT, p. 347. And again—THE ATHENIANS, *notwithſtanding the long poſſeſſion that Barbariſm hath had of this place,
ſeem to be much* MORE POLISHED *in point of* MANNERS *and* CON-
VERSATION, *than any other in theſe parts; being civil, and of reſpect-
ful behaviour to all, and highly complimental in their diſcourſe* †.

STUART ſays of the *preſent Athenians*, what *Spon* and *Wheeler* ſaid
of their forefathers;—he found in them the ſame addreſs, the ſame
natural acuteneſs, tho' ſeverely curbed by their deſpotic Maſters.

ONE cuſtom I cannot omit. He tells me, that frequently at their
convivial Meetings, one of the company takes, what they now call,
a Lyre, tho' it is rather a ſpecies of Guitar, and after a ſhort pre-
lude on the Inſtrument, as if he were waiting for inſpiration, accom-
panies his inſtrumental Muſic with his voice, ſuddenly chanting ſome
extempore Verſes, which ſeldom exceed two or three Diſtichs; that
he

---

* *Spon*, V. II. p. 76, 92, *Edit.* 8vo.   † *Wheeler*, p. 356, *Edit. Fol.*

he then delivers the Lyre to his neighbour, who, after he has done Ch. III.
the fame, delivers it to another; and that fo the Lyre circulates, till
it has paft round the table.

Nor can I forget his informing me, that, notwithftanding *the va-*
rious Fortune of ATHENS, as a *City*, ATTICA was ftill famous for
OLIVES, and Mount HYMETTUS for HONEY. *Human Inftitutions*
perifh, but Nature is permanent.

CHAP. IV.

Account of Byzantine Scholars continued — SUIDAS — JOHN STOBÆUS or of STOBA — PHOTIUS — MICHAEL PSELLUS — this last said to have commented twenty-four Plays of MENANDER — Reasons, to make this probable — EUSTATHIUS, a Bishop, the Commentator of HOMER — EUSTRATIUS, a Bishop, the Commentator of ARISTOTLE — PLANUDES, a Monk, the admirer and translator of LATIN Classics, as well as the Compiler of one of the present GREEK ANTHOLOGIES. — Conjectures concerning the duration of THE LATIN TONGUE at Constantinople.

Part III. THAT I may not be prolix, I hasten from the writers already mentioned to SUIDAS, who is supposed to have lived during the ninth or tenth Centuries. In his *Lexicon*, which is partly *Historical*, partly *Explanatory*, he has preserved many Quotations from Authors who lived in the earlier and politer ages, and from Poets in particular, whose works at present are for the greater part lost. KUSTER, an able Critic in the beginning of the present Century, gave a fine Edition of this Author, at *Cambridge*, in three Volumes Folio; and Mr. TOUPE *of Cornwall* (whom I have mentioned already, and cannot mention with too much applause) has lately favoured the learned world with many valuable Emendations *.

JOHN

---

* Concerning this little known Author see the Preface of his learned Editor, *Kuster*.

JOHN STOBÆUS or of *Stobo*, (whose name *John* makes it probable he was a *Christian*) is of an uncertain age, as well as *Suidas*; tho' some imagine him to have lived during an *earlier* period, by two or three Centuries*. His work is *not à Lexicon*, like that of the other, but *an immense Common-Place*, filled with Extracts upon various fubjects, both *Ethical* and *Physical*, which Extract, he had collected from the moft approved Writers. As this Book is highly valuable from containing such an incredible variety of Sentiments upon *interesting* Topics, and those taken from Authors, many of whom are loft; as it is at the fame time fo incorrectly printed, that in too many places it is *hardly intelligible:* it would be a labour well worthy of an able Critic, by the help of *Manuscripts*, and plaufible *Conjecture*, to restore it, as far as poffible, to its original Purity. The Speculations he chiefly gives us are neither trivial, nor licentious, but, in the language of *Horace*,

> ———— *quod magis ad nos*
> *Pertinet, et nescire malum eft.* ———

BUT to return from STOBÆUS to SUIDAS. If we confider the late age when *Suidas* lived; if we confider too the Authors, which he muft needs have ftudied, in order to form his work; Authors, who many of them wrote in the moft *refined* and *polished* Ages; it will be evident, that even in those *late* Centuries the Tafte for *a purer Literature was by no means extinct*, and that even *then* there were Readers, who knew its value.

IN

---

* See *Fabric. Biblioth. Græc.* T. VIII. 665.

In the *ninth Century*, lived Photius, *Patriarch of Conſtantinople.*
His moſt celebrated work may be called *a Journal of his Studies*; a
Journal, where we learn the various *Authors* he peruſed; the *Subjects*
they treated; the *Plans* of their Works; and where ſometimes alſo
we have *Extracts.* From him we are informed not only of many
Authors now loſt, but what was in his time the ſtate of many, that
are now remaining.

Among the Authors now loſt he peruſed Theopompus *the Hiſto-*
rian, and Hyperides *the Orator*; among thoſe, now mutilated and
imperfect, he peruſed intire Diodorus Siculus. Many others, if
neceſſary, might be added of either ſort.

'Tis ſingular with regard to Photius, that from a *Layman* he was
raiſed at once to be *Patriarch of Conſtantinople.* Yet his Studies evidently ſeem to have had ſuch a rank in view, being principally applied to *Theology*, to *Hiſtory*, and to *Oratory*; with *enough Philoſophy*,
and *Medicine*, not to appear deficient, if ſuch ſubjects ſhould occur.
As to *Poetry*, one might imagine, either that he had no reliſh for it,
or that, in the train of his inquiries, he did not eſteem it a requiſite *.

Michael Psellus, of the *eleventh Century*, was knowing in
the *Greek Philoſophy and Poetry* of the *purer* ages, and for his various
and extenſive Learning was ranked among the firſt and ableſt Scholars of his time.

Besides

---

* See *Fabric. Bibl. Græc.* T. IX. 369.

Besides his Treatise of *Mathematics*, his Comments upon *Aristotle*, and a number of other Works (many of which are printed) he is said to have commented and explained no less than *twenty-four Comedies* of Menander, a Treatise now lost, tho' extant as well as the Comedies in so *late* a period. He must have had a relish for that polite Writer, or otherwise 'tis not probable, he would have undertaken such a labour*.

Nor need we wonder this should happen. Why should not the polite Menander have had his Admirers in these Ages, as well as the licentious Aristophanes?—Or rather, why not as well as Sophocles, and Euripides? The *Scholia* upon these (tho' some perhaps may be more ancient) were compiled by Critics, who lived long after Psellus †.

We may add with regard to *all these Scholiasts* (whatever may have been their Age) they would never have undergone the *labours* of Compilation and Annotation, had they not been encouraged by the

---

* See *Fabric. Bibl. Græc.* T. I. 769.

In the passage, quoted by *Fabricius* upon this subject, its Author says, that the latter *Greek* Monks persuaded the latter *Greek* Emperors, to destroy *Menander* and many other of the *old Greek Poets*, from the looseness of their Morals, and their great Indecencies. That the Monks may have persuaded this, is not improbable—perhaps from Bigotry; perhaps from a consciousness of their own wretched Inferiority in every species of elegant Composition—but certainly from no indignation against Indecency and Immorality. For if so, why preserve *Lucian?* why preserve *Aristophanes?* why preserve Collections of Epigrams, more indecent and flagitious, than the grossest Productions of the most licent ous modern Ages?

† *Demetrius Triclinius*, the Scholiast on *Sophocles*, lived after *Planudes*, for he mentions him. See *Fabric. Bib. Græc.* p. 634.

Part III. the tafte of their *Contemporary* Countrymen. For who ever publifhed, without hopes of having Readers?

The fame may be afferted of the learned *Bifhop of Theffalonica*,
Eustathius, who lived in the *twelfth* Century. His admiration
of Homer muft have been *almoft* enthufiaftic, to carry him thro'
fo complete, fo minute, and fo vaft a Commentary, both upon *the
Iliad* and *the Odyffey*, collected from fuch an immenfe number both
of Critics and Hiftorians *.

Eustratius, *the Metropolitan of Nice*, who lived a *little* earlier
in the fame Century, convinces us that he ftudied Aristotle with
no lefs zeal; and that, not only in his *Logical* pieces, but in his
Ethical alfo, as may be feen by thofe minute and accurate Comments on the Nicomachean Ethics, which go under his name,
and in which, tho' *others* had their fhare, he ftill is found to have
taken fo large a Portion to himfelf †.

Planudes, a Monk of the *fourteenth* Century, appears (which
is fomewhat uncommon) to have underftood and admired THE
Latin Classics, *Cicero, Cafar, Ovid, Boethius*, and others, parts
of which Authors he tranflated, fuch as the Commentaries of *Cafar*,
relative to the *Gallic* Wars, the Dream of Scipio by *Cicero*, the
Metamorphofis of *Ovid*, the fine Tract of *Boethius de Confolatione*,
and (according to Spon) *St. Auguftine de Civitate Dei*. Befides this,
he

---

* See *Fabric. Biblioth. Græc.* T. I. p. 289, &c.

† See *Fabric. Biblioth. Græc.* T. II. p. 151.

he formed a GREEK ANTHOLOGY (that well known Collection printed by *Wechelius,* in 1600,) and compofed feveral *original* Pieces of his own*.

IT appears from *thefe* Examples, and will hereafter appear from *others,* how much the Caufe of *Letters* and *Humanity* is indebted to THE CHURCH.

HAVING mentioned *Latin Claffics,* I beg leave to fubmit a conjecture concerning the ftate and duration of the LATIN TONGUE at *Conftantinople.*

WHEN CONSTANTINE founded this *Imperial City,* he not only adorned it with curiofities from every part of the *Roman Empire,* but he induced, by every fort of encouragement, many of the Firft Families in *Italy,* and a multitude more of inferior rank, to leave their Country, and there fettle themfelves. We may therefore fuppofe, that LATIN was for a long time the *prevailing Language* of the Place, till in a courfe of years it was fupplanted by GREEK, the *common* Language of the neighbourhood, and the *fafhionable acquired* Language of every polite *Roman.*

WE are told, that foon after the End of the *fixth* Century LATIN ceafed to be fpoken at ROME†. Yet was it in the beginning of that Century that JUSTINIAN publifhed his *Laws* in LATIN at *Conftantinople;* and that the celebrated PRISCIAN in the fame City taught *the Principles of the Latin Grammar.*

IF

---

* See *Fabric. Biblioth. Græc.* T. X. p. 533.　　† See before, p. 416.

IF we defcend to a period ftill later, (fo late indeed as to the *tenth* and *eleventh* Centuries) we fhall find, in the Ceremonial of the *Byzantine* Court, certain Formularies preferved, evidently connected with this fubject.

As often as the Emperor gave an Imperial Banquet, 'twas the Cuftom for fome of his Attendants, at peculiar times during the Feaft, to repeat and chant the following Words—Κωνσέρβιτ Δέυς ἰμπέριυμ βέςρυμ—βήβητε, Δόμηνι ἰμπεράτωρες ἐν μυλτος ἄννος· Δέυς ὀμνήποτευς πρέςετθ—Ἠν γαυδίῳ πρανδεῖτε, Δόμηνι.

IT may poffibly for a moment furprife a learned Reader, when he hears that the meaning of this ftrange Jargon is—*May God pre-ferve your Empire—Live, imperial Lords, for many years; God al-mighty fo grant—Dine, my Lords, in joy.*

BUT his doubts will foon vanifh, when he finds this Jargon to be LATIN, and comes to read it exhibited according to A LATIN ALPHABET—

CONSERVET DEVS IMPERIVM VESTRVM—VIVITE, DOMINI IMPERATORES, IN MVLTOS ANNOS; DEVS OMNIPOTENS PRAESTET—IN GAVDIO PRANDETE, DOMINI*.

'Tis

---

* Thefe Formularies are felected from a Ceremonial of the *Byzantine* Court, drawn up by the Emperor *Conftantine Porphyrogenitus,* who reigned in the beginning of the eleventh Century. The Book, being a large Folio, was publifhed in the original *Greek,* with

'Tis evident from thefe inftances, that traces of LATIN were ftill Ch. IV.
remaining at *Conftantinople*, during thofe Centuries. 'Twill be then
perhaps lefs wonderful, if PLANUDES upon the fame fpot fhould,
in the *fourteenth* Century, appear to have underftood it. We may
fuppofe, that by degrees it changed from a *Common* Language to
a *Learned* one, and that, being thus confined to *the Learned Few*,
its valuable Works were by *their* labours *again* made known, and
diffufed among their Countrymen in *Greek Tranflations*.

THIS too will make it probable, that even to the *loweft* age of
the *Greek Empire* their great LIBRARIES contained many valuable
LATIN MANUSCRIPTS; perhaps had *entire* Copies of *Cicero*, of
Livy, of *Tacitus*, and many others. Where elfe did PLANUDES,
when he tranflated, find his *Originals?*

---

with a *Latin* Tranflation and Notes, by *Leichius* and *Reifkius*, at *Lipfie*, in the year
1751. See of this Book p. 215, 216. Many more Traces of this *Helleniftic Latin*
occur in other parts of it. In the *Latin Types* I have followed the *Commentator*, and
not *the Tranflator*; and as the *Greeks* have no Letter but B to denote the *Latin V*,
have preferred *Vivite* to *Bibite*.

C H A P. V.

Nicetas, the Choniate—his curious Narrative of the Mischiefs done by Baldwyn's Crusade, when they sackt Constantinople in the Year 1205—many of the Statues described, which they then destroyed—a fine Taste for Arts among the Greeks, even in those Days, proved from this Narrative—not so, among the Crusaders—Authenticity of Nicetas's Narrative—State of Constantinople at the last Period of the Grecian Empire, as given by contemporary Writers, Philelphus and Æneas Sylvius—National Pride among the Greeks not totally extinct even at this Day.

Part III. BESIDES Planudes a large number of the same nation might be mentioned, but I omit them all for the sake of Nicetas, the Choniate, in order to prove thro' him, that the more refined part of that ingenious people had not even in the *thirteenth* Century *lost their Taste;* a Taste not confined to *Literary* Works only, but extended to Works of *other* kinds and character.

This Historian (I mean Nicetas*) was present at the sacking of *Constantinople* by the Barbarians of *Baldwyn's Crusade,* in the year 1205. Take, by the way of Sample, a part only of his Enumeration of the noble Statues, which were probably brought thither by

Constantine,

---

* He was called the *Choniate* from *Chona,* a City of *Phrygia,* and possest, when in the Court of *Constantinople,* some of the highest Dignities. *Fabric. Biblioth. Græc.* T. XI. p. 401, 402.

Conſtantine, to decorate his new City, and which thefe *Adventurers* Ch. V.
then deſtroyed *.

AMONG others he mentions the *Coloſſian Statue* of JUNO, erected
in the *Forum* of *Conſtantine*; the Statue of PARIS ſtanding by
VENUS, and delivering to her the Golden Apple; a ſquare and
lofty OBELISK, with a Figure on it to indicate the Wind; the Figure of BELLEROPHON, riding upon PEGASUS; the PENSIVE HER-
CULES, made by no leſs an Artiſt than LYSIPPUS; the two celebrated *Figures* of THE MAN and THE ASS, erected by *Auguſtus*
after his Victory at *Actium*; the WOLF, ſuckling ROMULUS and
REMUS; an EAGLE *deſtroying* a SERPENT, ſet up by *Apollonius
Tyaneus*; and an *exquiſite* HELEN, in all the Charms of Beauty and
of Elegance.

SPEAKING of *the Wind-obeliſk*, he relates with the greateſt feeling
the curious work on its ſides; the rural Scene; *Birds* ſinging; *Ruſtics*
labouring, or playing on their Pipes; Sheep bleating; *Lambs* ſkip-
ping; *the Sea*, and a Scene of *Fiſh* and *Fiſhing*; little naked *Cupids*,
laughing, playing, and pelting each other with Apples; A FIGURE
on the ſummit, turning with the ſlighteſt blaſt, and thence denominated *the Wind's Attendant*.

Of

* A large part of this Chapter is extracted from the Hiſtory of *Nicetas*, as printed
by *Fabricius* in the Tome above quoted, beginning from p. 405, and proceeding to
p. 418.

The Author has endeavoured to make his tranſlated Extracts faithful, but he thought
the whole *Original Greek* too much to be inſerted, eſpecially as it may be found in
Fabricius's Bibliotheca, a Book by no means rare. A few particular paſſages he has
given in *the Original*.

 Of the *two Statues* brought from *Actium* he relates, that they were set up there by *Augustus* on the following Incident. As he went out by night to reconnoitre the Camp of *Antony*, he met *a Man, driving an Ass.* The Man was asked, *who he was, and whither he was going*—my *Name*, replied he, *is* NICO, *my Ass's name* NICAN- DER; *and I am going to* CÆSAR'S *Army.* The Story derives its force from the *good Omen of lucky names*, and may be found (tho' with some variation) both in *Suetonius* and *Plutarch.* The *real* Curiosity was, that Statues so celebrated should be *then* exi- sting.

If the Figures of *the Wolf* and *the Founders of Rome* were of the same age, they might probably have been the very *Work*, to which VIRGIL is supposed to have alluded, in describing the Shield of ÆNEAS:

——*illam tereti cervice reflexam*

Mulcere alternos, et corpora fingere lingua.

Æn. VIII. 633.

But no where does the Taste of NICETAS appear so strongly, as when he speaks of the HERCULES, and the HELEN.

THE HERCULES is exhibited to us, as if he were actually present —*immense in bulk*, and, with an Air of Grandeur, *reposing himself*— his *Lion's-skin* (that lookt formidable even in brass) *thrown over him* —himself *sitting* without a Quiver, a Bow, or a Club, but having *the right leg bent* at the knee; *his Head* gently *reclining on the hand of his left Arm*; and a *Countenance full of dejection*, as if he were
reflecting

reflecting with indignation on the many succeſſive labours, impoſed
on him by *Euryſtheus* [*].

For his *Perſon*, we are informed he was *ample* in the *Cheſt*; *broad*
in the *Shoulders*; had *Hair that curled*; *Arms* that were *ſtrong* and
muſcular; and a *Magnitude* ſuch, as might be ſuppoſed to belong
to the original Hercules, were he to revive; *a Leg* being equal
in length to the Stature of a *common* Man [†]. And yet adds Nicetas, filled with Indignation, " this Hercules, being ſuch as here
" repreſented, this very Hercules did not theſe men ſpare."

I can only ſubjoin, by way of digreſſion, that there is a fine *Greek*
Epigram deſcribing the Statue of a dejected Hercules, ſitting
without his Weapons, which exactly reſembles this of Nicetas, and
which is ſaid likewiſe to be the work of Lysippus, only there the
Poet imputes his Hero's *Dejection*, not to the Tyranny of *Euryſtheus*,
but to the love of *Omphale* [‡].

If *Nicetas* ſpeak with *admiration* of *this* Statue, 'tis with *rapture*
he mentions *the other*. " *What*," ſays he, " *ſhall I ſay of the beauteous*
" Helen; *of her, who brought together all Greece againſt Troy?*
" *Did ſhe* mitigate *theſe* immitigable, *theſe* iron-hearted
" *Men?*

---

[*] Εκάθητο δε, μὴ γωρυτὸν ἐξημμένος, μὴ τόξον ταῖν χεροῖν φέρων, μὴ, κ. τ. λ. *Fabr.* as above,
p. 408, 409.

[†] Ἦν δὲ τὸ ςέρνον εὐρὺς, τῆς ὤμας πλατὺς, τὴν τρίχα ἔλος, κ. τ. λ. *Ibid.* p. 409.

[‡] Vid. *Antholog.* L. IV. tit. 8.

Part III. " *Men? No,*" says he, " *nothing like it could even she affect, who had*
  " *before enslaved so many Spectators with her Beauty* *."

AFTER this he describes her Dress, and then proceeds to her
Person; which Description, as it is something singular, I have endeavoured to translate more strictly.

 " HER LIPS," says he, " *like opening Flowers, were gently parted,*
" *as if she was going to speak: and as for that* GRACEFUL SMILE,
" *which instantly met the beholder, and filled him with delight; those*
" *elegant* CURVATURES OF HER EYE-BROWS, *and the remaining*
" HARMONY OF HER FIGURE; *they were what no Words can de-*
" *scribe, and deliver down to Posterity* †."

He then breaks into an Exclamation — " *But O!* HELEN, *Thou*
" *pure and genuine Beauty; Offspring of the Loves; decorated by the*
" *Care of* VENUS; *most exquisite of Nature's Gifts; Prize of Contest*
" *between Trojans and Grecians: where was thy* NEPENTHES, *that*
" *soothing Draught, which thou learnedst in Egypt? — Where thy irre-*
" *sistible Love-charms? — Why didst Thou not employ them now, as thou*
" *didst in days of yore? Alas! I fear 'twas destined by Fate, that*
" *Thou shouldst perish by Flames; Thou, who didst not cease even in thy*
" *Statue to inflame beholders into Love. I could almost say that these*
" SONS OF ÆNEAS *had demolished Thee by* FIRE, *as a species of reta-*
              " *liation*

---

* Ἆρ' ἐμείλιξε τὰς δυσμειλίκτας; ἆρ', ἐμαλθαξε τὰς σιδηρόφρονας; ἃ μὴν ἂν ὅϊε ὅλως τοῦτόν τι δεδύνηται
ἢ πᾶσα θεατὴν τῷ κάλλει ὀφθαλμωτήσασα, καπερ, κ. τ. λ. Fabric. ut supra, p. 410. 413.

† Ἦν δὲ καὶ τὰ χείλη, καλύκων δίκην, ἠρέμα παρανοιγόμενα, ὡς καὶ δοκεῖν, κ. τ. λ. Ibid. p. 413.

" *liation for the* BURNING OF THEIR TROY, *as thofe Flames were*
" *kindled by thy unfortunate Amours**.*"

I HAVE been thus particular in thefe Relations, and have tranflated for the greater part the very *words* of the Hiftorian, not only
becaufe the Facts are little known, but becaufe they tend to prove,
that even in thofe *dark* Ages (as we have too many reafons to call
them) there were *Greeks ftill extant,* who had *a Tafte for the finer
Arts,* and an *Enthufiaftic Feeling* of their exquifite *Beauty.* At the
fame time we cannot without indignation reflect on thefe *brutal
Crufaders,* who, after many inftances of *facrilegious* Avarice, related
by *Nicetas* in confequence of their Succefs, could deftroy all *thefe,*
and many other precious *Remains of Antiquity, melting them down
(for they were of Brafs) into Money to pay their Soldiers, and exchang-
ing things of ineftimable Value for a poor pittance of contemptible Coin* †.
They furely were what NICETAS well calls them, Τῦ καλῦ ἀνέραςοι
βάρβαροι, BARBARIANS *devoid of tafte for the* BEAUTIFUL *and*
FAIR ‡.

AND yet 'tis remarkable, that thefe *fad* and *favage* Events happened *more than a Century after* thefe Adventurers had firft paft into
tho

---

* Ἀλλ' Ὦ Τυνδαρὶς Ἑλένη, κάλλος ἀντίθεν καλὸν, Ἐρώτων μόσχευμα, Ἀφροδίτης τιμενέχημα, πανά-
ριτον φύσεως δώρημα, Τρώων καὶ Ἑλλήνων βράβευμα, πῶ σοι τὸ Νηπ πνὲς, κ. τ. λ.   Ibid, p. 413.

† Κενβρασιν [ἀγάλματα] εἰς νομίσμα, ἀνταλασσόμενοι μικρῶν τὰ μεγάλα, καὶ τὰ δαπάναις ποιηθέντα
μεγίςαις ἐπιδανῶν ἀντιδιδόντες κερμάτων.   Ibid. p. 408.

‡ I have given the words of *Nicetas* himfelf, which precede the paffage juft quoted,
In another part of his Narrative he ftiles them ILLITERATE BARBARIANS, *who abfolutely did not know their A B C.*—παρ' ἀγραμμάτοις βαρβάροις, καὶ τίμαν ἀναλφαβήτοις—
p. 414.

Part III.   the Eaſt, above *four-ſcore years of which* time they had poſſeſſed *the*
           Sovereignty of Paleſtine. But—

          CŒLUM, *non* ANIMUM *mutant,* &c.   HOR*.

   THO' I have done with theſe Events, I cannot quit THE GREEKS
without adding a word upon CONSTANTINOPLE, as to *Literature*
and *Language,* juſt *before* the fatal period, when it was taken by the
TURKS. There is more ſtreſs to be laid upon my Quotations, as
they are tranſcribed from Authors, who lived at *the time,* or immediately after.

   HEAR what PHILELPHUS ſays, who was himſelf at *Conſtantinople*
in that part of the fifteenth Century, while the *Greek* Empire *ſtill*
ſubſiſted. " *Thoſe* GREEKS (ſays he) *whoſe Language has not been*
" *depraved, and whom we ourſelves both follow and imitate, ſpeak even*
" *at this time in their ordinary talk, as the Comic* ARISTOPHANES *did,*
" *or the Tragic* EURIPIDES *; as the Orators would talk; as the Hiſto-*
" *rians; as the Philoſophers themſelves, even* PLATO *and* ARIS-
" TOTLE†."

                                                  SPEAKING

---

* It ought to be obſerved, that tho' the NARRATIVE of *Nicetas,* whence theſe Extracts are taken, appear not in the printed Editions (being probably either thro' fraud,
of ſhame, or both, deſignedly omitted;) yet has it been publiſhed by that *honeſt* and
learned Critic FABRICIUS, in the *ſixth* Volume of his *Bibliotheca Græca* here quoted,
and is ſtill extant in a *fair* and *ancient Manuſcript* of the two laſt Books of *Nicetas,*
preſerved in THE BODLEIAN LIBRARY.

† *Græci, quibus lingua depravata non ſit, et quos ipſi tùm ſequimur, tùm imitamur,
ita loquuntur vulgo hâc etiam in tempeſtate, ut Ariſtophanes Comicus, ut Euripides Tra-
gicus, ut Oratores omnes, ut Philoſophi etiam ipſi et Plato et Ariſtoteles.* Philelph. Epiſt.
in Hodii de Græcis Illuſtribus, Lib. I. p. 188.

SPEAKING afterwards of the *Corruption* of the Tongue in that City by the Concourse of Traders, and Strangers, he informs us, that the People belonging *to the Court* still retained " *the* ANCIENT *Dig-* " *nity and Elegance of Speech, and above all* THE WOMEN OF QUA- " LITY, *who, as they were wholly precluded from Strangers,* STILL " PRESERVED *that genuine and pure Speech of the* ANCIENT GREEKS, " *uncorrupted* *."

ÆNEAS SYLVIUS, afterwards Pope by the name of PIUS THE SE- COND, was the Scholar of this *Philelphus.* A long Letter of his is extant upon the taking of *Constantinople by Mahomet,* a Letter ad- drest to a Cardinal, just after that fatal Event. Speaking of the for- tune of the City, he observes, that NEW ROME (for so they often called CONSTANTINOPLE) had subsisted, from its foundation to its capture, nearly the *same* number of years with OLD ROME — that

between

---

* The fame *Philelphus* in the fame Epiftle adds—*Nam* VIRI AULICI *veterem fermonis dignitatem atque elegantiam retinebant; in primifque* IPSÆ NOBILES MULIERES, *quibus cum nullum effet omnino cum viris peregrinis Commercium,* MERUS ILLE AC PURUS GRÆ- CORUM SERMO SERVADATUR INTACTUS. *Hod. ut fupra.*

'Tis fomewhat fingular, that what *Philelphus* relates concerning *the Women of Rank at the Court of Conftantinople,* fhould be related by *Cicero* concerning *the Women of Rank* in the polifhed days of the *Roman Commonwealth;* concerning *Cornelia,* Mother of the *Gracchi;* concerning *Lælia,* Daughter of the great *Lælius;* concerning the *Muciæ,* the *Licinia,* in fhort, the Mothers, Wives, and Daughters of the moft illuftrious *Romans* of that illuftrious age.

Cicero accounts for *the purity of their Language,* and for its being untainted with *vitious novelty,* precifely as *Philelphus* does.—*Facilius enim* MULIERES INCORRUPTAM ANTIQUITATEM CONSERVANT, *quod,* MULTORUM SERMONIS EXPERTES, *ea tenent femper, quæ prima didicerunt.*

This Paffage is no fmall ftrengthening of *Philelphus's* Authority. See *Cicer. de Oratore* III. 45. & *de Claris Orator.* f. 211.

3 N 2

Part III. between Romulus, the founder of *Old Rome*, and the Goth, Alaric,
who took it, was an interval of about *eleven hundred years*; and that
there was nearly the fame interval between Constantine and Mahomet the Great.

, He obferves that tho' this *laft City* had been taken before, it had
never before fuffered fo *total* and fo *fatal* a change. " *Till this period*
" (fays he) *the remembrance of* ancient wisdom *remained at* Con-
" stantinople; *and, as if it were the Manfion, the Seat of Letters,*
" *no one of the Latins could be deemed fufficiently learned, if he had*
" *not ftudied for fome time at* Constantinople. *The fame Reputa-*
" *tion for Sciences, which* Athens *had in the times of ancient Rome,*
" *did* Constantinople *appear to poffefs in our times.* '*Twas thence,*
" *that* Plato *was reftored to us;* '*twas thence, that the Works of* Aris-
" *totle,* Demosthenes, Xenophon, Thucydides, Basil, Dio-
" nysius, Origen *and others were, in our days, made known; and*
" *many more in futurity we hoped would become fo. But now, as the*
" *Turks have conquered,* &c.*"

A little farther in the fame Epiftle, when he expreffes his fears,
left the Turks fhould deftroy all Books but their own, he fubjoins
　　　　　　　　　　　　　　　　　　　　　　　　　— " *Now*

---

* —*itaque manfit in hunc diem vetuftæ fapientiæ apud* Constantinopolim *monu-
mentum: ac, velut ibi domicilium Literarum effet, et ars fummæ philofophiæ, nemo Lati-
norum fatis doctus videri poterat, nifi Conftantinopoli aliquandiù ftuduiffit; quodque
florente Româ doctrinarum nomen habuerunt Athenæ, id tempeftate noftra videbatur Con-
ftantinopolis obtinere. Inde nobis Plato redditus: inde Ariftotelis, Demofthenis, Xeno-
phontis, Thucididis, Bafilii, Dionyfii, Origenis et aliorum multa Latinis opera diebus
noftris manifeftata funt; multa quòque in futurum manifeftanda fperabamus. Nunc vero,
ftuentibus Turcis,* &c. *Æueæ Sylv. Epift.* p. 704, 705. *Edit. Bafil.* 1551.

—" *Now therefore both* HOMER, *and* PINDAR, *and* MENANDER,
" *and all the more illuſtrious Poets will undergo a ſecond Death. Now*
" *will a final deſtruction find its way to the* GREEK PHILOSOPHERS.
" *A little light will remain perhaps among the* LATINS; *but that I ap-*
" *prehend will not be long, unleſs* GOD *from Heaven will look upon us*
" *with a more favourable eye, and grant a better fortune either to the*
" *Roman Empire, or to the Apoſtolic See,* &c. &c. * "

It muſt be remarked that, in this Epiſtle, by LATINS † he means
the Weſtern Europeans, as oppoſed to THE GREEKS, or *Eaſtern*; and
that by the ROMAN Empire (juſt before mentioned) he means the
GERMANIC Body.

THE Author's apprehenſions for the fate of Letters *in the Weſt* was
premature; for, upon the Deſtruction of this *imperial* City, the number of *learned Greeks,* which this Event drove into thoſe Weſtern
parts of *Europe*; the Favour of the *Popes* and the *Medici* Family,
ſhewn at this period to Literature; together with the then recent *In-*
vention of Printing, which, by multiplying Copies of Books, made
them ſo eaſy to be purchaſed — all this (I ſay) tended to promote
the

---

* *Nunc ergo et Homero, et Pindaro, Menandro, et omnibus illuſtrioribus Poetis ſecunda*
mors erit; nunc Græcorum philoſophorum ultimus patebit interitus. Reſtabit aliquid
lucis apud Latinos; at, fateor, neque id erit diuturnum, niſi mitiori nos oculo Deus ex
alto reſpexerit, fortunamque vel imperio Romano, vel Apoſtolicæ ſedi præbuerit meliorem,
&c. &c. Ibid. p. 705, 706.

Thoſe who have not the old Edition of *Æneas Sylvius,* may find the above quotations
in *Hody de Græcis Illuſtribus,* Lond. 1751. 8vo.

† *Nicetas* had before called them, SONS OF ÆNEAS. See p. 456.

Part III. the Caufe *of Knowledge* and *of Tafte*, and to put things into that train, in which we hope they may long continue.

BESIDES *Philelphus*, *Æneas Sylvius*, and many others, who were *Italians*, I might mention two *Greeks of the fame age*, GEORGE GEMISTUS, and Cardinal BESSARIO, both of them deeply knowing in *Grecian Literature* and *Philofophy*.

BUT as fome account of thefe laft and of their Writings has been already given *, I fhall quit the *Greeks*, after I have related a fhort Narrative; a Narrative fo far curious, as it helps to prove, that even among the *prefent Greeks*, in the day of *Servitude*, the remembrance of their *ancient* Glory is *not yet* totally extinct.

WHEN the late Mr. *Anfon* (Lord *Anfon*'s Brother) was upon his Travels in *the Eaft*, he hired a Veffel, to vifit the Ifle of *Tenedos*. His Pilot, *an old Greek*, as they were failing along, faid with fome fatisfaction,—*There 'twas our Fleet lay.* Mr. *Anfon* demanded, *What Fleet?*—*What Fleet*, replied the old Man (a little piqued at the Queftion)—WHY OUR GRECIAN FLEET AT THE SIEGE OF TROY †.

BUT we muft now quit *the Greeks*, and, in confequence of our plan, pafs to the ARABIANS, *followers of Mahomet.*

---

* See Vol. I. p. 133, 134.

† This ftory was told *the Author* by Mr. *Anfon himfelf.*

CHAP. VI.

Concerning THE SECOND CLASS *of Geniuses during the middle Age,*
THE ARABIANS, *or* SARACENS—*at first, barbarous—their Cha-*
racter before the time of Mahomet — Their greatest Caliphs were from
among the ABASSIDÆ—ALMANZUR *one of the first of that race—*
ALMAMUM *of the same race, a great Patron of Learning, and learn-*
ed Men — ARABIANS *cultivated Letters, as their Empire grew settled*
and established — Translated the best Greek Authors into their own
Language — Historians, ABULPHARAGIUS, ABULFEDA, BOHADIN
— Extracts from the last concerning SALADIN.

THE ARABIANS* began ill. The Sentiment of their Caliph
OMAR, when he commanded the *Alexandrian Library* to be
burnt (a fact we have already related †) was natural to any Bigot,
when in the plenitude of Despotism. But they grew more rational,
as they grew less bigotted, and by degrees began to think, that
Science was worth cultivating. They may be said indeed to
have recurred to their *ancient* Character; that Character, which
they did not rest upon brutal Force alone, but which they boasted

Ch. VI.

---

* As many Quotations are made in the following Chapters from *Arabian* Writers,
and more particularly from ABULPHARAGIUS, ABULFEDA, and BOHADIN; a short
account of those three authors will be given in the Notes of *this* Chapter, where their
Names come in course to be mentioned.

† See before, p. 424.

Part III. ed to imply three capital things, *Hospitality, Valour,* and *Eloquence* *.

WHEN Succefs in Arms has defeated Rivals, and Empire becomes not only extended but *eftablifhed,* then is it that Nations begin to think of *Letters,* and to cultivate Philofophy, and liberal Speculation. This happened to *the Athenians,* after they had triumphed over the *Perfians;* to the *Romans,* after they triumphed over *Carthage;* and to the ARABIANS, after the *Caliphate* was eftablifhed at *Bagdad* †.

AND here perhaps it may not be improper to obferve, that after the four firft Caliphs, came the race of the OMMIADÆ. Thefe about thirty years after *Mahomet,* upon the deftruction of *Ali,* ufurped the Sovereignty, and held it ninety years. They were confidered by the *Arabic* Hiftorians as a race of Tyrants, and were in number fourteen ‡. Having made themfelves by their oppreffions to be much detefted, the laft of them, *Merwin,* was depofed by *Al-Suffah,* from whom began another race, the race of ABASSIDÆ §, who claimed to be related in blood to *Mahomet,* by defcending from his Uncle, *Abbas.*   **As**

---

* *Schultens* in his *Monumenta vetuftiora Arabiæ* (Lugdun. Batavor. 1740) gives us in his Preface the following Paffage from *Saphadius,* an *Arabic* Author. ARABES *antiquitus non habebant, quo gloriarentur, quam* GLADIO, HOSPITE, *et* ELOQUENTIA.

† See before, p. 426, 427.

‡ See *Herbelot* ↑ *Bibliotheque Orientale,* under the word OMMIADES, alfo *Abulpharagius,* p. 158, 160. and in particular *Abulfeda,* p. 138, &c.

§ *Abulphar.* p. 138—150, &c. *Abulfeda,* p. 143. *Herbelot's Bib. Orient.* under the word ABASSIDES.

' As many of thefe were far fuperior in character to their predeceffors, fo their Dominion was of much longer duration, lafting for
more than five Centuries.

The former part of this Period may be called the Æra of *the
Grandeur,* and *Magnificence* of the Caliphate.

Almanzur, who was among the firft of them, removed the imperial feat from *Damafcus* to *Bagdad,* a City which he himfelf
founded upon the banks of the *Tigris,* and which foon after became
one of the moft fplendid Cities throughout the *Eaft.*

Almanzur was not only a great Conqueror, but a lover of Letters
and learned Men. 'Twas under him that *Arabian* Literature, which
had been at firft chiefly confined to Medicine and a few other
branches, was extended to Sciences of every denomination *.

His Grandfon Almamun (who reigned about fifty years after)
giving a full Scope to his love of Learning, fent to the *Greek* Emperors for Copies of their *beft* Books; employed the ableft Scholars,
that could be found, *to tranflate* them; and, when tranflated, encouraged men of genius in their perufal, taking a pleafure in being
prefent at *literary Converfations.* Then was it that learned men,
in the lofty Language of *Eaftern* Eloquence, were called *Luminaries,*
*that difpel darknefs; Lords of human kind; of whom, when the World
becomes deftitute, it becomes barbarous and favage* †.

THE

---

* See *Abulfeda,* p. 144. *Abulpharag.* p. 139. 141. 160.

† See *Abulfeda,* p. 181. *Abulpharag.* p. 160, 161. The *lofty Language* alluded to
ftands thus in the *Latin* Verfion of the page laft quoted. *Docti tenebrarum lumina
funt, et generis humani domini, quibus deftitutus ferus evadit mundus,*

Part III.   THE rapid Victories of thefe *Eaftern* Conquerors foon carried their Empire from *Afia* even into the remote regions of *Spain*. Letters *followed* them, as they went. *Plato*, *Ariftotle*, and their beft Greek Commentators were foon tranflated into *Arabic*; fo were *Euclid*, *Archimedes*, *Apollonius*, *Diophantus*, and the other Greek *Mathematicians*; fo *Hippocrates*, *Galen*, and the beft profeffors of *Medicine*; fo *Ptolemy*, and the noted Writers on the fubject of *Aftronomy*. The ftudy of thefe Greeks produced others like them; produced others, who not only explained them in *Arabic* Comments, but compofed *themfelves* original pieces upon the fame Principles.

AVERROES was celebrated for his Philofophy in *Spain*; ALPHA-RABI and AVICENNA were equally admired thro' *Afia*[*]. Science (to fpeak a little in their own ftile) may be faid to have extended

> —— *a Gadibus ufque*
>
> *Auroram et Gangem* ——.

Nor, in this immenfe multitude, did they want *Hiftorians*, fome of which, (fuch as ABULFEDA, ABULPHARAGIUS, BOHADIN[†], and others)

---

[*] See *Herbelot*, under the feveral Names here quoted.

[†] ABULFEDA was an *Oriental Prince*, defcended from the fame Family with the great *Saladin*. He died in the year 1345, and publifhed *a General Hiftory*, in which however he is *moft particular* and diffufe in the Narrative of *Mahomet*, and his Succeffors.

Learned Men have publifhed different parts of this curious Author. *Gagnier* gave us in *Arabic* and *Latin* as much of him, as related to *Mahomet*. This was printed in a thin Folio at *Oxford*, in the year 1723.

The largeft Portion, and from which moft of the facts here related are taken, was publifhed by *Reifke*, or *Reifkius* (a very able Scholar) in *Latin only*, and includes the Hiftory of the *Arabians* and their *Caliphs*, from the firft year of the *Mahometan Æra*,

                            An.

others) have been tranflated, and are perufed, even in their Tranflations, both with pleafure and profit, as they give not only the outlines of amazing Enterprifes, but a fample of Manners, and Character, widely differing from our own.

No Hiftory perhaps can be more curious than the Life of Saladin by Bohadin, This Author was a conftant Attendant upon
the

An. Dom. 622, to their 406th year, *An. Dom.* 1015. This Book, a moderate or thin
Quarto, was printed at *Lipfic,* in the year 1754.

We have another Portion of a period *later ftill* than this, publifhed by *Schultens* in
Arabic and *Latin;* a Portion relative to the Life of *Saladin,* and fubjoined by *Schultens*
to the Life of that great Prince by *Bohadin,* which he (Schultens) publifhed. But more
of this hereafter,

Abulpharagius gave likewife *a general Hiftory,* divided into nine *Dynafties,* but is
far more minute and diffufe (as well as *Abulfeda)* in his Hiftory of *Mahomet* and the
Caliphs.

He was a Chriftian, and the Son of a Chriftian Phyfician—was an *Afiatic* by birth,
and wrote in *Arabic,* as did *Abulfeda.* He brought down his Hiftory a little below
the time of the celebrated *Jingez Chan,* that is to the middle of the thirteenth Century,
the time when he lived. A fine Edition of this Author was given in *Arabic* and *Latin,*
by the learned *Pococke,* in two fmall Quartos, at Oxford, 1663.

Bohadin wrote the Life of the celebrated *Saladin,* but more particularly that part
of it, which refpects the *Crufades,* and *Saladin's* taking of *Jerufalem. Bohadin* has
many things to render his Hiftory highly valuable; he was a *Contemporary* Writer;
was an *Eye-witnefs of almoft every Tranfaction;* and what is more, inftead of being an
obfcure Man, was *high in office,* a *favourite* of *Saladin's,* and *conftantly about his perfon.*
This author flourifhed in the twelfth Century, that is in the time of *Saladin* and King
Richard, Saladin's antagonift.

Bohadin's Hiftory in *Arabic* and *Latin,* with much excellent Erudition, was publifhed in an elegant Folio, by that accurate Scholar, *Schultens,* at *Leyden,* in the year
1755.

It muft be obferved that, tho' Abulpharagius was a *Chriftian,* yet Abulfeda and
Bohadin were both *Mahometans.* All three Hiftorians bear a great refemblance to
Plutarch, as they have enriched their Hiftories with fo many ftriking *Anecdotes.* From
Abulpharagius too, and Abulfeda, we have much curious information as to the
Progrefs and State of Literature in thofe Ages and Countries.

 the perfon of this great Prince thro' all his active and important
Life, down to his laft Sicknefs, and the very hour of his Death.
The many curious Anecdotes, which he relates, give us the ftriking
Picture of an Eaftern Hero.

TAKE the following Inftance of *Saladin*'s Juftice and Affability.

" HE was in company once with his intimate Friends, enjoying
" their converfation apart, the crowd being difmift, when a Slave of
" fome rank brought him a petition in behalf of a perfon oppreft.
" The Sultan faid, that he was then fatigued, and wifhed the matter,
" whatever it was, might for a time be deferred. The other did not
" attend to what was defired, but on the contrary almoft thruft the
" petition into the Sultan's face. The Sultan on this, opening and
" reading it over, declared he thought the Petitioner's Caufe a good
" one. — *Let then our Sovereign Lord*, fays the other, *fign it.* —*There*
" *is no Ink-ftand*, fays the Sultan (who, being at that time feated at
" the door of his Tent, rendered it impoffible for any one to enter)
" —*You have one*, replies the Petitioner, *in the inner part of your*
" *Tent*, (which meant, as the Writer well obferves, little lefs than
" bidding the Prince go and bring it himfelf.) The Sultan, looking
" back and feeing the Ink-ftand behind him, cries out, *God help me*,
" *the man fays true*, and immediately reached back for it, and figned
" the Inftrument."

HERE the Hiftorian, who was prefent, fpoke the language of a
good Courtier. " *God Almighty*, faid he, *bore this Teftimony to our*
" *Prophet, that HIS Difpofition was a fublime one: our Sovereign Lord*,
                                                    " *I perceive*,

" *I perceive, has a Temper like him.* The Sultan not regarding the
" Compliment, replied coolly.—*The Man did no harm; we have dif-*
" *patched his bufinefs, and the Reward is at hand* *."

AFTER this fact we fhall the more readily believe *Bohadin*, when
fpeaking of the fame illuftrious perfon, he informs us, that his Converfation was remarkably elegant and pleafing; that he was a perfect
mafter of the Arabian Families, of their Hiftory, their Rites, and
Cuftoms; that he knew alfo the Genealogies of their Horfes (for
which we know that to this hour Arabia is celebrated;) nor was he
ignorant of what was rare and curious in the world at large; that he
was particularly affable in his inquiries about the Health of his
Friends, their Illnefs, their Medicines, &c. that his Difcourfe was
free from all obfcenity and fcandal; and that he was remarkably
tender and compaffionate both to orphans and to perfons in years †.

I MAY add from the fame authority an inftance of his Juftice.

" As BOHADIN, the Hiftorian, was one day exercifing at *Jeru-*
" *falem* his office of a Judge, a decent old Merchant tendered him
" a Bill or Libel of Complaint, which he infifted upon having open-
" ed. *Who* (fays Bohadin) *is your Adverfary?—My Adverfary,* re-
" plies the Merchant, *is the Sultan himfelf: but this is the Seat of*
" *Juftice,*

---

* See *Bohadin*, p. 22.

† See *Bohadin*, p. 23. and at the end of *Bohadin*, the *Excerpta* from *Abulfeda*,
p. 62, 63.

 " *Juflice, and we have heard that you* (applying to Bobadin) *are not*
" *governed by regard to Perfons.* Bohadin told him the Caufe could
" not be decided without his Adverfary's being firft apprized. The
" Sultan accordingly was informed of the affair; fubmitted to ap-
" pear; produced his Witneffes; and, having juftly defended him-
" felf, gained the Caufe. Yet fo little did he refent this Treat-
" ment, that he difmift his Antagonift with a rich Garment and a
" Donation *."

His *Severity* upon occafions was no lefs confpicuous, than his
Clemency.

We learn from the fame Writer, that *Arnold*, Lord of *Cracho*,
(called *Reginald* by *M. Paris*, and *Rainold* by *Fuller)* had thought
proper, during the Truce between the *Chriftians* and the *Saracens*, to
fall upon the Caravan of Travellers going to *Mecca* from *Egypt*,
whom he cruelly pillaged and thruft into Dungeons, and when they
appealed to the Truce for better ufage, replied with fcorn, *Let your
Mahomet deliver you.*

Saladin, fired with indignation at this perfidy, vowed a Vow to
difpatch him *with his own hand*, if he could ever make him prifoner.
This Event happened at the fatal Battle of *Hittyn*, where *Guy*
King of *Jerufalem*, *Arnold*, and all the principal Commanders of
the *Chriftian* Army were taken. *Saladin*, as foon as his Tent could
be

---

* See *Bohadin*, p. 10.

be erected, in the height of his Feſtivity, orders King *Guy*, his Brother *Geoffry*, and prince *Arnold* into his preſence.

As *Guy* the King was nearly dying for thirſt, *Saladin* preſented him a delicious Cup, cooled with Snow, out of which the King drank, and then tranſmitted it to *Arnold*. *Tell the King, ſays the Sultan, turning to his Interpreter, tell him, Thou, King, art He, who haſt given the Cup to* THIS MAN, *and not I.*

Now it is a moſt admirable Cuſtom (obſerves *Bohadin*) among the *Arabians*, a cuſtom breathing their liberal and noble diſpoſition, that a Captive, the moment he has obtained meat or drink from his Captor, is by that very treatment rendered ſecure of Life, the *Arabians* being a people, by whom HOSPITALITY and the generous *point of honour* is moſt ſacredly obſerved.

THE Priſoners, being diſmiſt, were ſoon remanded, when only the Sultan and a few of his Miniſters were left. *Arnold* was the firſt brought in, whom the Sultan reminding of his irreverent Speech, ſubjoined, *See* ME *now act the part of Mahomet's Avenger.* He then offers *Arnold* to embrace the *Mahometan* Faith, which he refuſing, the Sultan with his drawn ſcymitar gave him a ſtroke, that broke the hilt, while the reſt of his attendants joined and diſpatched him. King *Guy* thought the ſame deſtiny was prepared for him. The Sultan however *bid him be of good cheer,* obſerving, that *it was not cuſtomary for Kings to kill Kings; but that this Man had brought deſtruction upon himſelf by paſſing the Bounds of all Faith and Honour* *.

WHEN

---

* See *Bohadin*, p. 27. 28. 70. 71.

 WHEN Princes are victorious, their Rigour is often apt to extend too far, especially where Religion, as in thefe Wars called HOLY, blends itfelf with the tranfaction.

MORE than fourfcore years before *Saladin's* time the Crufaders, when they took *Jerufalem*, had murdered every *Mahometan* they found there *,

WHEN *Saladin* took *Jerufalem*, he had at firft meditated putting all the *Franks* to the fword, as a fort of retaliation for what had been done there by thefe firft Crufaders. However he was perfuaded to change his intention, and fpare them; nay more, after he had turned the reft of their Churches into Mofques, he ftill left them one, in which they had Toleration to perform their worfhip †.

AFTER the fatal Battle of *Hittyn*, where *Guy* and *Arnold* (as above mentioned) were taken, *Saladin* divided his Prifoners; fome were fold; others put to death; and among the laft all the commanders of the *Hofpitalers* and *Templars*.

ON the taking of *Ptolemais* by the Crufaders, fome difference arifing between them and *Saladin* about the Terms of the Capitulation,

---

* See *Abulpharagius*, p. 243. *Matt. Par.* in anno 1099. p. 48. *Fuller's Holy Warre*, B. I. c. 24. p. 141.

† See *Abulpharagius*, p. 273. *Bohadin*, p. 73. *Abulfedæ Excerpta*, p. 42. *Matt. Paris*, p. 145. *Fuller's H. Warre*, B. II. c. 46. p. 106.

lation, the Crufaders led the Captive *Muffelmans* out of the City into a Plain, and there in cold blood murdered three thoufand *.

Cuftoms in all times, and in all Countries, have a fingular effect. When the French Ambaffadors were introduced to *Saladin*, he was playing with a favourite Son, by name *Elemir*. The Child no fooner beheld the Embaffadors with their Faces fhaved, their Hair cut, and their Garments of an unufual form, than he was terrified, and began to cry. A Beard perhaps would have terrified a Child in *France*: and yet, if Beards are the gift of Nature, it feems eafier to defend the little Arabian †.

BOHADIN, our Hiftorian, appears to have thought fo, who, mentioning a young *Frank* of high Quality, defcribes him to be a fine Youth, except that his Face was *fhaved*; a *Mark*, as he calls it, by which the *Franks* are diftinguifhed ‡.

WE cannot quit *Saladin*, without a word on his *Liberality*.

' HE ufed to fay, 'twas poffible there might exift a man (and by fuch man 'twas fuppofed he meant *himfelf*) who with the fame eye of contempt could look on *Riches* and on *Dirt* §.

THESE feem to have been his Sentiments, when fome of his Revenue-officers were convicted of putting into his Treafury Purfes

of.

---

* See *Bohadin*, p. 70, for the *Templars*, and p. 183, for the *Mufulmans*—alfo *Fuller's* H. *Warre*, B. II. c. 45. p. 105.

† See *Bohadin*, p. 270.   ‡ See *Bohadin*, p. 193.   § See *Bohadin*, p. 13.

Part III. of Brafs for Purfes of Gold. By the rigour of Eaftern Juftice
they might have immediately been executed; but *Saladin* did no
more than difmifs them from their office *.

When his Treafury was fo empty, that he could not fupply
his Largeffes, in order to have it in his power, he fold his very
furniture †.

When his Army was encamped in the Plains of *Ptolemaïs*, 'twas
computed he gave away no lefs than twelve thoufand Horfes; nay,
'twas faid he never mounted a Horfe, which was not either *given
away*, or *promifed* ‡.

Bohadin, whom he employed in moft of his acts of *Munificence*,
relates, that all who approached him, were fenfible of its effects;
nay that he exceeded in his Donations even the unreafonable wifhes
of the Petitioners, altho' he was *never heard to boaft* of any favour
that he had conferred §.

The effect of fuch immenfe *Liberality* was, that, when he died,
out of all the vaft revenues of *Egypt*, *Syria*, the *Oriental Provinces*,
and *Arabia Felix*, there was no more left in his Treafury, than forty
feven pieces of Silver, and one of Gold; fo that they were forced to
borrow money, to defray the expences of his Funeral ‖.

As

---

* See *Bohadin*, p. 27.   † See *Bohadin*, 12, 13.

‡ See *Bohadin*, p. 13.—The fame Book, in the Extract from *Abulfeda*, p 64.

§ See *Bohad.* p. 13.

‖ See *Bohadin*, p. 5. 13. and, in the fame Book, the Extracts from *Abulfeda*, p. 66.—
Abulpharagius, p. 277. See *Fuller's* Character of *Saladin*, *Holy Warre*, B. III. c. 14.
as alfo the above Extracts, and *Abulpharagius*, both under the fame pages.

As to the facts refpecting the Weftern Crufaders at this period, Ch. VI.
and particularly *Saladin's* great Antagonift, *Richard Coeur de Leon*,
thefe are fubjects referved, till we come to the *Latins* or *Franks*.

WE fhall now fay fomething concerning *Arabian* Poetry and
Works of *Invention*, adding withal a few more Anecdotes, relative
to their *Manners* and *Character*.

C H A P. VII.

Arabian Poetry, *and Works of Invention — Facts relative to their*
Manners and Characters.

Part III. ARABIAN Poetry is fo immenfe a Field, that he, who enters
it, is in danger of being loft. 'Twas their favourite ftudy long
before the time of *Mahomet*, and many Poems are ftill extant of an
earlier Æra *. So much did they value. themfelves upon the Elegance of their Compofitions, that they called their neighbours, and
more particularly the *Perfians*, Barbarians †. It feems unfortunate for thefe laft, that the *old Greeks* fhould have. diftinguifhed
them by the fame appellation ‡.

If we reckon among pieces of Poetry not the *Metrical* only, but
thofe alfo the mere efforts of *Invention* and *Imagination*, (fuch as the
incomparable *Telemachus*, of the truly eloquent *Fenelon)* we may
juftly range in this Clafs the *Arabian* Nights, and the *Turkifh* Tales.
They are valuable not only for exhibiting a picture of *Oriental* manners, during the fplendor of the *Caliphate*, but for inculcating in
many

---

* See *Schultens* in his *Monumenta vetuftiora Arabiæ*, Lugd. Bat. 1740, where there
will be found Fragments of Poetry *many Centuries before Mahomet*, and fome fuid to
be as ancient *as the days of Solomon*.

† Vid. *Pocockii Not. in Carmen Tograi*, p. 5.—and *Abulfed.* p. 19 t.

‡ See *Ifocrates, Plato, Demofthenes*, &c.

many inftances a ufeful and inftructive *Moral.* Nothing can be Ch. VII.
better written than *the Tale of Alnafchar*, to illuftrate that important
part of the *Stoic Moral*, the fatal confequence *of not refifting our
Fancies* *.

THEY were fond of the *Fabulous* and *Allegorical*, and loved to re-
prefent under that Form the doctrines they moft favoured. They
favoured no doctrine more than that of each individual's *inevitable
Deftiny.* Let us fee after what manner they conveyed this doctrine.

" THEY tell us, that as *Solomon* (whom they fuppofed a Magician
" from his fuperior Wifdom) was one day walking with a perfon in
" *Paleftine*, his Companion faid to him with fome horror, *what ugly
" Being is that which approaches us ?· I don't like his Vifage—fend me,
" I pray thee, to the remoteft Mountain of India.* Solomon complied,
" and the very moment he was fent off, the *ugly* Being arrived. So-
" *lomon* (faid the Being) *how came that fellow* HERE? *I was to have
" fetched him from the remoteft Mountain of India.* Solomon anfwer-
" ed—ANGEL OF DEATH, *thou wilt find him* THERE †."

I MAY

---

* A curious and accurate Verfion of this admirable Tale is printed at *Oxford*, in a
Grammar of the *Arabic* Language; a Verfion which gives us too much reafon to
lament our imperfect view of thofe other ingenious Fictions, fo *obfcurely* tranfmitted
to us thro' a *French Medium.*

† This Tale was told me by Dr. *Gregory Sharpe*, late Mafter of the Temple, well
known for his knowledge in *Oriental literature.*

I MAY add to this that elegant Fiction concerning the *self-taught* Philofopher *Hai Ebn Yokdan*, who, being fuppofed to have been caft an Infant on a defert Ifland, is made by various Incidents (fome poffible, but all ingenious) to afcend gradually, as he grew up *in Soli-tude*, to the Sublime of all Philofophy, Natural, Moral, and Divine*.

BUT this laft was the Production of a more refined Period, when they had adopted the Philofophy of other nations. In their earlier days of Empire they valued no Literature, but their own, as we have learnt from the celebrated Story, already related, concerning *Omar*, *Amrus*, and the Library at *Alexandria* †.

THE fame *Omar*, after the fame *Amrus* had conquered the vaft Province of *Egypt*, and given (according to the cuftom of thofe early times) many proofs of *perfonal* ftrength and valour, the fame *Omar* (I fay) was defirous to fee the Sword, by which *Amrus* had performed fo many Wonders. Having taken it into his hand, and found it no better than any other fword, he returned it with contempt, and averred, *it was good for nothing. You fay true, Sir,* replied *Amrus; for you demanded to fee the Sword, not the Arm that wielded it; while that was wanting, the Sword was no better than the fword of Pharezdacus.*

Now *Pharezdacus* was it feems a Poet, famous for his *fine defcription* of a Sword, but not equally famous for his *perfonal Prowefs* ‡.

"Tis

---

* See *Pococke's* Edition of this Work, Oxon. 1671.

† See before, p. 424. 463.   ‡ *Pocock. Notæ in Carm. Togr.* p. 184.

'Tis a fingular inftance of their attention to *Hofpitality*, that they
ufed to kindle Fires by night, upon Hills near their Camps, to conduct wandering Travellers to a place of refuge *.

Such an attention to this Duty naturally brings to our mind what
Eumæus in *the Odyffey* fays to *Ulyffes*.

> Ξεῖν', ὅ μοι θέμις ἐς', οὐδ' εἰ κακίων σέθεν ἔλθοι,
>
> Ξεῖνον ἀτιμῆσαι, πρὸς γὰρ Διός εἰσιν ἅπαντες
>
> Ξεῖνοι ——

> STRANGER, *I dare not with difhonour treat*
>
> *A* STRANGER, *tho' a ſhorſe, than thou, fhould come;*
>
> *For* STRANGERS *all belong to Jove* —— Ὀδυσ. Ξ. 56.

Nor are there wanting other inftances of Refemblance to the age
of *Homer*. When *Ibrahim*, a dangerous competitor of the Caliph
Almanzur, had in a decifive battle been mortally wounded, and his
friends were endeavouring to carry him off, a defperate conflict enfued, in which the Enemy prevailed, overpowered his Friends, and
gained what they contended for, the body of *Ibrahim*. The refemblance between this Story and that refpecting the Body of *Patroclus*,
is a fact too obvious, to be more than hinted †.

In an earlier period, when *Moawigea* (the competitor of the great
Ali) was preft in a battle, and had juft begun to fly, he is reported
to have rallied upon the ftrength of certain verfes, which at that
critical

---

* *Ejufd. Carm. Togral*, p. 111.   † See *Abulfeda*, p. 148.

Part III. critical inflant occured to his memory. The Verfes were thefe, as
we attempt to tranflate them.

> When direful Scenes of Death appear,
> And fill thy flutt'ring Heart with fear :
> Say — HEART! be firm; the ftorm endure;
> For Evils ever find a cure.
> Their Mem'ry, fhould we 'fcape, will pleafe;
> Or, fhould we fall, we fleep at eafe *.

THIS naturally fuggefts to every Lover of *Homer*, what is faid by
Ulyffes.

> Τέτλαθι δὴ κραδίη· κỳ κύντερον ἄλλο ποτ᾽ ἔτλης
> Ἥματι τῷ, ὅτε, κ. τ. λ.   Οδυς. Υ, 18.

> Indure it, HEART; for worfe thou haft indured
> In days of yore, when, &c.

Such Refemblances, as thefe, prove a probable connection be-
tween the manners of the *Arabians*, and thofe of the ancient *Greeks*.
There are other Refemblances, which, as they refpect not only *Greek*
Authors but *Roman*, are perhaps no more than *cafual*.

THUS an *Arabian* Poet —

> Horfes and Wealth we know you've none;
> Let then your Eloquence atone
> For Fortune's failure † ——

WHAT

---

* *Abulfeda*, p. 91.   † *Abulfeda*, p. 279.

WHAT the *Arabian* fays of his Friend, *Horace* fays of himfelf.   Ch. VII
      Donarem pateras, grataque commodus,
      Cenforine, meis &c.   Od. I.

ANOTHER of their Poets has the following Sentiment.
      Who fondly can himfelf deceive,
      And venture Reafon's rules to leave;
      Who dares, thro' ignorance, afpire
      To that, which no one can acquire;
      To fpotlefs fame, to folid health,
      To firm, unalienable, wealth:
      Each Wifh he forms, will furely find
      A Wifh denied to human kind *.

HERE we read *the Stoic* Defcription of *Things not in our power,* and
the confequence of purfuing them, as if they were *Things in our
power,* concerning which fatal miftake fee *Epictetus,* either in the Original, or in Mrs. *Carter's* valuable Tranflation. The *Enchiridion* we
know begins with this very doctrine.

THERE is a fine Precept among the *Arabians* — *Let him, to whom*
THE GATE *of Good Fortune is opened, feize his Opportunity; for he
knoweth not, how foon it may be fhut.*

COMPARE this with thofe admired Lines in *Shakfpeare* —
      There is A TIDE *in the affairs of men,*
      Which taken at the flood, &c.   Jul. Caef. Act IV. Sc. 5.

                                   THO'

---

                      * *Abulfeda,* p. 279.

 Tho' the *Metaphors differ*, the *Sentiment* is *the same* *.

In the Comment on the Verfes of *Tograi* we meet an *Arabic* Sentiment, which fays, that *a Friend is another felf*. The fame elegant thought occurs in *Ariflotle's* Ethics, and that in the fame words. Ἔϛι γὰρ ὁ φίλος ἄλλος αὐτός †.

After the preceding inftances of *Arabian* Genius, the following perhaps may give a fample of their *Manners* and *Charaɛter*.

On a rainy day the *Caliph Almotafem* happened, as he was riding, to wander from his attendants. While he was thus alone, he found an old Man, whofe Afs, laden with faggots, had juft caft his burden, and was mired in a flough. As the old Man was ftanding in a ftate of perplexity, *the Caliph* quitted his horfe, and went to helping up the Afs. *In the name of my father and my mother, I befeech thee*, fays the old Man, *do not fpoil thy cloaths*. *That is nothing to Thee*, replied the Caliph, who, after having helped up the Afs, replaced the faggots, and wafhed his hands, got again upon his horfe, the old Man in the mean time crying out, *Oh Youth, may God reward thee!* Soon after this the Caliph's company overtook him, whom he generoufly commanded to prefent the old Man with a noble largefs of gold ‡.

To this inftance of *Generofity* we fubjoin another of *Refentment*.

The

---

* *Bohadin Vit. Salad.* p. 73. Of this Work, p. 373.

† *Ariftl. Ethic. Nicom.* X. 4. and *Not. in Carm. Tograi*, p. 25.

‡ *Abulpharagius*, p. 166.

Ch. VII.

The *Grecian Emperors* ufed to pay *the Caliphs* a tribute. This the Emperor *Nicephorus* would pay no longer; and not only that, but requiring the *Caliph* in a haughty manner to refund all he had received, added that, if he refufed, the Sword fhould decide the Controverfy. The Caliph had no fooner read the Letter, than inflamed with rage he infcribes upon the back of it the following anfwer.

In the name of the moft merciful God: from Harun, Prince of the Faithful, to Nicephorus, Dog of the Romans: I have read thy Epiftle, Thou Son of an unbelieving Mother: to which, what thou fhalt BE-HOLD, and not what thou fhalt HEAR, fhall ferve for an anfwer.

HE immediately upon the very day decamped; marched as far as *Heraclia*, and, filling all things with rapine and flaughter, extorted from *Nicephorus* the performance of his Contract*.

THE following is an inftance of a calmer *Magnanimity*. In the middle of the third Century after *Mahomet*, one *Jacub*, from being originally a Brazier, had made himfelf Mafter of fome fine Provinces, which he governed at will, tho' profeffing (like the Eaftern Governors of later times) a feeming deference to his proper Sovereign.

THE *Caliph*, not fatisfied with this apparent fubmiffion, fent a Legate to perfuade him into a more perfect obedience. *Jacub,* who

---

* *Abulfeda,* p. 166, 167.

3 Q 2

Part III. who was then ill, fent for the Legate into his prefence, and there fhewed him three things, which he had prepared for his infpection; a Sword, fome black Barley Bread, and a Bundle of Onions. He then informed the Legate, that, fhould he die of his prefent diforder, the Caliph in fuch cafe would find no farther trouble. But if the contrary fhould happen, there could be then no Arbitrator to decide between them, excepting *that*, pointing to the *Sword*. He added, that if Fortune fhould prove adverfe, fhould he be conquered by the Caliph, and ftripped of his poffeffions, he was then refolved to return to his ancient frugality, pointing to the *Black Bread* and the *Bundle of Onions* *.

To former inftances of *Munificence* we add the following, concerning the celebrated *Almamun* †.

BEING once at *Damafcus*, and in great want of money, he complained of it to his Brother *Mottefem*. His Brother affured him he fhould have money in a few days, and fent immediately for thirty thoufand pieces of Gold from the revenues of thofe Provinces, which he governed in the name of his Brother. When the money arrived, brought by the Royal beafts of burden, *Almamun* invited *Jahia* the Son of *Actam*, one of his favourites, to attend him on horfeback, and view what was brought. They went accordingly, and beheld the Treafure arranged in the fineft order, and the Camels too, which had brought it, richly decorated. The Prince admired both the quantity of the money, and the elegance of the fhow;

and

---

* *Abulfeda*, p. 214.   † See p. 465.

and as his Courtier looked on with no lefs admiration, *he bid them*
be of good cheer. Then turning about to *Jahia:* O! *Abu Moham-*
med, fays he, *we fhould be fordid indeed, were we to depart hence with*
all this money, as if it were fcraped up for ourfelves alone, whilft our
longing friends look on to no purpofe. Calling therefore immediately
for a Notary, he commands him to write down for fuch a family fo
many thoufands; for fuch a family fo many; and fo on, never
ftopping till, out of the thirty thoufand pieces, he had given away
twenty-four thoufand, without fo' much as taking his foot out of
the ftirrup*.

FROM *Munificence* we pafs to another Quality, which, tho' lefs
amiable, is not lefs ftriking and popular, I mean *Magnificence.*

THE fplendour of the Caliph *Moctader,* when he received the
Ambaffador of the *Greek Emperor* at *Bagdad,* feems hardly credible.
We relate it from one of their Hiftorians, precifely as we find it.

THE Caliph's whole Army both Horfe and Foot were under
Arms, which together made a Body of one hundred and fixty
thoufand Men. His State-officers ftood near him in the moft fplendid apparel, their Belts fhining with Gold and Gems. Near them
were feven thoufand Eunuchs; four thoufand white, the remainder
of them black. The Porters or Door-keepers were in number feven
hundred. Barges and Boats with the moft fuperb decoration were
fwimming on the *Tigris.* Nor was the Palace itfelf lefs fplendid,
in

---

* *Abulfeda,* p. 189.

Part III. in which were hung up thirty-eight thoufand pieces of Tapeftry; twelve thoufand five hundred of which were of filk, embroidered with gold. The Carpets on the floor were twenty-two thoufand. An hundred Lions were brought out, with a Keeper to each Lion.

Among the other Spectacles of rare and flupendous luxury, was a Tree of Gold and Silver, which opened itfelf into eighteen larger branches, upon which, and the other lefs branches, fate Birds of every fort, made alfo of gold and filver. The Tree glittered with Leaves of the fame Metals, and while its branches thro' Machinery appeared to move of themfelves, the feveral Birds upon them warbled their proper and natural notes.

When the *Greek* Ambaffador was introduced to the *Caliph*, he was led by the Vifir thro' all this *Magnificence* *.

But befides *Magnificence* of this kind, which was at beft but *temporary*, the Caliphs gave inftances of *Grandeur* more *permanent*. Some of them provided public buildings for the reception of Travellers; fupplied the Roads with Wells and Watering Places; meafured out the diftances by columns of Stone, and eftablifhed Pofts and Couriers. Others repaired old Temples, or built magnificent new ones. The provifion of Snow (which in hot Countries is almoft a Neceffary) was not forgotten. Add to this Forums, or public Places for Merchants to affemble; Infirmaries; Obfervatories, with proper Inftruments, for the ufe of Aftronomers; Libraries, Schools,

and

---

* *Abulfeda*, p. 237. This, according to the *Chriftian Æra*, happened in the year 917.

and Colleges for Students; together with Societies, inftituted for Ch. VII.
Philofophical inquiry*.

In the account of the *Efcurial Arabic* Manufcripts, lately given by
the learned *Cafiri*, it appears that the *Public* Libraries in *Spain*,
when under the *Arabian* Princes, were no fewer than feventy: a
noble help this to Literature, when Copies of Books were fo rare and
expenfive †.

A transaction between one of the Caliph of *Bagdad*'s Ambaffadors and the Court of *Conftantinople*, is here fubjoined, in order to illuftrate the then *Manners* both of the Ambaffador and the Court.

As this Court was a remnant of the ancient Imperial one under
the *Cafars*, it ftill retained (as was natural) after its dominions were

fo

------

* Many things are enumerated in this Paragraph, to confirm which we fubjoin the
following References among many omitted.

For *Buildings to accommodate Travellers,* Abulfed. p. 154. *Abulphar.* p. 315, 316.

For *Wells upon the Road, Watering-places* and *Mile-ftones,* Abulfed. p. 154. for *Pofts
and Couriers,* the fame, p. 157. 289.

For *Temples,* Abulfed. p. 125. *Abulphar.* p. 210, 315, 316.

For *Snow,* Abulfed. p. 154. *Abulphar.* p. 261. *Bohadin,* p. 70.

For *Infirmaries,* Abulpher. p. 210, 343.

For *Obfervatories, Public Schools,* &c. *Abulphar,* p. 216.

For *Learned Societies,* Abulphar. p. 217. *Abulfed.* p. 181, 182, 183. 210. 274.
Bohadia. Vit Salad. p. 25.

Among their Philofophical Tranfactions was a Menfuration of the Earth's Circum-
ference, made by order of the Caliph *Almamun,* which they brought to about twenty-
four thoufand Miles.

† Vid. *Biblioth. Arabica-Hifpan.* Vol. II. p. 71. *Matriti,* 1770.

 fo much leffened, an attachment to that Pomp and thofe minute Ceremonials, which in the zenith of its Power it had been able to enforce. 'Twas an Affection for this fhadow of Grandeur, when the
fubftance was in a manner gone, that induced the Emperor Conftantine Porphyrogenitus to write no lefs than a large Folio Book upon
its Ceremonials *.

'Twas in confequence of the fame principles, that the above Ambaffador, tho' coming from the Caliph, was told to make a humble
Obeifance, as he approached the Grecian Emperor. This the Ambaffador (who had his national pride alfo) abfolutely refufing, it was
ingenioufly contrived, that he fhould be introduced to the Emperor
thro' a door fo very low, as might oblige him, however unwillingly,
to make the Obeifance required. The Ambaffador, when he arrived,
no fooner faw the door, than he comprehended the contrivance, and
with great readinefs turned about, and entered the Room backward †.

We have faid little concerning eminent Arabians during this
period in Spain. Yet that we may not be wholly filent, we fhall
mention one fact concerning Averroes, the famous Philofopher
and Lawyer, who was born at Corduba in the eleventh Century.

As he was lecturing one day in the College of Lawyers, a Slave,
belonging to one who was his Enemy, came and whifpered him.
Averroes turning round, and faying, *well, well*, the company believed

---

* See before, p. 450.   † Abulphar.

lieved the Slave had brought him a meſſage from his maſter. The
next day the Slave returned, implored his pardon, and publicly con-
feſſed that, when he whiſpered him, he had ſpoken a ſlander. *God
forgive thee*, replied AVERROES; *Thou haſt publicly ſhewn me to be a
patient man; and as for thy injury, 'tis not worthy of notice.* AVER-
ROES after this gave him money, adding withal this monition: *What
thou haſt done to* ME, *do not do to another* *.

AND here, before we conclude this Chapter, we cannot help con-
feſſing that the *Faɛts*, we have related, are not always arranged in the
ſtriɛt order of *Chronology*.

THE MODES indeed of *Hiſtory* (if theſe Chapters merit that
name) appear to be different. *There is a Mode* which we may call
Hiſtorical *Declamation*; a *Mode*, where the Author, dwelling little
upon *Faɛts*, indulges himſelf in various and copious *Reflections*.

WHATEVER Good (if any) may be derived from this Method, it
is not likely to give us much Knowledge of *Faɛts*.

Another Mode is that, which I call *General* or rather *Public* Hiſtory; a *Mode*, abundant in *Faɛts*, where Treaties and Alliances,
Battles and Sieges, Marches and Retreats are accurately retailed;
together with Dates, Deſcriptions, Tables, Plans, and all the colla-
teral helps both of *Chronology* and *Geography*.

                                                         IN

----

* *Fabric. Biblioth. Græc.* T. XIII. p. 283, 284.

Part III.   In this, no doubt, there is Utility. Yet *the famenefs* of the
Events refembles not a little the Samenefs of Human Bodies. One
Head, two Shoulders, two Legs, &c. feem equally to characterife an
European and an *African*; a native of old *Rome*; and a native *of
Modern*.

A third Species of Hiftory ftill behind is that, which gives a fample
of Sentiments and Manners.

If the account of *thefe laft* be faithful, it cannot fail being inftructive, fince we view thro' thefe *the interiour of human Nature.*
'Tis by thefe we perceive what fort of animal *Man* is; fo that while,
not only *Europeans* are diftinguifhed from *Afiatics,* but *Englifh* from
French, French from *Italians,* and (what is ftill more) every individual
from his neighbour; we view at the fame time one Nature, *which
is common to them all.*

Horace informs us that a *Drama,* where the Sentiments and
Manners are well preferved, will pleafe the Audience more than a
Pompous Fable, where they are *wanting* *. Perhaps, what is true
in *Dramatic* Compofition, is not lefs true in *Hiftorical.*

Plutarch, among the *Greek* Hiftorians, appears in a peculiar
manner to have merited this praife. So likewife Bohadin among
the *Arabians,* and to Him we add Abulpharagius, and Abulfeda, from whom fo many facts in thefe Chapters are taken.

Nor

---

* Sup. p. 398. in the Note.

Nor ought I to omit (as I shall soon refer to them) some of our best Monkish Historians, tho' prone upon occasion to degenerate into *the incredible.* As they often lived during the times which they described, 'twas natural they should paint *the life* and THE MAN-NERS, which *they saw.*

A single Chapter more will finish all we have to say concerning the *Arabians.*

C H A P. VIII.

Arabians favoured MEDICINE *and* ASTROLOGY —*facts, relative to
these two subjects* — *they valued* KNOWLEDGE, *but had no Ideas of*
CIVIL LIBERTY — *the mean Exit of their last Caliph,* MOSTASSEM
— *End of their Empire in* ASIA, *and in* SPAIN — *their present
wretched degeneracy in* AFRICA — *an Anecdote.*

Part III.
THE ARABIANS favoured MEDICINE and ASTROLOGY, and
many of their Princes had Profeffors of each fort ufually near
their perfons. *Self-Love,* a natural Paffion, led them to refpect the
Art of Healing; *Fear,* another natural Paffion, made them anxious
to know *the Future,* and *Superftition* believed there were men, who,
by *knowing the Stars,* could difcover it.

WE fhall firft fay fomething concerning MEDICINE *, which we
are forry to couple with fo futile an impofture.

'TIS commonly fuppofed that *the Prefcriber* of Medicines, and
the Provider, that is to fay in common words, *the Phyfician* and *the
Apothecary,* were characters anciently *united* in *the fame* perfon. The
following fact proves the contrary, at leaft among *the Orientals.*

IN an Army commanded by *Aphfhin,* an Officer of the *Caliph Al-
Motaffem,* it happened that *Aphfhin* and the Army Phyfician, *Zacharias,*

* *
* *Abulphar,* p. 160.

charias, were difcourfing together. *I affert*, fays *Zacharias, you can* Ch. VIII.
fend for nothing from an Apothecary, but, whether he has it or has it
not, he will affirm that he has. *Aphfhin*, willing to make the trial,
bids them bring him a catalogue of unknown *people*, and tranfcribing
out of it about twenty of their *names*, fends Meffengers to the Apo-
thecaries to provide him thofe Medicines. A few confeft they knew
no fuch medicines; others affirmed *they knew them well*, and taking
the money from the Meffengers, gave them fomething out of their
fhops. *Aphfhin* upon this, called them together, permitted thofe,
who faid they knew nothing of the Medicines, to remain in the
Camp, and commanded the reft that inftant to depart *.

THE following ftory is more interefting.

THE Caliph, *Mottawakkell*, had a Phyfician belonging to him,
who was a CHRISTIAN, named *Honaïn*. One day, after fome other
incidental converfation, *I would have thee*, fays the Caliph, *teach me*
a Prefcription, by which I may take off any Enemy I pleafe, and yet at
the fame time it fhould never be difcovered. *Honaïn*, declining to give
an anfwer, and pleading ignorance, was imprifoned.

BEING brought again, after a year's interval, into the *Caliph's* prefence, and ftill perfifting in his ignorance, tho' threatened with death,
the *Caliph* fmiled upon him and faid, *Be of good cheer, we were*
only willing to try thee, that we might have the greater confidence in
thee.

As

---

* *Abulphar*, p. 167.

As *Honaïn* upon this bowed down and kiffed the Earth, *What hindered thee,* fays the *Caliph, from granting our requeft, when thou fawcft us appear fo ready to perform what we had threatened? Two things,* replied *Honaïn,* MY RELIGION, *and* MY PROFESSION: MY RELIGION, *which commands me to do good to my Enemies;* MY PRO-FESSION, *which was purely inflituted for the benefit of Mankind.* TWO NOBLE LAWS, faid the *Caliph,* and immediately prefented him (accord-ing to the Eaftern Ufage) with rich Garments and a fum of Money *.

THE fame *Caliph* was once fitting upon a Bench with another of his Phyficians named *Baétifh,* who was dreft in a Tunic of rich filk, but which happened on the edge to have a fmall Rent. The *Caliph,* entering into difcourfe with him, continued playing with this rent, till he had made it reach up to his girdle. In the courfe of their converfation, the *Caliph* afked him, *How he could determine, when a Perfon was fo mad, as to require being bound? — We bind Him,* replies *Baétifh, when things proceed to that extremity, that he tears the Tunic of his Phyfician up to the girdle.* The *Caliph* fell backward in a fit of laughing, and ordered *Baétifh* (as he had ordered *Honaïn)* a Prefent of rich Garments, and a Donation in Money †.

THAT fuch Freedom of Converfation was not always checked, may appear from the following, as well as the preceding Narrative.

THE *Caliph, Al-wathick,* was once fifhing with a rod and line, upon a Raft in the River *Tigris.* As he happened to catch nothing, he
turned

---

* Abulpharag. p. 172, 173.   † Abulpharag. p. 171.

turned about to his Physician *John, the Son of Mifna,* then fitting Ch. VIII.
near him, and faid a little fharply, *Thou unlucky fellow, get thee gone.*
Commander of the Faithful, replies his Physician, *fay not what is ab-*
furd.   That John, the Son of Mifna, whofe Father was an obfcure Man,
and whofe Mother was purchafed for a few pieces of Silver; whom For-
tune has fo far favoured, that he has been admitted to the fociety and
familiarity of Caliphs; who is fo overpowered with the good things of
life, as to have obtained from them that, to which even his hopes did not
afpire; that He (I fay) *fhould be an* UNLUCKY FELLOW, *is furely fome-*
thing moft abfurd.—

However, if the Commander of the Faithful would have me tell him,
WHO IS UNLUCKY, *I will inform him.—And who is he,* fays the
Caliph?—The Man, replied JOHN, *who being fprung from four Ca-*
liphs, and being then raifed thro' God to the Caliphate HIMSELF, *can*
leave his Caliphate and his Palaces, and in the middle of the Tigris fit
upon a paultry raft twenty cubits broad, and as many long, without the
leaft affurance that a ftormy blaft may not fink him; refembling too by
his employ the pooreft, the worft fellows in the world, I mean Fifhermen.

THE Prince on this fingular difcourfe only remarked—*My Com-*
*panion I find is moved, if my prefence did not reftrain him**.

ANOTHER inftance of lenity I muft not omit, tho' in a later period, and in another Country. When *Al-azis* was Sultan of Egypt,
a Poet there wrote a fcandalous invective upon *Him* and *his Vizir.*
                                                              The

---

* *Abulpharag.* p. 108.

Part III. The Vizir complained and repeated the Verses to *Al-azis*, to whom the Sultan thus replied: *I perceive*, says he, *that in this invective I have my share along with* You; *in pardoning it,* You *shall have your share along with* Me' *.

We are now, as we promised, to mention Astrology, which seems to have been connected in its origin with *Astronomy*. Philosophers, men of veracity, studied the Heavenly Bodies; and 'twas upon *their* labours, that Impostors built *Astrology*.

The following Facts however, notwithstanding its temporary credit, seem not much in its favour.

When *Al-wathick* (the *Caliph*, whom we have just mentioned) was dangerously ill, he sent for *his Astrologers*, one of whom, pretending to inquire into his destiny, pronounced that from that day he would live fifty years. He did not however live beyond ten days †.

A few years after, the same Pretenders to Prediction said, that a vast number of Countries would be destroyed by floods; that the Rains would be immense, and the Rivers far exceed their usual boundaries.

Men began upon this to prepare; to expect Inundations with terror; and to betake themselves into places, which might protect them by their altitude.   The

---

* *Abulpharag.* p. 219.   † *Abulpharag.* p. 168.

The Event was far from corresponding either to the *threats* of Ch. VIII. the Prophets, or to the *fears* of the Vulgar. The Rain that feason was fo remarkably fmall, and fo many Springs and Rivers were abforbed by the Drought, that Public Supplications for Rain were many times made in the City of *Bagdad**.

We muft however confefs that notwithftanding thefe and many other fuch failures, *Aftrologers* ftill maintained their ground, gained admittance for many years into the Courts of thefe Princes, and were confulted by many, who appear not to have wanted abilities.

As the *Weft* of *Europe* learnt *Aftronomy* from thefe *Arabians*, fo Astrology appears to have attended it, and to have been much efteemed during Centuries not remote, thro' *Germany*, *Italy*, *France*, &c.

Even fo late as the days of Cardinal *Mazarine*, when that Minifter lay on his death-bed, and a Comet happened to appear, there were not wanting Flatterers to infinuate, that it had reference to *Him*, and his deftiny. The Cardinal anfwered them with a manly pleafantry—" *Meffieurs, la Comète me fait trop d'honneur* †.

We cannot quit thefe Orientals without obferving that, tho' they eagerly coveted the fair Fruit of Knowledge, they appear to have

had

---

* *Abulpharag.* p. 181. *Abulfeda*, p. 222.

† *Bayle, fur la Comète.*

 had little relish for the fairer Fruit of Liberty. This valuable Plant seems to have rarely flourished beyond the bounds of *Europe*, and seldom even there, but in *particular* regions.

It has appeared indeed from the facts already alledged, that these *Eastern* Princes often shewed many eminent Virtues; the Virtues I mean of Candour, Magnanimity, Affability, Compassion, Liberality, Justice, and the like. But it does not appear, that either *they* or their *subjects* ever quitted those ideas of *Despotism* and *Servitude*, which during all ages appear to have been *the Characteristic* of *Oriental* Dominion.

As all things human naturally decay, so, after a period of more than five Centuries, did the illustrious race of the Abassidæ. The last *reigning* Caliph of that Family, *Al-Moßaßem*, wasting his time in idleness and luxury, and that without the least Judgment, or Consistency in the conduct of his Empire; when he was told of the formidable approach of the *Tartars*, and how necessary it was, either to sooth them by Submission, or to oppose them by Force, made, in answer to this advice, the following mean reply—*For Me Bagdad suffices; which they will not surely think too much, if I yield them the other Provinces. They will not invade me, while I remain there; for this is my Mansion, and the place of my abode.*

Little did these poor Sentiments avail. *Bagdad* soon after was taken, and he himself, having basely asked permission to approach the *Tartar* Prince, appeared, and offered him dishes, filled with Pearls and precious Stones. These *the Tartar* distributed among

his

his Attendants, and a few days after put the unhappy *Caliph* to death*.

Bagdad being loft, by this fatal Event the *Dignity* and *Sovereignty* of the *Caliphs* were no more.

THE Name indeed remained in *Egypt* under the *Mamlucs*, but it was a name merely of *Honour*, as thofe other Princes were abfolute.

IT even continued in the fame Family to the time of *Selim*, Emperor of the *Turks*. When that Emperor in 1520 conquered *Egypt*, and deftroyed the *Mamlucs*, he carried the *Caliph*, whom he found there, a Prifoner to *Conftantinople*. 'Twas partly in this laft City, and partly in *Egypt* that this *Caliph*, when degraded, lived upon a Penfion. When he died, the Family of THE ABASSIDÆ, once fo illuftrious, and which had borne the Title of *Caliph* for almoft eight hundred years, funk with Him from Obfcurity into Oblivion†.

WHEN the *Tartars* and the *Turks* had extinguifhed the Sovereignty of thefe *Arabians* in the Eaft, and the Defcendants of the
ancient

---

* *Abulpharag.* p. 318, 337, 338, 339. Thefe Events happened in the middle of the thirteenth Century.

† See the Supplement of that excellent Scholar, *Pococke*, to his Edition of *Abulpharagius*. In this Supplement we have a fhort but accurate Account of the *Caliphs* who fucceeded *Moftaffem*, even to the time of their Extinction.

See alfo *Herbelot's Biblioth. Orientale,* under the Word *Abaffides*, with the feveral references to other Articles in the fame Work.

Part III. ancient *Spaniards* had driven them out of *Spain*, the remainder in *Africa* soon degenerated; till at length under the celebrated Muly Ismael, in the beginning of this Century, they sunk into a State of *Ignorance*, *Barbarity*, and *abject Servitude*, hardly to be equalled either in ancient or in modern History.

But I say nothing concerning them during this unhappy Period. That which I have been treating, tho' in Chronology a *middle* Period, was to them, in many respects, a truly *Golden* one.

I conclude this Chapter with the following Anecdote, so far curious, as it proves that, even in our own Century, the Taste among *the Orientals* for Philosophy was not *totally* extinguished.

In the year 1721 a Turkish Envoy came to the Court of *France*. As he was a Man of Learning, he searched thro' *Paris* (tho' in vain) for the Commentary of *Averroes upon Aristotle*, a large Work in *Latin*, containing five Folio Volumes, printed at *Venice* by the *Junta*, in the years 1552, 1553. It happened that, visiting the King's Library, he saw the Book he wanted; and seeing it, he could not help expressing his ardent wish to possess it. The King of *France*, hearing what had happened, ordered the Volumes to be magnificently bound, and presented him by his Librarian, the Abbe *Bignon* *.

---

* *Vid. Reimanni Histor. Atheismi et Atheorum*, 8vo. p. 597.

CHAP. IX.

Concerning the LATINS *or* FRANKS—BEDE, ALCUIN, JOANNES ERIGENA, *&c.* GERBERTUS *or* GIBERTUS, *travelled to the Arabians in Spain for improvement—suspected of* MAGIC—*this the misfortune of many superior Geniuses in dark Ages; of* BACON, PETRARCH, FAUST, *and others—Erudition of* THE CHURCH; *Ignorance of* THE LAITY—INGULPHUS, *an Englishman, educated in the Court of Edward the Confessor—attached himself to the Duke of Normandy—accomplished Character of* QUEEN EGITHA, *Wife of the Confessor—Plan of Education in those Days—*THE PLACES *of Study,* THE AUTHORS *studied—Canon Law, Civil Law, Holy War, Inquisition—Troubadours—*WILLIAM OF POICTOU—*Debauchery, Corruption, and Avarice of the Times—*WILLIAM THE CONQUEROR, *his Character and Taste—his Sons,* RUFUS *and* HENRY—*little Incidents concerning them—*HILDEBERT, *a Poet of the times—fine Verses of his quoted.*

I PASS now to another Race, THE LATINS, or *Inhabitants of* WESTERN EUROPE, who in this middle age were often by the Arabians, their Contemporaries, called FRANKS.

IGNORANCE was their *general* Character, yet *Individuals* we except in the enumeration, which follows.

BEDE, called *the Venerable* from his respectable Character, was *an Englishman;* was born in the seventh Century, but flourished in the eighth;

Part III. eighth; and left many Works, Critical, Hiſtorical, and Theological, behind him.

ALCUIN (ſometimes called *Alcuinus*, ſometimes *Flaccus Albinus*) was *Bede's* Diſciple, and like him an *Engliſhman*. He was famous for having been Preceptor to *Charlemagne*, and much in his favour for many years [*].

JOANNES ERIGENA, a Native of *Scotland*, and who about the ſame period, or a little later, lived ſometimes in *France*, and ſometimes in *England*, appears to have underſtood *Greek*, a rare accompliſhment for *thoſe* Countries in thoſe days.

IT is related of him, that when he was once ſitting at table over againſt the Emperor *Charles the Bald*, the Emperor aſked him— *How far diſtant* A SCOTT *was from* A SOTT?—*As far, Sir*, replied he, *as the Table's length* [†].

A TREATISE of his, which appears to be *Metaphyſical*, intitled *De Diviſione Naturæ*, was printed in a thin Folio at OXFORD, in the year 1681.

ABELARD,

---

[*] The *Grammatical* Works of theſe two, together with thoſe of other Grammarians, were publiſhed in Quarto by *Putſchius*, at *Hanover*, in the year 1605. Thoſe, who would learn more concerning them, may conſult *Fabricius* and *Cave*.

[†] In the original, taken from *Roger de Hoveden, Annal. pars prior*, it is—*Quid diſtat inter* SOTUM *et* SCOTUM?—The Anſwer was—*Tabula tantum*.

We have tranſlated SOTUM, SOTT, in order to preſerve the Emperor's dull Pun, tho' perhaps not quite agreeably to its proper meaning.

The word SCOTUM plainly decides the Country of this learned man, which ſome ſeem, without reaſon, to have doubted.

ADELARD, a Monk of *Bath*, for the fake of *Mathematical* Knowledge travelled into *Spain*, *Egypt*, and *Arabia*, and tranflated *Euclid* out of *Arabic* into *Latin*, about the year 1130. ROBERT OF READING, a Monk, travelled into *Spain* on the fame account, and wrote about the year 1143 *.

THEY found, by fatal experience, that little Information was to be had *at home*, and therefore ventured upon thefe perilous journies abroad.

GERBERTUS or GIBERTUS, a Native of *France*, flourifhed a little before them in the *tenth* Century, called, (tho' not on his account) *Sæculum obfcurum*, *the dark Age*. His ardent Love for *Mathematical Knowledge* carried *Him* too from his own Country into *Spain*, that he might there learn Science from the learned *Arabians*.

AFTER an uncommon proficiency in the *Mathematics*, and after having recommended himfelf for his Learning and Abilities both to *Robert*, King of *France*, and to the Emperor *Otho*, he became firft Archbifhop of *Rheims*, then of *Ravenna*, and at length *Pope*, by the name of SYLVESTER THE SECOND.

His three capital Preferments being at *Rheims*, *Ravenna*, and *Rome*, each beginning with an R, gave occafion to the following barbarous Verfe —

Tranfit ab R Gerbertus ad R, poft Papa viget R †.

'TIS

---

* See *Wallis's* Preface to his *Algebra*, *Fol. Lond.* 1685. p. 5.

† See *Brown's Fafciculus rerum expetendar. et fugiendar.* Vol. II. p. 83.

'Tis fingular that not his *Sacerdotal*, nor even his *Pontifical* Character could fcreen him from the imputation of Magic, incurred merely, as it fhould feem, from his *fuperior Ingenuity.*

A Bishop *Otho*, who lived in the next Century, gravely relates of him, that he obtained the *Pontificate* by *wicked Arts*, for in his youth, when he was nothing more than a fimple Monk, having left his Monaftery, *he gave himfelf up wholly to the Devil,* on condition *he might obtain* that, which he defired.

Soon after this, the fame Hiftorian, having given an account of his gradual Rife, fubjoins——that at length, *by the Devil's help,* he was made *Roman Pontiff,* but then it was upon *Compact,* that after his deceafe, he fhould wholly in *Body* and *Soul* belong to Him, thro' whofe frauds he had acquired *fo great* a Dignity *.

A Cardinal *Benno*, of nearly the fame age with this Bifhop *Otho*, fpeaking of the fame great man *(Gerbertus* I mean) informs us, *his Demon* had affured him, that he fhould not die, till he had celebrated Mafs at *Jerufalem* — that *Gerbertus,* miftaking this for *the City* fo called, unwarily celebrated Mafs *at Rome*, in *a Church* called *Jerufalem,*

---

* *Hic* (fcilicet *Gerbertus) malis artibus Pontificatum obtinuit, eo quod ab adolefcentia, cum Monachus effet, relicto Monafterio, fe totum Diabolo obtulit, modo quod optabat obtineret.*—And foon after, a fhort narrative of his Rife being given, the Hiftorian fubjoins—*Poftremò Romanus Pontifex Diabolo adjuvante fuit conftitutus; hâc tamen lege, ut poft ejus obitum totus* ILLIUS *in anima et corpore effet,* CUJUS *fraudibus tantaɴ adeptus effet dignitatem.* See Bifhop Otho, in *Brown's Fafciculus,* juft quoted, V. II. p. 88.

falem, and, being deceived by the *Equivocation of the Name*, met a Ch. IX.
fudden and a wretched end *.

As to thefe Stories, they are of that *vagabond* fort, which wander from Age to Age, and from Perfon to Perfon; which find their way into the Hiftories of diftant periods, and are fometimes transferred from *Hiftories* to the *Theatre*.

THE JERUSALEM TALE may be found in *Shakfpeare's* HENRY THE FOURTH; and for THE COMPACT, we have all feen it in the Pantomime of DR. FAUSTUS.

ONE thing we cannot but remark: the dull Contemporaries of thefe fuperior Geniufes, not fatisfied with referring their Superiority to Pre-eminence *merely natural*, recurred abfurdly to Power *fupernatural*, deeming nothing lefs could fo far exceed themfelves.

SUCH was the Cafe of *the able Scholar* juft mentioned. Such, fome centuries afterward, was the Cafe of ROGER BACON, of FRANCIS PETRARCH, of JOHN FAUST, and many others.

BACON'S Knowledge of Glaffes, and of the *Telefcope* in particular, made them apply to Him *literally*, what *Virgil* had faid *poetically* —

> *Carmina vel Cælo poffunt deducere Lunam.*

VIRGIL

 VIRGIL himself had been foolishly thought a *Magician*, and therefore, becaufe PETRARCH was delighted with the ftudy of fo capital an author, even PETRARCH alfo was fufpected of MAGIC.

FOR JOHN FAUST, as he was either the Inventor, or among the firft Practifers of the Art of *Printing*, 'tis no wonder the ignorant vulgar fhould refer to *Diabolical* Affiftance a Power, which multiplied Books in a manner to them fo incomprehenfible.

THIS Digreffion has led us to Examples rather againft *Chronological Order*; tho' all of them included within that Age, of which we are writing *. For the honour too of the CHURCH, thefe *falfly accufed Geniufes* were all of them *Ecclefiaftics*. Indeed the reft of *Weftern Europe* was in a manner *wholly barbarous*, compofed of ignorant *Barons*, and their more ignorant *Vaffals*; men like *Homer's Cimmerians*,

> Ἠέρι κ᾿ νεφέλῃ κεκαλυμμένοι ——
> *With Fog and Cloud envelop'd* ——

FROM thefe we pafs, or rather go back, to INGULPHUS, an *Ecclefiaftic*, and an *Hiftorian*, valuable for having lived during an interefting *Time*, and in interefting *Places*.

HE was by birth an *Englifhman*, and had been educated in the Court of *Edward the Confeffor*; went thence to the Court of the
Duke

---

* BACON lived in the thirteenth Century; PETRARCH, in the fourteenth; FAUST, in the fifteenth. See a curious Book of *Gabriel Naude*, a learned *Frenchman* of the laft Century, intitled *Apologie pour les grand Hommes, accufées de* MAGIE.

Ch. IX.

Duke of Normandy, to whofe favour he was admitted, and there preferred. Some time after this, when the fuccefsful Expedition of that Duke had put him in poffeffion of the *Crown of England,* the Duke (then *William the Conqueror)* recalled him from *Normandy;* took him into favour here, and made him at length *Abbot of Croyland,* where he died advanced in years *.

INGULPHUS tells us, that King *Edward's* Queen, EGITHA, was admirable for her *Beauty,* her *literary Accomplishments,* and her *Virtue.*

HE relates, that being a Boy he frequently faw *Queen Egitha,* when he vifited his Father, in King *Edward's* Court;—that many times when he met her, as he was coming from School, fhe ufed to difpute with him about his Learning, and his Verfes—that fhe had a peculiar pleafure to pafs from *Grammar* to *Logic,* in which fhe had been inftructed; and that, when fhe had entangled him there with fome fubtle Conclufion, fhe ufed to bid one of her Attendants give him two or three pieces of money, and carry him to the Royal Pantry, where he was treated with a Repaft †.

As to *the Manners of the times,* he tells us, that the whole Nation began to lay afide the *Englifh Cuftoms,* and in many things to *imitate the Manners of the French;* all the Men of Quality to fpeak the *Gallic Idiom* in their Houfes, as a high ftrain of Gentility; to

draw

---

* See *Ingulphus's Hiftory,* in the Preface to the *Oxford* Edition of the year 1684. See alfo p. 75, of the Work itfelf.

† See the fame *Ingulphus,* p. 62.

3 T 2

Part III. draw their Charters and public Inftruments after the manner of
the *French*; and in thefe and many other things *to be afhamed of
their own Cuftoms* *.

SOME years before the Conqueft, *the Duke of Normandy* (whom
INGULPHUS calls *moft illuftrious* and *glorious)* made a vifit to *England*, attended with a grand retinue. King *Edward* received him
honourably, kept him a long while, carried him round to fee his
Cities and *Caftles,* and at length fent him home with many rich
Prefents †.

INGULPHUS fays, that at this time *Duke William* had no hopes
of *the Succeffion*, nor was any mention made of it; yet confidering
the Settlement of the Crown made upon him foon afterward, and
the Reception he then found, this fhould hardly feem probable.

KING *Edward*, according to INGULPHUS, had great merit in
remitting the DANE-GELT, that heavy Tax impofed upon the people by the *Danifh Ufurpers*, his immediate Predeceffors ‡.

As to LITERARY MATTERS, it has appeared that *the Queen*,
befides the ufual Accomplifhments of the times, (which fhe undoubtedly poffeft) had been inftructed alfo in fuperior forts of Knowledge. She may be fuppofed therefore to have furpaft, not only
her own Court, but perhaps other Courts *fince*, as they have feldom
more to boaft, than the fafhionable Polifh.

For

---

* See the fame Author, in the fame page.

† See the fame Author, p. 65, 58.   ‡ See the fame Author, p. 65.

For the Literary Qualifications of our *Hiſtorian* himſelf, we perceive ſomething of his Education in what we have already quoted from him. He is more particular afterwards, when he tells that he was firſt bred at *Weſtminſter*, and then ſent to *Oxford*—that in the firſt he learnt *Grammar*, in the laſt he ſtudied *Ariſtotle* and the *Rhetoric of Cicero*:—that finding himſelf ſuperior to many of his Contemporaries, and diſdaining the littleneſs of his own Family, he left home, ſought the Palaces of Kings and Princes, &c. &c. 'Twas thus that, after a variety of Events, he became Secretary to *the Duke of Normandy*, afterwards *William the Conqueror*, and ſo purſued his Fortune, till he became *Abbot of Croyland**.

We ſhall only remark on this Narrative, that Westminster and Oxford ſeem to have been *deſtined to the ſame purpoſes then, as now*; that the Scholar at Westminster was to *begin*, and at Oxford was to *finiſh*; a Plan of Education which ſtill exiſts; which is not eaſy to be mended; and which can plead ſo ancient and ſo uninterrupted a Preſcription.

Nearly the ſame time a Monk, by name Gratian, collecting the numerous Decrees of Popes and Synods, was the firſt who publiſhed a Body of Canon Law †. 'Twas then alſo, or a little earlier, that *Amalfi*, a City of *Calabria*, being taken by the *Piſans*, they diſcovered there by chance an original MS. of *Juſtinian's* Code, which had been in a manner unknown from the time of that Emperor‡.

This

---

* See the ſame Author, p. 73, 75.

† This happened in the year 1157. See *Duck De Auctoritate Juris Civilis Romanor.* p. 66, 88. Edit. Lond. 1679.

‡ See the ſame author, p. 66.—*Amalfi* was taken by the *Piſans* in the year 1127.

Part III. This curious Book was brought to *Pifa*, and, when *Pifa* was taken by the *Florentines*, was transferred to *Florence*, and there has continued even to this day.

And thus it was that by fingular fortune the Civil and Canon Law, having been about the fame time promulged, gradually found their way into moft of the *Weftern* Governments, changing more cr lefs their Municipal Laws, and changing with thofe Laws the very forms of their Conftitutions.

'Twas foon after happened that *wild Enthufiafm*, which carried fo many thoufands from the *Weft* into the *Eaft*, to profecute what was thought, or at leaft called a Holy War*.

After the numerous Hiftories ancient and modern of thefe Crusades, it would be fuperfluous to fay more, than to obferve that, by *repeating* them, men appear to have grown worfe; to have become more favage, and *greater barbarians.* It was fo late as during one of the *laft* of them, that thefe Crufaders facked the *Chriftian* City of *Conftantinople* †, and that while *thefe* were committing unheard-of cruelties in that *Capital of Chriftendom, another* party of them, *nearer home,* were employed in maffacring the innocent *Albigeois* ‡.

                   So

---

* It began in the year 1095. See *Fuller's Holy Warre*, Book I. ch. 8. *William of Malmefbury*, Lib. IV. c. 2. among the *Scriptores poft Bedam.*

† In the year 1204. See the fame *Fuller*, B. III. chap. 17. and *Nicetas* the *Choniate*, already quoted at large, from p. 452 to p. 458.

‡ The Crufades againft them began in the year 1206; the Maffacres were during the whole courfe of the war; fee *Fuller's Holy Warre*, B. III. from chap. 18 to ch. 22. efpecially chap. 21. and *Mofheim's Church Hiftory*, under the article *Albigenfes.*

So great was the zeal of Extirpation, that when one of thefe *home Crufades* was going to ftorm the City of *Bezieres*, a City filled with *Catholics*, as well as *Heretics*, a fcruple arofe that, by fuch a meafure, *the Good* might perifh as well as *the Bad*. *Kill them all*, faid an able Sophift — *kill them all, and God will know his own* [*].

To difcover thefe *Albigeois*, the home Crufades were attended by a *Band of Monks*, whofe bufinefs was TO INQUIRE after Offenders, called *Heretics*. When the *Crufade* was finifhed, the *Monks*, like the Dregs of an empty Veffel, ftill remained, and deriving from *the Crufade* their *Authority*, from the *Canon Law* their *judicial* Forms, became by *thefe two* (I mean *the Crufade* and *Canon Law)* that formidable Court, THE COURT OF INQUISITION.

BUT in thefe latter events we rather anticipate, for they did not happen, till the beginning of *the thirteenth* Century, whereas the firft Crufade was towards the End of *the eleventh* †.

ABOUT the beginning of the eleventh Century, and for a Century or two after, flourifhed the Tribe of TROUBADOURS, or PROVENÇAL

POETS,

---

[*] *Tuez. les tous: Dieu connoit ceux, qui font a lui.* Hiftoire de Troubadours, Vol. I. p. 193.

† In the year 1095 or 1096.—*Fuller's H. Warre*, p. 21. And *William of Malmefbury*, before quoted, p. 510.

'Tis to be remarked, that thefe two Events, I mean the facking of *Conftantinople*, and the Muffacres of the *Albigeois*, happened more than *a hundred years* after this *Holy War* had been begun, and after its *more fplendid* Parts were *paft*, that is to fay, the taking of *Jerufalem*, the eftablifhment of *a Kingdom* there, (which lafted eighty years) and the *gallant Efforts* of *Coeur de Leon* againft *Saladin*. All againft the *Saracens*, that followed, was languid, and, for the greater part of it, adverfe.

Part III. POETS [*], who chiefly lived in the Courts of thofe Princes, that had Sovereignties in or near PROVENCE, where the *Provençal Language* was fpoken. 'Twas in this Language they wrote, a Language, which, tho' obfolete now, was then efteemed the beft in Europe, being prior to the *Italian* of *Dante* and *Petrarch*.

THEY were called TROUBADOURS from *Trouver*, *to find* or *to invent* [†], like the *Greek Appellation*, POET, which means (we know) A MAKER.

THEIR Subjects were moftly *Galantry* and *Love*, in which their *licentious* Ideas we are told were excefﬁve. Princes did not difdain [‡] to be of their number, fuch among others as our RICHARD COEUR DE LÉON, and the celebrated WILLIAM, COUNT *of* POICTOU, who was a Contemporary with *William the Conqueror* and his Sons.

A SONNET or two, made by RICHARD, are preferved, but they are obfcure, and as far as intelligible, of little value [§].

THE Sonnets of WILLIAM *of Poiƈtou*, now remaining, are (as we are informed) of the moft *licentious* kind, for a more *licentious man* never exifted [‖].
HISTORIANS

---

[*] See a Work, 3 Vol. 12mo. intitled, *Hiftoire Litteraire de Troubadours*, printed at *Paris* 1774, where there is an ample detail both of them, and their Poems.

[†] See *Hift. de Troub.* Vol. I. Difcours prelim. p. 25.

[‡] See the fame Work in the fame page.   [§] See *Hift. de Troub.* Vol. I. p. 54.

[‖] See *Hift. de Troub.* Vol. I. p. 7.

As to his famous Abbey or Nunnery, foon after mentioned, fee the fame Work, p. 3, 4. but more particularly and authentically, fee *William of Malmeſbury*, a writer nearly contemporary.

HISTORIANS tell us, that near one of his Castles he founded a fort of Abbey for Women of Pleafure, and appointed the moft celebrated among his Ladies to the Offices of Abbefs, Priorefs, &c. that he difmift his Wife, and, taking the Wife of a certain Vifcount, lived with her publicly,—that being excommunicated for this by *Girard Biſhop of Angoulefme*, and commanded to put away his unlawful Companion, he replied, *Thou ſhalt ſooner curl Hair upon that bald Pate of thine, than will I ſubmit to a divorce from the Viſcounteſs*—that having received a like rebuke, attended with an Excommunication from his *own Biſhop, the Biſhop of Poiƈlou*, he ſeized him by the Hair, and was about to diſpatch him, but fuddenly ſtopt by faying, *I have that Averſion to Thee, Thou ſhalt never enter Heaven thro' the aſſiſtance of* MY *Hand* *.

IF I might be permitted to digreſs, I would obſerve that HAMLET has adopted precifely *the ſame* fentiment. When he declines the opportunity offered him *of killing the King at his Prayers*, he has the following Expreſſions among many others:

> *A Villain kills my Father, and for that*
> *I, his ſole ſon, do this ſame Villain* SEND
> *To* HEAV'N—*O! THIS is Hire and Salary,*
> NOT REVENGE.—— *Hamlet, Act III. Sc. X.*

"TIS

---

contemporary, and from whom the Narrative here given is taken. The paſſage in *Malmeſbury* begins with the words—*Erat tum Willielmus, Comes Piƈlavorum*, &c. &c. p. 96. Edit. Londin. Fol. 1596.

* The Words in *Malmeſbury* are—*Nec cælum unquam intrabis meæ manus miniſterio*, P. 96.

 'Tis hard to defend fo ftrange a fentiment either in HAMLET, or THE COUNT. We fhall only remark that HAMLET, when he delivered it, was perfectly *cool*; THE COUNT, agitated *by impetuous Rage.*

This Count, as he grew older, became, as many others have done, from *a Profligate a Devotee*; engaged in one of the *firft Crufades*; led a large body of Troops into the Eaft; from which however, after his Troops had been routed, and moft of them deftroyed, he himfelf returned with ignominy home[*].

THE loofe Gallantry of thefe *Troubadours* may remind us of the Poetry during the Reign of *our fecond Charles* — nor were the *Manners* of one *Court* unlike thofe of the other, unlefs that thofe of the Court of *Poiĉou* were more abandoned of the two.

BE that as it may, we may fairly I think conclude, if we compare the two Periods, there were Men as *wicked* during the *early* period, as during the *latter*, and not only fo, but *wicked* in Vices of *exactly the fame* Character.

IF we feek for Vices of *another* character, we read *at the fame æra* concerning a neighbouring Kingdom to *Poiĉou*, that " All the peo-
" ple of rank were fo blinded with AVARICE, that it might be truly
" faid of them (according to JUVENAL) .

> *Not one regards the method,* HOW HE GAINS,
> *But fix'd his Refolution,* GAIN HE MUST.

                                  " THE

---

[*] See the fame *William of Malmefbury,* p. 75. 84.

" The more they difcourfed about Right, the greater their Inju-
" ries. Thofe, who were called the Jufticiaries, were the Head
" of all Injuftice. The Sheriffs and Magiftrates, whofe Duty was
" Juftice and judgment, were more atrocious than the very Thieves
" and Robbers, and were more cruel than others, even the moft
" cruel. The King himfelf, when he had leafed his Domains as
" dear, as was poffible, transferred them immediately to another
" that offered him *more*, and then again to another, neglecting
" always his former agreement, and labouring ftill for *bargains* that
" were greater, and more profitable *."

Such were *the* good old times of good old England, (for
'tis of *England* we have been reading) during the reign of our
Conqueror, William.

And yet if we meafure Greatness (as is too often the cafe
with *Heroes*) by any other Meafure, than that of *Moral Rectitude*,
we cannot but admit that he *muft* have been Great, who could
conquer a Country fo much larger than his own, and tranfmit the
permanent Poffeffion of it to his Family. The numerous *Norman*
Families, with which he filled this Ifland, and the very few *Saxon*
ones, which he fuffered to remain, fufficiently fhew us the Extent
of this Revolution.

                                                          As

* See *Henrici Huntindonienfis Hiftor.* L. *VII.* p. 212, *inter Scriptores poft Bedam—*
Edit. London, 1594, beginning from the Words, *Principes omnes*, &c. The Verfe from
Juvenal is—

   Unde habeat, quærit nemo, fed oportet habere.

Part III. As to his TASTE, (for 'tis *Taſte* we inveſtigate, as often as we are able) there is a curious Fact, related of him by JOHN OF SALISBURY, a learned Writer, who lived as early as the times of *Stephen* and *Henry the Second*.

THIS Author informs us, that WILLIAM, after he was once ſettled in the peaceable poſſeſſion of his Kingdom, ſent Ambaſſadors to Foreign Nations, that they ſhould collect for him, out of all the celebrated Manſions, whatever ſhould appear to them *magnificent* or *admirable*.

OUR Author cannot help allowing that this was the laudable project of a great man, deſirous of pouring into *his own* Dominions all, that was excellent in *others**.

IT does not appear what theſe Rarities were, but it ſufficiently ſhews *the Conqueror* to have had a Genius ſuperior to the Barbarity of his Age.

ONE may imagine he was not ignorant of *Ovid*, and the ancient *Mythology*, by his anſwer to *Philip* King of France.

William,

---

* *Simile aliquid feciſſe viſus eſt Rex Anglorum* VILHELMUS PRIMUS, *cujus virtuti Normannia et tandem major Britannia ceſſit. Aſſumpto namque regni diademate, et pace compoſita, legatos miſit ad exteras nationes, ut a præclaris omnium domibus, quicquid eis magnificum aut mirificum videretur, afferrent. Defluxit ergo in inſulam opulentam, et quæ fere ſola bonis ſuis eſt in orbe contenta, quicquid magnificentiæ, imo luxuriæ potuit inveniri. Laudabile quidem fuit magni viri propoſitum, qui virtutes omnium orbi ſuo volebat infundere.* Joan. Saliſb. de *Nugis Curialium,* p. 480. Edit. Lugd. 8vo. 1595.

William, as he became old, grew to an *unweildy* Bulk. The king of *France*, in a manner not very polite, afked of him, (with reference to this bulk) " *When, as he had been fo long in breeding, he expeƈted* " *to be brought to bed?"*—" *Whenever that happens,"* replied *William,* " *it will be, as* SEMELE *was, in Flames and Thunder."* France foon after that felt his Devaftations *.

His Son RUFUS feems more nearly to have approached the character of the times.

WE have a Sample of his Manners in the following Narrative. Being immenfely fond of expence in drefs, when one of his attendants brought him new Shoes, and was putting them on, he demanded, " *How much they coft?"*—" *Three Shillings, Sir,"* replied his Attendant—" *Son of a Whore,"* fays Rufus,—" at *fo pitiful a* " *price to provide Shoes for a King!—Go and purchafe me fome for a* " *mark of Silver* †."

Matthew Paris writes, that he was once told of a formidable dream, relative to his death, which had been dreamed by a certain Monk. RUFUS, on hearing it, burft into laughter, and faid, " *The* " *Man's*

---

* *Quærente, fc. Philippo, numquidnam tandem pareret* GUILIELMUS, *qui tam diu geffiffet* UTERUM: *fe pariturum, fed inftar* SEMELES, *refpondit, cum flaminis et fulmine. Panciroll. Nova Reperia,* Tit. x. p. 219. Edit. Francofurt. 1631. See this faƈt fomewhat differently told by *Matthew Paris,* p. 13. *Edit. Fol. London,* 1640. The devaftations, here mentioned, are related in the fame page.

† *Will. of Malmefbury,* p. 69. The words of *Rufus* were—*Fili meretricis, ex quo habet Rex caligas tam exilis pretii! Vade et affer mihi emptas marcâ argenti.*

Part III.   " Man's a Monk, and Monk-like has dreamed to get a little money—
            " give him a hundred Shillings, that he may not think he has been
            " dreaming for nothing *."

His Historian *Malmesbury*, after having related other Facts of him, adds, *that he had neither Application enough, nor Leisure, ever to attend to Letters* †.

It was not so with his Brother, *Henry* the First. He (as this Historian informs us ‡) spent his Youth in the schools of liberal Science, and so greedily imbibed the sweets of *Literature*, that in aftertimes, (as the same Writer rather *floridly* relates) *no Tumults of War, no Agitation of Cares, could ever expel them from his illustrious Mind*.

Soon after we meet the well-known saying of *Plato*, that 'twas then States would be happy, if *Philosophers* were to reign, or *Kings* were to philosophize. Our Historian, having given this Sentiment, tells us, (to use his own expressions) that *Henry* fortified his Youth with *Literature* in a view to the Kingdom, and ventured even in his Father's hearing, to throw out the Proverb, *Rex illiteratus, Asinus coronatus, that an illiterate King was but an Ass crowned* §.

THAT

---

* *Matthew Paris*, p. 53. Rufus's words were—*Monachus est, & lucri causa monachiliter somniavit; da ei centum solidos, ne videatur inaniter somniasse.*

† *William of Malmesbury*, p. 70.

‡ The same, p. 87.

§ The same, p. 87, b.

THAT the King his Father, from perceiving his Son's Abilities, had something like *a Presentiment* of his future Dignity, may appear from the following Story.

WHEN *Henry* was young, one of his Brothers having injured him, he complained of his ill-treatment to his Father with tears. *Don't cry, Child*, says his Father, *for Thou too shalt be King* *.

As *Henry* was a learned Prince, we may suppose he was educated by learned men; and perhaps, if we attend to the account given by *Ingulphus* of his own Education † in the time of *Edward* the Confessor, 'tis probable there may have been *among the Clergy* a succession of learned men from the time of *Venerable Bede*.

'Tis certain that in *England at least*, during these *middle* Ages, LEARNING never flourished more, than from the time of *Henry the First* to the reign of his Grandson *Henry the Second*, and for some years after.

THE learned Historian of the Life of *Henry the Second* (I mean the First Lord Lyttelton) has put this beyond dispute.

PERHAPS too *the Times, which followed*, were *adverse* to the Cause of Literature. THE CRUSADES had made the Laity greater Barbarians,

---

* The Words of *William* were—*Ne fleas, Fili; quoniam et Tu Rex eris.* See *William of Malmesbury*, p. 87.

† P. 507, 8, 9.

Part III. barians, if poſſible, than they were before. Their Cruelty had been ſtimulated by acting againſt *Greeks*, whom they hated for *Schiſmatics*; and againſt *Saracens*, whom they hated for *Infidels*; altho' it was from *theſe alone* they were likely to *learn*, had they underſtood (which *few* of them did) a ſyllable of *Greek* or *Arabic*.

ADD to this, THE INQUISITION being then * eſtabliſhed in all its terrors, *the Clergy* (from whom *only* the Cauſe of *Letters* could hope any thing) found their Genius inſenſibly checkt by its gloomy terrors.

THIS *depraved* Period (which laſted for a Century or two) did not mend, till *the Invention of Printing*, and the *Taking of Conſtantinople*. Then 'twas that theſe, and other hidden Cauſes, rouſed the Genius of *Italy*, and reſtored to Mankind thoſe *Arts* and that *Literature*, which to *Weſtern Europe* had been ſo long unknown.

BEFORE I conclude this Chapter, I cannot but remark, that, during theſe inauſpicious times, ſo *generally* taſteleſs, there were even LATINS as well as GREEKS †, whom *the very Ruins of Antique Arts* carried to *Enthuſiaſtic Admiration*.

HILDEBERT, Arch-Biſhop *of Tours*, who died in the year 1139, in a fine Poem, which he wrote upon the City of *Rome*, among others

has

---

* See before, p. 511.

† See before, what has been quoted from NICETAS THE CHONIATE, p. 452, &c.

has the following Verses, in praise of the then remaining Statues and **Ch. IX.**
Antiquities.

> *Non tamen annorum series, nec flamma, nec ensis,*
> *Ad plenum potuit tale abolere decus,*
> *Hic Superum formas Superi mirantur et ipsi,*
> *Et cupiunt fictis vultibus esse pares.*
> *Nec potuit Natura Deos hoc ore creare,*
> *Quo miranda Deum signa creavit Homo.*
> *Vultus* adest his Numinibus, potiusque coluntur*
> *Artificum studio, quam Deitate sua †.*

'Tis worth observing, that the *Latinity* of these Verses is in general pure, and that they are wholly free from the *Leonine jingle*.

They are thus attempted in *English*, for the sake of those, who do not read the original.

> *But neither passing Years, nor Fire, nor Sword*
> *Have yet avail'd such Beauty to annul.*
> *Ev'n Gods themselves their mimic Forms admire,*
> *And wish their own were equal to the feign'd.*
> *Nor e'er could Nature Deities create*
> *With such a Countenance, as Man has giv'n*
> *To these fair Statues, Creatures of his own.*
> *Worship they claim, tho' more from* HUMAN ART,
> *Than from* THEIR OWN DIVINITY, *ador'd.*

---

* *Forsan Cultus.*

† *William of Malmesbury,* p. 76.—*Fabricii Bibliotheca med. et infim. ætat. in voce,* HILDEBERT.

CHAP. X.

SCHOOLMEN—*their Rife, and Character—their Titles of Honour—
Remarks on fuch Titles—*ABELARD *and* HELOISA—JOHN *of* SA-
LISBURY—*admirable Quotations from his two celebrated Works—*
GIRALDUS CAMBRENSIS—WALTER MAPPS—RICHARD COEUR
DE LEON—*his Tranfactions with Saladin—his Death, and the fin-
gular Interview, which immediately preceded it.*

Part III. WE are now to confider the ftate of LITERATURE with refpect
to *other* Geniufes, both before the *Conqueft*, and after it, follow as to the times of our *Firft Richard*.

'TWAS during this Period began the Race of SCHOOLMEN, a Race
much admired, and followed in their day. Their *fubtlety* was great,
and though that fubtlety might fometimes have led them into Refine-
ments rather *frivolous*, yet have they given eminent famples of *penetrating Ingenuity.*

THEY began in the eleventh Century, and lafted to the fourteenth,
when *new Caufes* leading to *new Events*, they gradually decreafed,
and were no more.

THAT they had fome merit muft be allowed, when we are told
that the learned Bifhop *Saunderfon* ufed conftantly to read the SE-
CUNDA

cunda Secundæ of Thomas Aquinas [*], and that *this Treatife*, together with Aristotle's Rhetoric, and Cicero's Offices, were *three Books*, which he always had with him, and never ceafed to peruse. The *Scholaftic* Tract muft have been no bad one, which was fo well affociated.

Various Epithets at the time were beftowed upon thefe Schoolmen. There was *the Irrefragable* doctor, *the Subtle, the Seraphic, the Angelic,* &c.

There is certainly fomething exaggerated in the *Pomp* of thefe Appellations. And yet, if we reflect on our *modern* Titles of *Honour*; on our common *fuperfcriptions of Epiftles*; on our common modes of *concluding* them; and mark how *gravely* we admit all this; may we not fuppofe thofe *other* Epithets appear ridiculous, not fo much from their being *abfurd*, as from their being *unufual* [†]?

Before we quit thefe *Schoolmen*, we cannot omit the famous Peter Abelard, who, when he taught at *Paris*, was followed by thoufands, and was confidered almoft as an Oracle in difcufling the abftrufeft of fubjects. At prefent he is better known for his unfortunate Amour with the celebrated Heloisa, his Difciple, his Miftrefs, and at length his Wife.

Her

---

[*] This able and acute man died, aged 48 years, in the year 1274.

[†] For a fuller account of thefe *Schoolmen* fee *Scholaftica Theologia Syntagma*, by *Prideaux* Bifhop of *Worcefter, Mofheim's* Hiftory, and *Cave's Hiftor. Lit.* V. 2. p. 275.

Part III. Her *Ingenuity* and *Learning* were celebrated alſo, and their *Epiſtolary* Correſpondence, remarkably, curious, is ſtill * extant. The Religion of the times drove them at length to finiſh their days in two ſeparate Convents. When Abelard died (which happened about the year 1134), his Body was carried to Heloiſa, who buried it in the Convent of the *Paraclete*, where ſhe preſided.

My Countryman, John of Salisbury, comes next, who lived in the reign of *Stephen*, and *Henry the Second*. He appears to have been converſant in *all the Latin Claſſics*, whom he not only quotes, but appears to underſtand, to reliſh, and to admire †.

How far they ſunk into his Mind, and inſpired him with ſentiments ſimilar to their own, the following paſſages may ſuffice to ſhew.

Take his Ideas of Liberty and Servitude.

" *For as the true and only* Liberty *is to ſerve Virtue, and diſcharge*
" *its various duties; ſo the only true and eſſential* Slavery *is to be in*
" *ſubjection to the Vices. He therefore is evidently miſtaken, who*
" *imagines that either of theſe Conditions can proceed from any other*
" *Cauſe: for indeed (if we except the difference of* Virtue *and* Vice)
" *all men throughout the world proceed from a ſimilar beginning; con-*
                                                          " *ſiſt*

---

* An octavo Edition of their Letters in *Latin* was publiſhed at *London*, in the year 1718.

† See p. 256 (Philoſophical Arrangements) of this Volume.

" _sist of, and are nourished by the same elements; draw from the same_
" _principle the same vital breath; enjoy the same cope of heaven; all_
" _alike live; all alike die_ *."

TAKE his idea concerning the extensive influence of PHILO-
SOPHY.

" 'Tis PHILOSOPHY, _that prescribes a just measure to all things; and_
" _while she arranges moral_ Duties, _condescends to mix with such as are_
" _plebeian and vulgar.— No otherwise, indeed, can any thing be said_
" _to proceed rightly, unless she herself confirm by_ DEEDS, _what she_
" _teaches us in_ WORDS †."

SPEAKING of VIRTUE and FELICITY, he thus explains himself.—

" _But these_ (two possessions) _are more excellent than any other, be-_
" _cause_ VIRTUE _includes all things, that are to be done;_ FELICITY,
" _all things that are to be wished._ Yet does FELICITY _excel_ VIRTUE,
" _because in all things the End is more excellent than the Means._
" _Now_

---

* _Sicut enim vera et unica_ LIBERTAS _est, servire virtuti, et ipsius exercere officia; ita
unica et singularis_ SERVITUS _est vitiis subjugari. Errat plane quisquis aliunde condi-
tionem alterutram opinatur accidere. Si quidem omne hominum genus in terris simili ab
ortu surgit, eisdem constat et alitur elementis, eundemque spiritum ab eodem principio
carpit, eodemque fruitur cælo, æque moritur, æque vivit._ De Nugis Curialium, p. 510.
Edit. Lugdun. 1595.

† _Ipsa_ (PHILOSOPHIA) _est, quæ universis præscribit modum, et dum disponit officia,
etiam plebeis, et vulgaribus interesse dignatur. Alioquin nihil aliud recte procedit, nisi
et ipsa rebus asserat, quod verbis docet._ De Nugis Curial. p. 489.

Part III. " *Now no one is* HAPPY, *that he may act* rightly ; *but he acts* RIGHTLY,
" *that he may live* happily *."

THE following Diftich is of his own Age, but being difficult to
tranflate, is only given in its original, as a fample of elegant and
meritorious Poetry.

IT expreffes a *refined* thought; that *as the Soul of Man animates
the Body, fo is the Soul itfelf animated by God.*
    Vita Animæ DEUS *eft; hæc, Corpóris; hac fugiente,*
    Solvitur hoc; perit hæc, deftituente Deo †.

THE preceding Quotations are taken from his Tract *De Nugis
Curialium :* thofe, which follow, are from another Tract called ME-
TALOGICUS, fo named from being fubfequent to *Logic,* as META-
PHYSICS are to *Phyfics.*

HE makes *three* things requifite to the exiftence of every ART, and
thefe are GENIUS, MEMORY, and THE REASONING FACULTY, and
thefe *three* he thus *defines —*

" GENIUS *is a certain Power, naturally implanted in the Mind, and
" which is of itfelf* ORIGINALLY CAPABLE ‡.
                                  " MEMORY

---

* *Sunt autem hæc omnibus aliis præftantiora, quia* VIRTUS *omnia agenda,* FELICITAS *omnia optanda complectitur. Felicitas tamen Virtuti præftat, quia in omnibus præftantius eft propter quod aliquid, quam quod propter aliquid. Non enim felix eft quis, ut recte agat; fed recte agit, ut feliciter vivat.* De Nugis Curial. p. 367, 368.

† Ibid. p. 127.

‡ *Eft autem* INGENIUM *vis quædam, animæ naturaliter infita, per fe valens.* Metalog. p. 756.

" MEMORY *is (as it were)* THE MIND'S ARK *or* CHEST; *the firm*
" *and faithful preserver of things perceived* *.

" THE REASONING FACULTY *is a power of the Mind, which exa-*
" *mines things, that have occurred either to* THE SENSES, *or to* THE
" INTELLECT, *and fairly decides in favour of the better; which, well*
" *weighing the* SIMILITUDES *and* DISSIMILITUDES *of things, at*
" *length (after due discussion) establishes* ART, *and shews it to be (as*
" *it were)* A FINITE SCIENCE OF THINGS INFINITE †."

OUR Author concludes with telling us, that " *As* NATURE *is the*
" MOTHER *of all* ARTS, *so the Contempt of them surely redounds to*
" *the Injury of their* PARENT ‡."

I MUST

---

* MEMORIA *vero quasi* MENTIS ARCA, *firma et fidelis custodia perceptorum.* Metalog.
p. 757.

† RATIO *eorum, quæ Sensibus aut animo occurrunt, examinatrix animi vis est, et fidelis
arbitra potiorum; quæ, rerum similitudines dissimilitudinesque perpendens, tandem* ARTEM
statuit quasi quandam INFINITORUM FINITAM ESSE SCIENTIAM. Metalog. 757.

This may be illustrated from *the Arts* of ARITHMETIC and GRAMMAR.

Numbers, which are INFINITE, being reduced to the FINITE GENERA of *Even* and
Odd; and these again being divided into the FEW SUBORDINATE SPECIES: in this
limited *Reduction* we behold the Rise of ARITHMETIC, and of all the various Theorems
contained in that Art.

Sounds Articulate, which are INFINITE, being reduced to the FINITE GENERA of
Vowels and *Consonants;* and *Vowels* again being enlarged into the species of *Long,
Short,* and *Middle;* *Consonants* into the Species of *Mutes* and *Liquids:* In these *limited
Reductions* we behold the Rise of GRAMMAR; thro' which, by about twenty *Simple
Sounds* called *Letters,* we form *Articulate Sounds* by Millions.

‡ *Quia* ARTIUM NATURA *mater est, merito in injuriam parentis redundat contemptus
earum.* Metalog. 757.

I must not omit some of his *Grammatical* ideas, because they are of a superior sort, that is to say, they are *Logical* and *Philosophical.*

He tells us—*For as* [IN NATURE] ACCIDENTS *cloath* SUB-STANCES, *and give them a* FORM; *so* [IN LANGUAGE] *through a similar correspondence are* SUBSTANTIVES *vested with a* FORM *by* ADJECTIVES. *And that this* [grammatical] *Institution of* REASON *may the more easily coincide with* NATURE, *in the same manner as the* SUBSTANCE OF EVERY NATURAL BEING *knows nothing of* INTENSION *and* REMISSION: *so likewise in* LANGUAGE SUBSTANTIVES *admit no* DEGREE OF COMPARISON *.

AFTER this he proceeds to shew that *this Imitation of Nature* not only exists in *Nouns,* but in *the other Parts of Speech.* He tells us, that VERBS, as they denote TIME, are necessarily provided with TENSES; and, as they always express *something else* in their *original meaning,* he calls the *additional denoting of Time* by a truly *philosophic* Word, a CONSIGNIFICATION †.

THE writer of these Remarks cannot say he has transferred any of them into his *Hermes,* because *Hermes* was written long before he knew *John of Salisbury.* But, that both Writers drew from the same source,

---

* *Sicut enim* ACCIDENTIA SUBSTANTIAM *vestiunt, et informant:* sic quadam proportione RATIONIS ab ADJECTIVIS SUBSTANTIVA *informabtur. Et, ut familiarius* RATIONIS *Institutio* NATURÆ *cohæreat,* sicut SUBSTANTIA *cujusque rei* INTENSIONIS *et* REMISSIONIS *ignara est:* sic SUBSTANTIVA ad COMPARATIONIS GRADUM *non veniunt.* Metalog. 561.

† MOTUS *non est* sine TEMPORE, nec VERBUM *esse potuit* sine TEMPORIS CONSIGNIFICATIONE. Metalog. 561. *Aristot. de Interpret. c.* 3.

fource, he thinks fufficiently clear from the fimilitude of their fentiments *.

I FEAR, I have dwelt too long on my *Countryman*, perhaps,
becaufe a countryman; but more in truth, becaufe his Works are
little known, and yet are certainly curious and valuable.

I SHALL only mention, that there were other refpectable Geniufes
of *the fame Century*, fuch as the *Epic Poet*, JOSEPH OF EXETER;
the pleafant Archdeacon of Oxford, WALTER MAPPS; GIRALDUS
CAMBRENSIS, &c.

BUT the eloquent *Author of the Life of Henry the Second* has in
his third Volume handled the ftate of our Literature *during this
period* in fo mafterly a way, that the writer of thefe obfervations
would not have faid fo much, had not the Arrangement of his
Remarks made it in fome degree neceffary †.

WE muft not conclude this Chapter without relating a few Facts,
relative to the gallant RICHARD, called from his *Magnanimity Cœur
de Leon*. Other *Heroes*, long before him, had been likened to
Lions; and the celebrated *Ali*, in the lofty language of *Arabia*, was
called *the Lion of God*.

WHAT *Bohadin* fays of RICHARD is remarkable. " He was," as
that Hiftorian relates, " uncommonly active; of great fpirit and
" firm Refolution; one, who had been fignalized by his Battles,
" and

---

* See Vol. I. p. 267, 268.   † See Lord Lyttelton's Life of Henry the Second.

Part III. " and who was of intrepid courage in War. By thofe, whom he
" led, he was efteemed *lefs than the King of France* on account of
" his Kingdom, and Dignity, but more abundant in Riches, and
" *far more illuftrious for military Valour* *."

This Teftimony receives no fmall weight, as it comes from a
contemporary writer, who was *prefent*; and who, being likewife a
faft Friend to *Saladin*, *Richard's* great Antagonift, can hardly be
fufpected of flattering *an Adverfary*.

In the following Extracts from the fame Author, which Extracts
contain *Different* Conferences between *Richard* and *Saladin*, we
have a fample of their *fentiments*, and of *the manner* in which they
exprefs them.

When Richard in *Paleftine* was ill, he longed for Fruit and
Ice, and the fruits he defired were Pears and Peaches. He fent
for them to *Saladin*, and they were immediately given him. *Richard*
in return was equally bountiful, and entertained the Sultan's people
magnificently. War between great men feldom extinguishes Humanity †.

After a long and various War, Richard fent to Saladin the
following Message.

" When you have greeted the Prince, you will lay what follows
" before him —The *Muffulmans* and *Francs* are both perifhing;
" their

---

* *Bohadin, cit. Salad.* p. 160.   † *Bohadin,* p. 176.

" their countries laid waſte, and completely paſſing to ruin; the Ch. X.
" wealth and Lives of their people conſumed on either ſide. To
" this Conteſt and *Religious War* its proper Rights have been now
" paid. Nothing remains to be ſettled, but the affair of *the Holy*
" *City*, of *the Croſs*, and of *the ſeveral Regions* or Countries. As
" to *the Holy City*, it being the ſeat of our Worſhip, from *that*
" indeed we can by no means recede, altho' not a ſingle man of
" us were to ſurvive the attempt. As to *the Countries*, thoſe on
" this ſide *Jordan*, ſhall be reſtored to us. As to *the Croſs*, it being
" *with you only a uſeful piece* of Wood, altho' *to us* of value ineſti-
" mable, This *the Sultan* will give us; and thus Peace being eſtabliſh-
" ed, we ſhall all of us reſt from this our uninterrupted fatigue.*"

SALADIN'S ANSWER TO RICHARD.

" THE HOLY CITY is as much holy to *us*, as to *you*; nay, is
" rather of greater worth and dignity *to us*, than *to you*; as 'twas
" *thence* that *our Prophet* took his Journey by night to Heaven;
" 'tis *there the Angels* are wont ſolemnly to aſſemble themſelves.
" Imagine not therefore that we ſhall ever depart thence. We
" dare not among *the Muſſulmans* appear ſo abandoned, ſo neg-
" lectful of our Affairs, as to think of this. As to THE REGIONS
" or COUNTRIES, theſe alſo you know were originally ours, which
" you indeed have annexed to your Dominions by the Imbecillity
" of *the Muſſulmans* at the period, when you attacked them. God
" has not ſuffered you to lay a ſingle ſtone there, ever ſince the
                                                        " War

____

* *Bohadin,* p. 207.

Part III. " War began; while we, 'tis evident, enjoy all the produce of our
" Countries to the full. Laſtly, as to the Cross, that in truth is
" *your* Scandal, and a great diſhonour to the Deity; which, how-
" ever, it does not become us, by giving up, to neglect, unleſs it
" be for ſome more important advantage, accruing thence to the
" Faith of *Mahomet* *."

It muſt be obſerved, that *the Croſs* here mentioned was ſuppoſed
to have been that, on which *Chriſt* was crucified; and which being
in *Jeruſalem*, when it was taken, had been from that time in the
hands of *Saladin*.

Tho' no Peace was now made, it was made ſoon after, yet
without reſtoration either of *Jeruſalem*, or of *the Croſs*.

. 'Twas uſual in thoſe days to ſwear to Treaties, and ſo did the
inferior Parties; but the *two Monarchs* excuſed themſelves, ſaying,
" *it was not uſual for Kings to ſwear* †."

When Richard was returning home, he was baſely ſeized by
a *Duke of Auſtria*, and kept priſoner for more than a year, till by
a large ſum raiſed upon his people he was redeemed ‡.

This gallant Prince, after having eſcaped for years the moſt
formidable perils, fell at length unfortunately by the Arrow of an
obſcure hand, in beſieging an obſcure Caſtle, within *his own French*
Domains.   He

---

* *Bohadin*, p. 208.   † *Bohadin*, p. 261.
‡ See the Hiſtories of *Richard's* Life, *Rapin, Hume*, &c.

Ch. X.

HE did not immediately die; but, as the wound began to mortify, and his end to approach, he ordered the person, who had shot him (his name was *Bertram de Gurdun*), to be brought into his presence.

WHEN he arrived, the King thus addrest him. " *What harm have*
" *I ever done thee? for what reason hast thou slain me?*" Bertram replied — " *Thou hast slain my Father and two Brothers with thy own*
" *hand; and now 'twas thy desire to slay* ME. *Take then any Ven-*
" *geance upon me thou wilt; I shall freely suffer the greatest tortures*
" *thou canst invent, so that thou art but dispatched, who hast done the*
" *world so much mischief.*"

THE King, on this, intrepid answer, commanded his Chains to be taken off; forgave what he had done, and dismist him with a Present.

BUT the King's servants were not so generous, as their master; for, when the King was dead, (which soon happened) they put the prisoner to a cruel death.

A POET of the time compares, not improperly, the Death of RICHARD to that of a *Lion*, killed by an *Ant*. The *sentiment* is better than the *Metre*.

Istius in morte perimit Formica Leonem[*].

'TIS

---

[*] *Rogeri de Heredon Annalium pars posterior*, p. 791, Edit. Francof. 1601. We have transcribed from the original the Discourse, which past between *Richard* and *Bertram*, as it appears to be curious, and the *Latinity* not to be despised.

Quid

 'T is somewhat singular, that in thefe Periods, confidered as dark and barbarous, *the fame Nations* fhould ftill retain their *fuperiority of Tafte,* tho' not perhaps in its original purity. During the reign of *Henry the Third,* (which foon followed) when Bifhop *Poore* erected *the Cathedral of Salifbury* (which confidering its lightnefs, its uniformity, and the height of its Spire, is one of the completeft *Gothic* buildings now extant) we are informed he fent into Italy for the beft Architects*.

Long before this, in the eighth Century, when one of the *Caliphs* erected a moft *magnificent Temple or Mofque* at *Damafcus*, he procured for the building of it the moft fkilfull Architects, and thofe not only from his own Dominions, but (as the Hiftorian informs us) from Greece†.

From thefe accounts it is evident, that fome Knowledge of the Fine Arts, even during this *middle Age,* exifted both in Italy and Greece.

Should it be demanded, *to which Nation, in this refpect, we give the Preference,*—it is a Queftion to be decided by recurring to Facts.

Italy

Quid mali tibi feci?   Quare me interemifti?—Cui ille refpondit—Tu intcremifti patrem meum, et duos fratres manu tuâ, et ME *nunc interimere voluifti. Sume ergo de me vindictam, quamcunque volueris: libenter enim patiar, quæcunque excogitaveris majora tormenta, dummodo Tu interficiaris, qui tot et tanta mala contulifti mundo.*

* *Matthew Paris.*   † *Abulfed.* p. 125.

Ch. X.

Italy at the beginning of her History was barbarous; nor did she emerge from her Barbarity, till Greece, which she had conquered, gave her Poets, Orators, Philofophers, &c.

Græcia capta ferum Victorem cepit——— Hor.

After a fucceffion of Centuries the *Roman Empire* fell. By this fatal Event the *Finer Arts* fell alfo, and lay for years in a kind of torpid ftate, till they revived through the genial warmth of Greece.

A few Greek Painters, in the *thirteenth* Century, came from *Greece* into *Italy*, and taught their Art to Cimabue, a *Florentine*[*]. Cimabue was the Father of *Italian Painters*, and from him came a Succeffion, which at length gave the *Raphaels*, the *Michael Angelo's*, &c.

The *Statues*, and ruined *Edifices*, with which *Italy* abounded, and which were all of them by Greek Artifts, or after Grecian Models, taught the *Italians* the *Fine Arts* of *Sculpture* and *Architecture*[†].

The Greek Fugitives from *Conftantinople*, after it's unhappy Cataftrophe, brought that fuperior *Literature* into *Italy*, which enabled

---

[*] *Cimabue died in* 1300.

[†] *How early* thefe fine Remains begin to excite their admiration, we learn from thofe warm Verfes of *Hildebert*, quoted before, p. 521.

Part III. enabled the *Italians* to read in the original the capital Authors of *Attic Eloquence* [*].

WHEN *Literature, Sculpture, Architecture,* and *Painting* had thus attained a perfection in *Italy,* we learn from History, they were transplanted into *the North,* where they lived, tho' it was rather like *Exotics,* than *Natives.*

As therefore *Northern Europe* derived them from *Italy,* and this last from *Greece,* the conclusion is evident, that NOT ITALY, but GREECE WAS THEIR COMMON PARENT. And thus is the Question concerning *Preference* to be decided.

---

[*] Sup. p. 461.

C H A P. XI.

Concerning the POETRY of the LATTER LATINS, or WESTERN Eu-
ROPEANS—Accentual Quantity—RHIME—Samples of RHIME in
Latin—in Claffical Poets, accidental; in thofe of a later age, de-
figned—RHIME among the Arabians—ODILO, HUCBALDUS, HIL-
DIGRIM, HALABALDUS, Poets or Heroes of Weftern Europe—
RHIMES in MODERN Languages—of Dante, Petrarch, Boccaccio,
Chaucer, &c.—Sannazarius, a pure Writer in Claffic Latin, without
Rhime—Anagrams, Chronograms, &c. finely and accurately defcribed
by the ingenious Author of the SCRIBLERIAD.

A ND here, as we are about to fpeak upon the POETRY of thefe
times; we wifh our Readers previoufly to review, what we
have already faid upon the *two Species of verbal Quantity*, the *Syllabic*
and the *Accentual* *.

·IT will there appear that till *Greek* and *Latin* degenerated, *Accen-*
tual Quantity was hardly known. But tho' *Degeneracy* fpread it
thro' thefe two Languages, yet, with regard to *modern* Languages,
'twas the beft that could be attained. Their harfh and rugged *Dia-*
lects were in *few* inftances fuited to the *Harmonious Simplicity* of the
Syllabic Meafure.

AND

---

* See from p. 321 to p. 332.

And yet, tho' this more perfect and elegant *Prosody* was rarely attainable, so strong was the Love of Mankind for Rhythm, so connate (if I may so say) with their very Being, that Metre *of some sort* was every where cultivated, and even these *northern* Tribes had their *Bards*, their *Minstrels*, their *Troubadours*, and the like.

Now, tho' in the latter Latinity *Syllabic Quantity* was little regarded, and the *Accentual* more frequently supplied its place, they did not esteem even *this last* always sufficient *to mark the Measure*. An Expedient was therefore found (flattering to the Ear, because it had something of *Harmony)* and this was, *to mark the last Syllables* of different Verses with *Sounds that were Similar*, so that the Ear might not doubt a moment, where every Verse *ended*.

And hence in *Modern* Verse *these last Syllables*, which Poets of *a purer* Age in a manner *neglected*, came to claim a peculiar and *superior* regard, as helping to mark the Rhythm thro' the medium of the Rhime.

> *Si Sol spendescat Mariá purific*ante,
> *Major erit glacies post festum, quam fuit* ante *.

Nor was this practised in *Heroics only*, but in *Trochaics* also. ——

> *Suscitavit igitur* ‖ *Deus Hebræo*rum
> *Christianos principes,* ‖ *et robur* eorum
> *Vindicare scilicet* ‖ *Sanguinem Sanct*orum,
> *Subvenire filiis* ‖ *Mortifica*torum †.   Nay

---

* Rhime *is the* Similitude of Sound *at the Ends of two Verses.* Rhythm *is* Measured Motion, *and exists in Verses of every sort, whether Classical or not Classical, whether Blank Verse, or Rhime. In short,* without Rhythm *no Verse can exist of any species;* without Rhime *they may, and often do,*

† *Roger Hoveden, Annal.* p. 379, b.

Ch. XI.

Nay fo fond were thofe Poets of their Jingle, that they not only infufed it into *different* Verfes, but into *one and the fame* Verfe; making *the Middle* of each Verfe to rhime with *its End*, as well *as one Verfe* to rhime with *another*.

Thus in *St. Edmund's* Epitaph we read—
> *Hic erat* EDMUNDUS, *animâ cum corpore* MUNDUS,
> *Quem non* IMMUNDUS *potuit pervertere* MUNDUS *.

And again in thofe verfes tranfcribed from an old monument——
> *Hic funt* CONFOSSA *Bernoldi præfulis* OSSA;
> *Laudet cum* GLOSSA, *dedit hic quia munera* GROSSA.

To thefe may be added the Infcription upon the three Wife Men of the Eaft, buried (as they tell us) at *Cologn* in the Weft,
> *Corpora fanctorum recubant hic terna* MAGORUM,
> *Ex his fublatum nihil eft, alibive* LOCATUM.

Verses of this fort, of which there are innumerable ftill extant, have been called *Leonine* Verfes, from *Leo*, a writer of the 12th Century, who is fuppofed to have been their inventor. But this fhould feem a miftake, if the Infcription upon the Image of a King *Dagobert*, who lived in *the feventh* Century, be of the fame period with that Monarch.
> *Fingitur hac fpecie, bonitatis odore* REFERTUS,
> *Iftius Ecclefiæ fundator, Rex* DAGOBERTUS.

Tis

---

* *Waverly*, p. 202.

3 Z 2

Part III.   'TIS true there are Verſes of this ſort to be found even among
Poets, *the firſt in claſſical rank.*

Thus VIRGIL,

> *Trajicit: i,* VERBIS *virtutem illude* SUPERBIS.

Thus HORACE,

> *Fratrem mœrentis, rapto de fratre* DOLENTIS.

Thus even HOMER himſelf,

> Ἐκ γὰρ κρηΤΑΩΝ ξένος ἔυχομαι ἐυρειΑΩΝ.

THE difference ſeems to have been, THE RHIMES, falling from
theſe *ſuperior* Geniuſes, fell ('twas probable) *accidentally;* with the
latter race of Poets they were the Work of *labour* and *deſign.* They
may well indeed be called Works *of labour and deſign,* when we reflect on the immenſe pains, which their makers muſt have taken,
where *their Plan of Rhiming* was ſo *complicated,* as they ſometimes
made it.

TAKE a ſingular example of no fewer than *three* RHIMES to each
Verſe.

> *Crimina* CRESCERE *flete;* TEPESCERE *jus, decus,* ÆQUUM;
> *Flete,* GEMISCITE; *denique* DICITE, *dicite* MECUM,
> *Qui regis* OMNIA, *pelle tot* IMPIA, *ſurge,* PERIMUS,
> *Nos, Deus,* ASPICE, *ne fine* SIMPLICE *lumine* SIMUS.

Fabricius, who gives theſe Verſes, remarks, that they were written
in the *Dactylic Leonine;* that is, they had every Foot *a Dactyl,* excepting

cepting the laft, and contained *three Rhimes* in each Verfe, TWO *within the Verfe* itfelf, and ONE *referring to the Verfe that followed.* He adds, that their Author, *Bernardus Morlanenfis*, a Monk of the eleventh Century, compofed no lefs than *three* Books of this wonderful Verfification. What leifure muft he have had, and how was it employed * ?

BEFORE we quit the fubject of RHIME we may add, that RHIME was ufed not only by the *Latin*, but by the *Arabian* Poets, as we may fee by a tract upon the *Arabic* Profody, fubjoined by Dr. *Pococke* to his *Carmen Tograi.*

RHIME however was not fo ftrictly followed, but that fometimes they quitted it. In the following *Heroics*, the Monk *Odilo*, addreffing himfelf to his Friend *Hucbaldus*, appears fo warm in his wifhes, as not only to forget *Rhime*, but even *Claffical* Quantity.

> *Hucbaldo Sŏpho Sŏphiă sĭt femper amica;*
> *Hucbaldus Sŏphus Sŏphiæ femper amicus:*
> *Expofco hoc Odĭlo, peccator cernuus ēgo.*

THIS Genius (over whofe Verfes I have occafionally marked the *accentual* Quantity in contra-diftinction to the *Syllabic*) is fuppofed to have written in the *tenth* Century.

OTHERS, *rejecting Rhime*, wrote *Elegiacs*; as that Monk, who celebrated *Hildĭgrim* and *Halabuldus*; the one for building a Church, the other for confecrating it.   *Hildĭgrim*

---

* See *Fabric. Biblioth. med. et infim. ætatis*, under the word *Bernardus Morlanenfis.*

Hildigrim ſtruxit; Hālābaldus Epiſcopus Archi
Sanctificavit: honor certus utrumque manet.

In the firſt of theſe two Verſes the word *Archi-Epiſcopus* is, by a pleaſant *tranſpoſition*, made into a *Dactyl* and *Spondree*, ſo as to complete the Hexameter [*].

'Twas upon *theſe* Principles of Verſification, that the early Poets of this Æra wrote much bad *Verſe* in much bad *Latin*. At length they tried their ſkill in their *Vernacular*. tongues, introducing *here* alſo their *Rhime* and their *Accentual quantity*, as they had done before in *Latin*.

Thro' the Southern parts of *France* the Troubadours (already mentioned) [†] compoſed Sonnets in the *Provençal* Tongue. Soon after them Dante, Petrarch, and Boccaccio wrote Poems in *Italian*; and ſoon after theſe, Chaucer flouriſhed in *England*. From *Chaucer*, thro' *Rowley*, we paſs to Lords *Surry* and *Dorſet*; from them to *Spencer*, *Shakſpeare*, and *Johnſon*: after whom came *Milton*, *Waller*, *Dryden*, *Pope*, and a ſucceſſion of Geniuſes, down to the preſent time.

The three Italian Poets, we have mentioned, were capital in their kind, being not only ſtrong and powerful in *Sentiment*, but, what

---

[*] See *Recueil de divers Ecrits pour ſervir de l'Eclairciſſements a l'Hiſtoire de France par L'Abbe de Beuf*, p. 115.—p. 106.

[†] See before, p. 511.

what is more furprifing, elegant in their *Diction* at a time, when
the *Languages of England* and *France* were barbarous and unpolifhed. This in *Englifh* is evident from our Countryman, CHAUCER,
who, even to an *Englifh* Reader appears fo uncouth, and who yet
wrote later than the lateft of thefe three.

IT muft, however, be acknowledged, that, if *we except his Language*, for LEARNING and WIT he appears equal to the beft of his
Contemporaries, and I may add even of his *Succeffors*.

I CANNOT omit the following *fample of his* LITERATURE, in the
Frankelein's Tale. In that Poem the fair *Dorigen* is made to lament
the abfence of her much loved *Arveragus;* and, as fhe fits upon a
Cliff, beholding the Sea, and the formidable Rocks, fhe breaks
forth with terror into the following Exclamation.

> *Eternal* GOD! *that thro' thy Purveyaúnce*
> LEADEST *the World by* CERTAIN *Governaúnce;*
> IN IDLE, *as men fayn,* YE NOTHING MAKE.
> *But, Lord, thofe griefly, fendly,* ROCKIS, *blake,*
> *That feem rathir a* FOUL CONFU'SIÓN
> *Of Work, than any* FAIR CREA'TIÓN
> OF SUCH *a* PERFECT GOD, *wife, and full ftable:*
> WHY *have ye wrought this work unrfafonáble?*

Dorigen, after more expoftulation of the fame fort, adds —

> *I wote well Clerkis woll fayn, as 'hem lefte,*
> *By Arguments, that* ALL IS FOR THE BESTE,

Tho'

Tho' I ne cannot well the Caufes know —
But thilke God, that made the Winds to blow,
Ay keep my Lord, &c.

THERE is an elegant Pathos in her thus quitting thofe deeper Speculations, to addrefs a Prayer for the fafety of her *Arveragus*.

The Verfe, before quoted,

To LEAD *the World by* CERTAIN *Governaunce*,

is not only a *philofophical Idea*, but *philofophically* expreft.

The next Verfe,

IN IDLE, *as Men fayn*, YE NOTHING MAKE,

is a fentiment tranflated literally from ARISTOTLE, and which that Philofopher fo much approved, as *often* to repeat it.

TAKE one Example —
Ὁ δὲ Θεὸς ϰ̓ ἡ φύσις ᾽ὐδὲν μάτην ποῦσαν —
GOD *and* NATURE MAKE NOTHING IN VAIN.

Arift. de Cælo, Lib. I. *Cap.* 4.

As to what follows, *I mean that fpeculation of learned men, that* ALL IS FOR THE BEST, this too we meet in *the fame* Philofopher, annexed (as it were) to *the fentiment juft alleged*.

Ἡ φύσις ἔθεν δημιεργεῖ μάτην, ὥσπερ εἴρηται πρότερον, ἀλλὰ πάντα πρὸς τὸ βέλτιον ἐκ τῶν ἐνδεχομένων. NATURE, *(as has been faid before)* CREATES NOTHING IN VAIN, *but* ALL THINGS FOR THE BEST, *out of the contingent materials*. *De Animal. inceſſu.* C. 12.

It

It may be fairly doubted, whether CHAUCER took this from the *original Greek*—'tis more probable he took it from the *Latin Version* of the *Spanish Arabic Version*, which *Latin* was then current, and admitted thro' *Western Europe* for the *Aristotelic Text*.

The *same thought* occurs in one of our most elegant *modern* Ballads; tho', whence the Poet took it, I pretend not to decide.

> *How can they say, that* NATURE
>   HAS NOTHING MADE IN VAIN?
> *Why then beneath the Water*
>   *Do* HIDEOUS ROCKS *remain?*
> THOSE ROCKS *no eyes discover,*
>   *Which lurk beneath the deep,*
> *To wreck, &c.*

BUT to return to CHAUCER—

IF in *the Tale* we have just quoted; if in the Tale of the *Nun's Priest*, and in many other of his works, there are these sprinklings of *Philosophy*; if to these we add the extensive Knowledge of *History, Mythology,* and various other subjects, which he every where shews: we may fairly, I think, arrange him among our *learned* Poets, and take from HIM *an Estimate of the Literature of the Times,* as far at least as possest by men of *superior* Education.

AFTER having mentioned (as we have lately done) PETRARCH and some of the *Italians,* I can by no means omit their countryman SANNAZARIUS, who flourished in the Century following, and whose

Part III. Eclogues in particular, formed on the Plan of *Fishing* Life inftead
of *Paftoral*, cannot be enough admired both for their *Latinity* and
their *Sentiment*. His fourth *Eclogue*, called *Proteus*, written in imitation of *Virgil's* Eclogue called *Silenus*, may be juftly valued as a
mafter-piece in its kind. The following flight fketch of it is fubmitted to the Reader.

" Two Fifhermen, failing during a dark night from *Caprea* into
" the Bay of Naples, as they filently approach the Promontory
" of *Minerva*, hear PROTEUS from the Shore, finging a marvelous
" Narrative of the ftrange Events, of which *thofe Regions* had been
" the well-known Scene. He concludes with the unhappy fate of
" the Poet's Friend and Patron, *Frederic King of Naples*, who,
" having been expelled his Kingdom, died an Exile in *France*."

IF I might be pardoned a digreffion, it fhould be on the Elegance
of the *Numbers*, by which this unfortunate part of the Tale is
introduced.

> *Addit triftia fata, et te, quem luget ademptum*
> *Italia*, &c.

THE Omiffion of the *ufual Cæfura*, in the firft of thefe verfes,
naturally throws it into that *Anapaftic Rhythm*, fo finely fuited to
folemn Subjects.

> *Addit — triftia — fata et — te quem*, &c.*

IT

---

* So *Homer*,

　　Πότνα - θία μὴ - μοι τόδε - χώεο,　　*Odyff.* E. 215.

It may be obferved alfo, in how *pathetic*, and yet withal, in how
manly a way *Sannazarius* concludes. *Frederic* died in a remote
region, and was buried, where he died. " *'Tis pleafing*, fays Pro-
" teus, *for a man's remains to reft in his own Country; and yet for*
" *a Tomb every Land fuffices*."

   Grata quies patriæ, fed et omnis terra Sepulcrum.

Ch. XI.

Those, who know how much fooner *Italy* emerged from Barbarity, than the reft of *Europe*, may chufe to place Sannazarius
rather at the *beginning* of a *good* age, than at the *conclufion* of a
bad one. Their opinion, perhaps, is not without foundation, and
may be extended to Fracastorius, Politian, Poggius, and
many other eloquent Authors, which that Century then produced,
when Eloquence was little known elfewhere.

Before we quit *Poetry*, we fhall fay fomething upon its *loweft*
Species, upon *Acroftics, Chronograms, Wings, Altars, Eggs, Axes,*
&c.

These were the poor Inventions of men *devoid of Tafte*, and yet
abfurdly aiming at Fame by thefe defpicable whims. Quitting the
paths of Simplicity and Truth (of which 'tis probable they were
wholly ignorant) they afpired, like Rope-dancers, to Merit, which
only lay in *the difficulty*. The *Wings*, the *Axes*, the *Altars*, &c.
were *wretched Forms*, into which they tortured poor *Words*, juft as
poor *Trees* in our Gardens were formerly mangled into Giants,
Flower-Pots, Peacocks, Obelifcs, &c.

4 A 2

Whoever

Part III. WHOEVER remembers that ACROSTICS, in Verſification, are formed from the *Initial Letter* of every Verſe, will ſee the Force and Ingenuity of the following deſcription.

> *Firm and compact, in three fair Columns wove,*
> *O'er the ſmooth plain the bold* ACROSTICS *move:*
> *High o'er the reſt* THE TOW'RING LEADERS RISE,
> *With* LIMBS GIGANTIC *and* SUPERIOR SIZE.

CHRONOGRAMS, by a different conceit, *were not confined to* INITIAL LETTERS, but, as they were *to deſcribe Dates,* THE NUMERAL LETTERS, *in whatever part of the Word they ſtood,* were diſtinguiſhed from *other* Letters *by being written in* CAPITALS.

FOR example, I would mark by a CHRONOGRAM the Date 1506. I take for the purpoſe the following Words,

> *—feriam ſidera vertice;*

and by *a ſtrange Elevation of* CAPITALS I compel even *Horace* to give me *the Date required.*

> *—ſeriaM ſiDera VertIce,* MDVI.

THE Ingenious Author, whom I have quoted before, thus admirably deſcribes this *ſecond* ſpecies of folly.

> *Not thus the loofer* CHRONOGRAMS *prepare;*
> *Careleſs their Troops, undiſciplin'd to War;*
> *With* RANK IRREGULAR, CONFUS'D *they ſtand,*
> THE CHIEFTAINS MINGLING *with the vulgar band.*

IF

If I have dwelt too long on thefe trifles, it is not fo much for their *merit* (of which they have none) as for thofe *elegant* Lines, in which they are fo well defcribed.

On the fame motive I conclude this Chapter with felecting a few more Lines from the fame ingenious Poem.

> *To join thefe fquadrons, o'er the champain came*
> *A numerous race, of no ignoble name;*
> *RIDDLE, and REBUS, Riddle's deareft Son,*
> *And falfe Conundrum, and infidious Pun;*
> *Fustian, who fcarcely deigns to tread the ground,*
> *And Rondeau, wheeling in repeated round.*
> *On their fair ftandards, by the winds difplay'd,*
> *Eggs, Altars, Wings, Pipes, Axes, were pourtray'd*.*

---

* See THE SCRIBLERIAD, (Book II. V. 151, &c.) of my valuable Friend, Mr. *Cambridge* of *Twickenham*.

C H A P. XII.

Paul *the Venetian, and* Sir John Mandeville, *great Travellers*—
Sir John Fortescue, *a great Lawyer—his valuable Book, addreſſ*
to his Pupil, the Prince of Wales—King's College Chapel *in*
Cambridge, founded by Henry the Sixth.—

Part III.　'TWAS during this middle Period lived thoſe celebrated Tra-
　　　　　vellers, Paul the Venetian, and our Countryman, Sir
John Mandeville.

We have mentioned Chaucer before them, tho' he flouriſhed
after both; for *Chaucer* lived till paſt the year 1400, Paul began
his Travels in the year 1272, and Mandeville began his in the
year 1322. The Reaſon is, *Chaucer* has been arranged with *the*
Poets, already ſpoken of.

Marc Paul, who is the firſt Writer of any Note concerning
the *Eaſtern* Countries, travelled into thoſe remote Regions as far
as the Capital and Court of *Cublai Chan*, the ſixth from that
tremendous Conqueror *Jingiz Chan* *.　Paul is a curious and minute
Relator of what he ſaw there.

He deſcribes *the Capital,* Cambalu, to be a ſquare walled in, of
Six miles on every ſide, having to each ſide three Gates, and the
ſeveral ſtreets rectilinear, and croſſing at right angles.

The

---

* See *Abulpharagius,* from p. 281 to p. 306.

The Imperial Palace, he tells us, was inclofed within a fquare Ch. XII.
wall of *a mile* on every fide, and was magnificently adorned with
Gilding and Pictures. 'Twas a piece of ftate, that thro' the grand
or principal gate no one could enter but the Emperor *himfelf*.

WITHIN the walls of this Square there were extenfive Lawns,
adorned with Trees, and ftockt with wild animals, ftags, goats,
fallow deer, &c. not to mention a River, which formed a Lake,
filled with the fineft fifh.

BESIDES this, at a League's diftance from the Palace, he defcribes a fmall Mountain or Hill, planted with Ever-greens, in cir-
cumference about a mile. " Here (he tells us) the Emperor had
" all the fineft trees that could be procured, brought to him, em-
" ploying his Elephants for that purpofe, as the trees were extracted
" with their roots.

" THE Mountain, from its verdure, was called THE GREEN
" MOUNTAIN." On its fummit ftood a fine Palace, diftinguifhed
" alfo by its *Green* Colour, where he *(the Great Chan)* often retired
" to enjoy himfelf *."

SPEAKING

---

* The preceding Extracts are taken from a *Latin* Edition of PAULUS VENETUS,
publifhed, in a fmall Quarto, *Coloniæ Brandenburgicæ, ex officina Georgii Schulzii, anno*
1679.

As the Book is not rare, nor the ftile curious, we have only given the feveral Pages,
by way of reference.

For *the Capital*, CAMBALU, fee p. 68. *Lib.* 2. *Cap.* 10.

For *the Imperial Palace, Lawns* adjoining, and *the Green Mountain*, fee p. 66, 67,
Lib. 2. *Cap.* 9.

 Speaking of *the Person of Cublai*, the then Monarch, he thus describes him.

> " He is remarkably handsome; of a moderate stature; neither
> " too corpulent, nor too lean; having a Countenance ruddy and
> " fair; large eyes; a beautiful Nose; and all the lineaments of
> " his Body formed in due proportion *."

We here quit our Traveller, only observing, as we conclude, that learned men have imagined this Cambalu to be Pekin in *China*, founded there by *Jingiz Chan*, soon after he had conquered it.

When we consider the immense Power of this mighty Conqueror, who in a manner subdued the vast Tract of *Asia*; we are *the less difficult* in believing such marvellous Relations. The City, the Palace, and the Territory around teach us, what was the *Taste* of him and his Family, whose boundless Empire could admit of *nothing minute*.

It is too an additional argument for *Credibility*, that, tho' the Whole is *Vast*, yet nothing appears either *Foolish*, or *Impossible*.

One thing is worthy of notice, that, tho' Paul resided in *China* so long, he makes no mention of the *celebrated* Wall.—Was this *forgetfulness?* or was it not *then* erected?

As

---

* *Rex* Cublai *est homo admodum pulcher, staturâ mediocri, non nimis pinguis, nec nimis macilentus, faciem habens rubicundam atque candidam, oculos magnos, nasum pulchrum, et omnia corporis lineamenta debitâ proportione consistentia.* Mar. Pauli Lib. 2, Cap. 8. p. 65.

As to our Countryman, Sir John Mandeville, tho' he did Ch. XII.
not travel fo far as *Marc Paul*, he travelled into many Parts of
Afia and *Africa*; and, after having lived in thofe Countries for
thirty-three years, died at *Liege* in the year 1371.

He wrote his Travels in three Languages, *Latin*, *French*, and
Englifh, from the laft of which Languages we quote, taking the
liberty, in a few inftances, to modernize the *Words*, tho' not in the
minuteft degree to change the *Meaning*.

We confine ourfelves for brevity to a fingle fact.

Travelling thro' *Macedonia*, he tells us, as follows—" In this
" Country was Aristotle born, in a City, that men call *Stra-*
" *geris* *, a little from the City of *Tragie* or *Trakys*; and at *Strageris*
" is *Ariftotle* buried, and there is an Altar at his Tomb, where
" they make a great Feaft every Year, as tho' he was a Saint.
" Upon this Altar the Lords (or Rulers) hold their Great Councils
" and Affemblies, for they hope, that, thro' the infpiration of God
" and of Him, they fhall have the better counfel †."

Such was the Veneration (for it was more than Honour) paid by
the *Stagirites* to their Countryman, more than *eighteen hundred years*
after his death ‡.   From

---

* Its ancient name in *Greek* was Στάγειρα, whence *Ariftotle* was often called, by way
of eminence, The Stagirite, as being a Citizen there.

† See *Maudeville's* Voyages, Chap. 2.

‡ Thofe, who defire a tafte of this great Man's Philosophy in *Englifh*, may
find their curiofity amply gratified in the laft work of that learned and acute *Grecian*,
Lord Monboddo, which work he ftiles Antient Metaphysics, publifhed in Quarto
at *Edinburgh*, 1779.

 FROM thefe times we pafs over the triumphant reign of *Henry the Fifth* (a reign rather of *Action* than of *Letters*) to that of his unfortunate Son. This was a Period, difgraced by unfuccefsful wars abroad, and by fanguinary diforders at home. *The King himfelf* met an *untimely* End, and fo did his hopeful and high fpirited *Son*, the *Prince of Wales*. Yet did not even thefe Times keep one Genius from emerging, tho' plunged by his rank into their moft tempeftuous part. By this I mean SIR JOHN FORTESCUE, Chancellor of *England*, and Tutor to *the young Prince*, juft mentioned. As this laft office was a Truft of the greateft importance, fo he difcharged it not only with confummate *Wifdom*, but (what was more) with confummate *Virtue*.

His Tract IN PRAISE OF THE LAWS OF ENGLAND *, is written with the nobleft view that man ever wrote; written to infpire his Pupil with a Love of the Country he was to govern, by fhewing him that, To GOVERN BY THOSE ADMIRABLE LAWS, would make him a FAR GREATER PRINCE, than the moft UNLIMITED DESPCTISM †.

THIS

---

* This Book, which he ftiles DE LAUDIBUS LEGUM ANGLIÆ, is written in Dialogue between himfelf, and the young Prince his Pupil, and was originally in *Latin*. The great *Selden* thought it worthy of a Commentary, and fince that it has been publifhed and enriched with additional Notes by Mr. *Gregor*. A new Edition was given ann. 1775, and the Latin Text fubjoined.

† See of *Fortefcue's* Work, Chap. IX. and XIII. and, above all, Chap. XIV. where he tells us *the Poffibility of doing amifs*, (which is the only Privilege an *abfolute* Prince enjoys above a *limited* one) *can be called* AN ADDITION OF POWER *no other, than we fo call* A POSSIBILITY TO DECAY, OR TO DIE. See p. 41 of the Englifh Verfion.

'Tis worth obferving that *Fortefcue*, in his dialogue, gives thefe fine fentiments to the *young Prince*, after he has heard much and due Reafoning upon the excellence of our Conftitution. See Chap. XXXIV, p. 119.

. Tuis he does not only prove by a detail of *particular Laws*, but by an accurate comparifon between the ftate of *England* and *France*, one of which he makes a Land of *Liberty*, the other of *Servitude*. His thirty-fifth and thirty-fixth Chapters upon this fubjeƈt are invaluable, and fhould be read by every ENGLISHMAN, *who honours that* NAME.

THRO' thefe and the other Chapters, we perceive an *interefting Truth*, which is, that the capital parts of our Conftitution, the *Trial by Juries*, the *Abhorrence of Tortures*, the *Sovereignty of Parliament* as well in the granting of *Money*, as in the making and repealing of *Laws*, I fay, that all thefe, and many other ineftimable privileges, exifted THEN, as they do NOW; were not *new* projeƈts of the Day, but SACRED FORMS, to which *Ages* had given a venerable *Sanc-tion* *.

As for the LITERATURE of this Great Man (which is more imme-diately to our purpofe) he appears to have been a Reader of *Ariftotle*, *Diodorus Siculus*, *Cicero*, *Quinƈtilian*, *Seneca*, *Vegetius*, *Boethius*, and many other ancients; to have been not uninformed in the Authors and Hiftory of *later Ages;* to have been deeply knowing not only in *the Laws of his own Country* (where he attained the higheft dignity they could beftow) but in *the Roman* or *Civil Law*, which he holds to be

---

* For trial by *Juries*, fee of this *Author* Chap. XX, XXI, and XXII.—For his abhorrence of *Torture*, fee Chap. XXIII.—For the *fovereignty of Parliament*, fee Chap. IX, XIII, XVIII, XXXVI, particularly p. 118 of the *Englifh Verfion*.—For the high antiquity of our *Laws* and *Conftitution*, fee Chap. XVII.

Part III. be far inferior*; we muſt add to this a maſterly inſight into the *State* and *Policy* of the *neighbouring Nations*.

PERHAPS a perſon of Rank, *even at preſent*, need not wiſh to be better inſtituted, if he had an ambition to ſoar above the Faſhionable Poliſh.

WE muſt not conclude, without obſerving that the Taſte for *Gothic Architecture* ſeems never to have been ſo *elegant*, as during this period; witneſs that exquiſite ſtructure, built by *Henry the Sixth*, I mean THE CHAPEL OF KING's COLLEGE in *Cambridge*.

---

* The inferiority of the *Roman* Law to *our own*, is a Doctrine he ſtrongly inculcates. See above all Chap. IX, XIX, &c. alſo Chap. XXXIV, where he nobly reprobates, as he had done before in Chap. IX, that infamous maxim, *Quod* PRINCIPI *placuit*, LEGIS *habet Vigorem*; a Maxim, well becoming an *Oriental Caliph*, but hardly decent even in a *degenerate Roman Law-giver*.

C H A P. XIII.

Concerning NATURAL BEAUTY — *its Idea the same in all Times —* THESSALIAN TEMPE — *Taste of* VIRGIL, *and* HORACE — *of* MILTON, *in describing Paradise — exhibited of late years first in Pictures — thence transferred to* ENGLISH *Gardens — not wanting to the enlightened Few of the middle Age — proved in* LELAND, PETRARCH, *and* SANNAZARIUS, — *comparison between the Younger* CYRUS, *and* PHILIP LE BEL *of France.*

BUT let us pass for a moment from the elegant Works of ART to the more elegant Works of NATURE. The two subjects are so *nearly* allied, that *the same Taste* usually relishes them *both.*

Now there is nothing more certain, than that the Face of *inanimate Nature* has been at all times captivating. *The Vulgar,* indeed, look no farther than to Scenes of *Culture,* because all their Views merely terminate in *Utility.* They only remark, that 'tis fine Barley; that 'tis rich Clover; as an Ox or an Afs, if they could speak, would inform us. But *the Liberal* have *nobler* views, and tho' they give to *Culture* it's due Praise, they can be delighted with *natural Beauties,* where *Culture* was *never* known.

AGES ago they have celebrated with enthusiastic rapture " a deep " retired Vale, with a River rushing thro' it; a Vale having it's sides " formed by two immense and opposite Mountains, and those sides di-
" verfified

Part III. " *verified by Woods, Precipices, Rocks and romantic Caverns.*" Such
was the Scene, produced by the River *Peneus*, as it ran between the
Mountains, *Olympus* and *Ossa*, in that well known Vale, the THESSA-
LIAN TEMPE[*].

VIRGIL and HORACE, the first for Taste among the *Romans*, appear to have been enamoured with Beauties of this character. Ho-
RACE prayed for a Villa, where there was *a Garden, a Rivulet*, and
above these *a little Grove.*

> *Hortus ubi, et tecto vicinus jugis aquæ fons,*
> *Et paulúm Silvæ super his foret.*　　　　　Sat. VI. 2.

VIRGIL wished to enjoy *Rivers*, and *Woods*, and to be hid under
immense shade in the cool *valleys* of Mount *Hæmus* —

> *—O! qui me gelidis in Vallibus Hæmi*
> *Sistat, et ingenti ramorum protegat umbra?*
>
> Georg. II. 486.

THE great ELEMENTS of *this* species of Beauty, according to *these*
Principles, were WATER, WOOD, and UNEVEN GROUND; to which
may be added a fourth, that is to say, LAWN. 'Tis the happy
Mixture of these four, that produces every Scene of *natural Beauty*,

as

---

[*] *Est nemus Hæmoniæ, prærupta quod undique claudit*
Silva; vocant TEMPE. *Per quæ Penëus ab imo*
Effusus Pindo spumosis volvitur undis,
Dejectuque gravi, &c.　　　　　Ovid, Metam. Lib. I. 568.

A fuller and more ample account of this beautiful spot may be found in the *First*
Chapter of the *Third Book of Ælian's Various History.*

as 'tis a more myſterious Mixture of *other* Elements (perhaps as *ſimple*, and *not more* in number) that produces a *World* or *Univerſe*.

Ch. XIII.

Virgil and *Horace* having been quoted, we may quote, with equal truth, our great countryman, MILTON. Speaking of the Flowers of *Paradiſe*, he calls them *Flowers*,

>——*which* NOT NICE ART
>*In beds and curious Knots, but* NATURE BOON
>*Pours forth profuſe on hill, and dale, and plain.* P. L. IV. 242.

Soon after this he ſubjoins —

>——*this was the Place,*
>*A happy rural Seat, of* VARIOUS VIEW.

HE explains this VARIETY, by recounting the Lawns, the Flocks, the Hillocks, the Valleys, the Grotts, the Waterfalls, the Lakes, &c. &c. and in another Book, deſcribing the approach of *Raphael*, he informs us, that this divine Meſſenger paſt

>——*Thro' Groves of Myrrh,*
>*And flow'ring Odors, Caſſia, Nard and Balm,*
>*A* WILDERNESS *of Sweets; for Nature here*
>*Wanton'd as in her prime, and play'd* AT WILL
>*Her Virgin-fancies, pouring forth more ſweet,*
>*Wild* ABOVE RULE *or* ART, ENORMOUS BLISS. —

P. L. V. 292.

THE *Painters* in the preceding Century ſeem to have felt the power of theſe *Elements*, and to have transferred them into their

Landſcapes

 Landſcapes with ſuch amazing force, that they appear not ſo much to have *followed*, as to have *emulated* Nature. *Claude de Lorraine, the Pouſſins, Salvator Roſa*, and a few more, may be called *ſuperior Artiſts* in this exquiſite Taſte.

Our Gardens in the mean time were taſteleſs and inſipid. Thoſe, who made them, thought *the farther they wandered from Nature*, the nearer they approached *the Sublime.* Unfortunately, where they travelled, *no Sublime was to be found*; and the farther they went, the farther they left it behind.

But *Perfection*, alas! was not the work of a day. Many Prejudices were to be removed; many gradual Aſcents to be made; Aſcents from Bad to Good, and from Good to Better, before the *delicious Amenities* of a *Claude* or a *Pouſſin* could be rivalled in a *Stourhead*, a *Hagley*, or a *Stow*; or *the tremendous Charms* of a *Salvator Roſa* be equalled in the Scenes of a *Peircefield*, or a *Mount Edgecumb*.

Not however to forget the ſubject of our Inquiry.—Tho' 'twas not before the *preſent* Century, that we eſtabliſhed a chaſter Taſte; tho' our neighbours at this inſtant are but learning it from us; and tho' to the Vulgar every where it is totally incomprehenſible (be they Vulgar in rank, or Vulgar in capacity): yet, even in the darkeſt periods we have been treating, periods, when Taſte is often thought to have been loſt, we ſhall ſtill diſcover *an enlightened few*, who were by no means inſenſible to the power of *theſe* beauties.

How

How warmly does LELAND describe *Guy's Cliff*; SANNAZARIUS, Ch.XIII.
his Villa of *Mergilline*; and PETRARCH, his favourite *Vauclufe?*

TAKE GUY's CLIFF from *Leland* in his own *old Englifh*, mixt with
Latin—" It is a place meet for the *Mufes*; there is *Sylence*; a praty
" wood; antra in vivo faxo; (Grottos in the living Rock) the River
" roling over the ftones with a praty noyfe." His *Latin* is more elegant
—Nemufculum ibidem opacum, fontes liquidi et gemmei, prata florida,
antra mufcofa, rivi levis et per faxa decurfus, nec non folitudo et quies
Mufis amiciffima*.

MERGILLINE, the Villa of *Sannazarius* near *Naples*, is thus
fketched in different parts of his Poems :

> Excifo in fcopulo, fluctus unde aurea canos
> Defpiciens, celfo fe culmine MERGILLINE
> Attollit, nautifque procul venientibus offert.
>
> Sannaz. De partu Virgin. I. 25.

> Rupis O! facræ, pelagique cuftos,
> Villa, Nympharum cuftos et propinquæ
> Doridos ——
> Tu mihi folos nemorum receffus
> Das, et hærentes per opaca lauros
> Saxa; Tu, fontes, Aganippedumque
> Antra recludis.   Ejufd. Epigr. I. 2.
>
> —— quæque

---

* See *Leland's Itinerary*, Vol. IV. p. 66.

—— quæque in primis mihi grata miniſtrat
Otia, Muſarumque cavas per ſaxa latebras,
MERGILLINA ; novos fundunt ubi citria flores,
Citria, Medorum ſacros referentia lucos.

               Ejuſd. De partu Virgin. III. ſub fin.

De Fonte Mergillino.

Eſt mihi rivo vitreus perenni
Fons, arenoſum prope littus, undè
Sæpe deſcendens ſibi nauta rores

      Haurit amicos. &c.   Ejuſd. Epigr. II. 36.

'TWOULD be difficult to tranſlate theſe elegant Morſels —'Tis ſufficient to expreſs what they mean, *collectively* —" that the Villa of " MERGILLINA had ſolitary WOODS ; had GROVES of Laurel and " Citron; had GROTTOS in the Rock, with RIVULETS and SPRINGS; " and that from ITS LOFTY SITUATION it lookt down upon the Sea, " and commanded an extenſive proſpect."

'TIS no wonder that *ſuch a Villa* ſhould enamour *ſuch an Owner.* So ſtrong was his affection for it, that, when during the ſubſequent Wars in *Italy,* it was demoliſhed by the Imperial Troops, this unfortunate Event was ſuppoſed to have haſtened his end *.

VAUCLUSE *(Vallis Clauſa)* the favourite retreat of PETRARCH, was a romantic Scene, not far from *Avignon.*

                                    " IT

---

* So we learn from *Paulus Jovius,* the writer of his Life, publiſhed with his Poems by *Grævius,* in a ſmall Edition of ſome of the *Italian* Poets, at *Amſterdam,* in the year 1695.

" It is a VALLEY, having on each hand, as you enter, immense
" Cliffs, but *closed up* at one of its Ends by a semi-circular Ridge of
" them; from which incident it derives *its name*. One of the most
" stupendous of these Cliffs stands in the front of the semi-circle,
" and has at its foot an opening into an immense *Cavern*. Within
" the most *retired and gloomy part* of this Cavern is a *large oval*
" *Bason*, the production of Nature, filled with pellucid and unfa-
" thomable Water; and from this reservoir issues a River of respect-
" able magnitude, dividing, as it runs, the Meadows beneath, and
" winding thro' the Precipices, that impend from above *."

THIS is an imperfect sketch of that spot, where PETRARCH spent
his time with so much delight, as to say that *this alone* was Life to
him, the rest but a state of punishment.

IN the two preceding Narratives I seem to see an anticipation of
that Taste for *natural* Beauty, which now appears to flourish thro'
Great Britain in such perfection. It is not to be doubted that the
Owner of Mergillina would have been charmed with *Mount Edgecumb*;
and *the Owner of Vauclufe* have been delighted with *Piercefield*.

WHEN we read in XENOPHON†, that the *younger* CYRUS had
with his own hand planted *trees for Beauty*, we are not surprised,

tho'

---

* See *Memoires pour la Vie de François Petrarque*, Quarto, Tom. I. p. 231, 341, 342.
See also *Plin. Nat. Hist.* L. XXVIII. c. 22.

† See the *Oeconomics of Xenophon*, where this Fact is related.

4 C 2

 tho' pleafed with the Story, as *the Age* was *polifhed*, and *Cyrus* an accomplifhed Prince. But, when we read that in the beginning of the 14th Century, *a King of France* (PHILIP LE BELL) fhould make it penal to cut down a Tree, *qui a efte gardè pour fa beautè, which had been preferved* FOR ITS BEAUTY; tho' we praife the Law, we cannot help being furprifed, that the Prince fhould at fuch a period have been fo far enlightened *.

---

* See a valuable Work, intitled *Obfervations on the Statutes, chiefly on the ancient,* &c. p. 7, by the Honble. Mr. *Barrington;* a work, concerning which it is difficult to decide, whether it be more entertaining, or more inftruétive.

CHAP. XIV.

Superior Literature *and* Knowledge *both of the Greek and Latin* Clergy, *whence —* Barbarity *and* Ignorance *of the* Laity, *whence — Samples of Lay-manners, in a Story from* Anna Comnena's *History—*Church Authority *ingeniously employed to check Barbarity—the same Authority employed for other good purposes — to save the poor Jews — to stop Trials by Battle — more suggested concerning Lay-manners — Ferocity of the* Northern Laymen, *whence — different Causes assigned —* Inventions *during the dark Ages — great, tho' the Inventors often unknown — Inference arising from these Inventions.*

BEFORE I quit the Latins, I shall subjoin two or three Observations on the Europeans in general. Ch. XIV.

The *superior* Characters for *Literature* here enumerated, whether in the *Western* or *Eastern Christendom* (for 'tis of *Christendom only* we are now speaking) were by far the greater part of them Ecclesiastics.

In this number we have selected from among the Greeks *the Patriarch of Constantinople,* Photius; Michael Psellus; Eustathius *and* Eustratius, *both of Episcopal Dignity;* Planudes; *Cardinal* Bessario —from among the Latins, *Venerable* Bede; Gerbertus, *afterwards* Pope Sylvester the Second; Ingulphus, *Abbot of Croyland;* Hildebert, *Archbishop of Tours;* Peter Abelard; John of Salisbury, *Bishop of Chartres;* Roger Bacon;

Part III. con; Francis Petrarch; *many Monkiſh Hiſtorians*; Æneas Sylvius, afterwards Pope Pius the Second, &c.

Something has been already ſaid concerning each of *theſe*, and other *Eccleſiaſtics**.   At preſent we ſhall only remark, that 'twas neceſſary, *from their very Profeſſion*, that they ſhould *read* and *write*; accompliſhments, at that time *uſually confined to themſelves*.

Those of the *Weſtern* Church were obliged to acquire ſome knowledge of Latin; and for Greek, to thoſe of the *Eaſtern* Church it was ſtill (with a few Corruptions) their *native* Language.

If we add to theſe Preparations *their mode of Life*, which, being attended moſtly with a decent competence, gave them immenſe leiſure; 'twas not wonderful that, *among ſuch a multitude, the more meritorious* ſhould emerge, and ſoar by dint of Genius above the common herd. Similar Effects proceed from ſimilar Cauſes. The Learning of *Egypt* was poſſeſt by their *Prieſts*; who were likewiſe left from their inſtitution to a life of leiſure†.

For the Laity on the other ſide, who, from their mean Education, wanted all theſe Requiſites, they were in fact no better than what *Dryden* calls them, *a tribe of Iſſachar*; a race, from their cradle bred in *Barbarity* and *Ignorance*.

A Sample

---

* Thoſe, who wiſh to ſee more particulars concerning theſe learned Men, may recur to their Names in the Index, or, if he pleaſe, may conſult the *Third* Part of theſe Inquiries, in Chapters IY. IX. X. XI. XIV.

† *Ariſtotle*, ſpeaking of *Egypt*, informs us—ἐκεῖ γὰρ ἠφείθη σχολάζειν τὸ τῶν ἱερέων ἔθνος— *For there* (meaning in *Egypt*) the Tribe of Prieſts *were left* to lead a Life of Leisure. *Ariſt. Metaph.* L. I. c. 1.

A Sample of thefe illuftrious *Laymen* may be found in Anna Ch. XIV.
Comnena's Hiftory of her Father *Alexius*, who was *Grecian Emperor*
in the *eleventh* Century, when the firft Crusade arrived at *Conftantinople*. So promifcuous a Rout of rude Adventurers could not fail
of giving umbrage to the *Byzantine Court*, which was ftately and ce-
remonious, and confcious withal of its internal debility.

After fome altercation, the Court permitted them to pafs into
Afia thro' the *Imperial* Territories, upon their *Leaders* taking *an Oath
of Fealty* to the Emperor.

What happened at the performance of this Ceremonial, is thus
related by the fair Hiftorian above-mentioned.

" All the Commanders being affembled, Godfrey of Bul-
" loign himfelf among the reft, as foon as the Oath was finifhed,
" one of the *Counts* had the audacioufnefs to feat himfelf *befide the
" Emperor* upon his throne. *Earl Baldwin,* one of *their own* people,
" approaching, took *the Count* by the hand; made him rife front the
" throne; and rebuked him for his Infolence.

" The *Count* rofe, but made no reply, except it was in his own
" unknown Jargon to mutter abufe upon the Emperor.

" When all things were difpatched, the *Emperor* fent for this man,
" and demanded, *who he was, whence he came, and of what Lineage?*
" — His anfwer was as follows — *I am a genuine* Frank, *and in the
" number of their Nobility. One thing I know, which is, that in a
" certain part of the Country I came from, and in a place, where three*
" *ways*

Part III. " ways meet, there stands an ancient Church, where every one, who has
" a desire to engage in single Combat, having put himself into fighting
" order, comes and there implores the assistance of the Deity, and then
" waits in expectation of some one, that will dare attack him. On this
" spot I MYSELF waited a long time, expecting and seeking some one,
" that would arrive, and fight me. But THE MAN, THAT WOULD
" DARE THIS, was no where to be found *."

THE *Emperor*, having heard this strange Narrative, replied pleasantly — " If at the time, when you sought War, you could not find it,
" a Season is now coming, in which you will find Wars enough. I there-
" fore give you this advice: not to place yourself either in the Rear of
" the Army, or in the Front, but to keep among those, who support the
" Centre; for I have long had knowledge of the Turkish method in their
" Wars †."

THIS was one of those COUNTS, or BARONS, the petty Tyrants of
Western Europe; men, who, when they were not engaged in *general*
wars, (such as the ravaging of a neighbouring Kingdom, the mas-
sacring of Infidels, Heretics, &c.) had no other method of filling up
their

---

* Those, who attend to *this* Story, and who have perused any of the Histories of
Chivalry, in particular an ingenious *French* Treatise upon the subject, in two small
Volumes 8vo. published at *Paris*, in the year 1759, intitled, *Mémoires sur l'ancienne
Chevalerie*, will perceive that the much admired *Don Quixote* is not an *Imaginary
Character*, but a Character, drawn after the *real Manners* of the times. 'Tis true indeed,
the Character is somewhat *heightened;* but even *here* the witty Author has contrived
to make it *probable*, by ingeniously adding a certain mixture of *Insanity*.

These *Romantic Heroes* were not wholly extinct even in periods *far later* than the
Crusades. THE CHEVALIER BAYARD flourished under *Francis the First of France*, and
LORD HERBERT OF CHERBURY under *James* and *Charles the First of England*.

† See *Anna Comnena's* History of her Father, *Fol. Gr. Lat.* p 300.

their leifure, than, thro' help of their *Vaffals*, by waging war upon one Ch. XIV.
another.

And here the *Humanity* and *Wifdom* of the Church cannot enough be *admired*, when by *her authority* (which was then mighty) fhe endeavoured to *fhorten* that fcene of Bloodfhed, which fhe could not *totally* prohibit. The Truce of God (a name given it *purpofely* to render the meafure more *folemn*) enjoined *thefe ferocious Beings*, under the terrors of *Excommunication*, not to fight *from Wednefday Evening to Monday Morning*, out of reverence to the *Myfteries*, accomplifhed on the other four days; the *Afcenfion* on Thurfday; the *Crucifixion* on Friday; the *Defcent to Hell* on Saturday; and the *Refurrection* on Sunday*.

I hope a farther obfervation will be pardoned, when I add that *the fame Humanity* prevailed during the fourteenth Century, and that *the terrors of* Church Power were then held forth with an intent *equally* laudable. A dreadful plague at that period defolated all *Europe*. *The Germans*, with no better reafon than their own *fenfelefs Superftition*, imputed this calamity to *the Jews*, who then lived among them in great opulence and fplendour. Many thoufands of thefe unhappy people were inhumanly maffacred, till *the Pope* benevolently interfered, and prohibited by the fevereft Bulls fo mad and fanguinary a proceeding†.

I could

---

* See any of the Church Hiftories of the time, in particular an ingenious French Book, entitled *Hiftoire Ecclefiaftique*, in two Volumes, 12mo. digefted into *Annals*, and having the feveral years marked in the courfe of the Narrative. Go to the years 1027, 1031, 1041, 1068, 1080.

† See the Church Hiftories about the middle of the fourteenth Century, and *Petrarch's Life*.

Part III.   I could not omit *two* such *salutary* exertions of *Church Power,* as they both occur within the period of this Inquiry. I might add *a third,* I mean the oppofing and endeavouring to check that abfurdeft of all Practices, the Trial by Battle, which *Spelman* exprefsly tells us that the Church in all ages *condemned* *.

. It muft be confeffed, that the Fact juft related concerning the *unmannered* Count, at the Court of *Conftantinople,* is rather againft the order of *Chronology,* for it happened during the firft Crufades. It ferves however to fhew *the Manners* of the *Latin* or *Weftern Laity,* in the beginning of *that Holy War.* They did not, in a fucceffion of years, grow *better,* but *worfe.*

"Twas a Century *after,* that *another Crufade,* in their march againft Infidels, facked *this very City;* depofed the then Emperor; and committed *Devaftations,* which no one would have committed, but *the moft ignorant, as well as cruel Barbarians.* If we defcend not at prefent to particulars, it is, becaufe we have already quoted fo largely from *Nicetas,* in a former Chapter †.

But a Queftion here occurs, eafier to propofe, than to anfwer.—— " *To what are we to attribute this character of* Ferocity, *which feems* " *to have then prevailed thro'* the Laity of Europe ?"

Shall we fay, 'twas Climate, and the Nature of the Country?—Thefe we muft confefs have in fome inftances great Influence.   *The*

---

* *Truculentum morem in omni ævo acriter infectarunt* Theologi, &c. See before, p. 418.

† See Part III. chap. 5, and *Abulpharagius,* p. 282, who defcribes their *indifcriminate Cruelty,* in a manner much refembling that of their *Brother Crufaders* at *Bezieres,* and that nearly about the fame time. See before, p. 511.

The Indians, feen a few years fince by Mr. *Byron* in the fouthern Ch. XIV. parts of *South America,* were brutal and favage to an enormous excefs. One of them, for a trivial offence, murdered his own Child (an infant) by dafhing it againft the Rocks. *The Cyclopes,* as defcribed by *Homer,* were much of the fame fort; each of them gave Law to *his own* Family, without *regard for one another;* and befides this, they were *Atheifts* and *Man-eaters.*

MAY we not fuppofe, that a ftormy fea, together with a frozen, barren, and inhofpitable fhore, might work on the Imagination of thefe *Indians,* fo, as by banifhing all *pleafing* and *benign* Ideas, to fill them with *habitual* Gloom, and a Propenfity to be cruel?—or might not the *tremendous* Scenes of *Etna* have had a like Effect upon the *Cyclopes,* who lived amid Smoke, Thunderings, Eruptions of Fire, and Earthquakes? If we may believe *Fazelius,* who wrote upon *Sicily* about two hundred years ago, the *Inhabitants* near *Etna* were in *his* time a fimilar Race *.

IF therefore thefe *limited* Regions had fuch an effect upon their *Natives,* may not a fimilar Effect be prefumed from *the vaft Regions of the North?* May not its cold, barren, uncomfortable *Climate* have made its numerous Tribes *equally rude* and *favage?*

IF this be not enough, we may add *another* Caufe, I mean their *profound Ignorance.* Nothing mends THE MIND more than CUL-TURE, to which thefe Emigrants had no defire, either from Example or Education, to lend a patient Ear.

WE

---

* See *Fazelius de Rebus ficulis,* L. II. c. 4.

Part III. WE may add *a farther Caufe ftill*, which is, that, when they had
acquired Countries better than their own, they *fettled under the
fame Military Form*, thro' which they had *conquered*; and were in
fact, when fettled, *a fort of Army after a Campaign, quartered*
upon the wretched remains of *the ancient Inhabitants*, by whom
they were attended under the different names of *Serfs, Vaffals, Vil-
lains*, &c.

'TWAS not likely the Ferocity of thefe *Conquerors* fhould abate
with regard to their *Vaffals*, whom, as ftrangers, they were more
likely to fufpect, than to love.

'TWAS not likely it fhould abate with regard to one another,
when the *Neighbourhood* of their Caftles, and the *Contiguity* of their
Territories, muft have given occafions (as we learn from Hiftory)
for endlefs Altercation.   But this we leave to the learned in
FEUDAL TENURES.

WE fhall add to the preceding Remarks one more fomewhat
fingular, and yet perfectly *different*; which is, that tho' the Darknefs in *Weftern Europe*, during the Period here mentioned, was (in
Scripture Language) *a Darknefs that might be felt*, yet is it furprifing
that, during a Period fo obfcure, many *admirable Inventions* found
their way into the world; I mean fuch as *Clocks, Telefcopes, Paper,
Gunpowder, the Mariner's Needle, Printing*, and a number here
omitted*.

'TIS

---

* See two ingenious Writers on this Subject, *Polydore Virgil, De Rerum Invento-
ribus*; and *Pancirolius, De Rebus perditis et inventis.*

'Tis furprifing too, if we confider the *importance* of thefe arts, and Ch. XIV.
their *extenfive utility*, that it fhould be either *unknown*, or *at leaft*
doubtful, by whom they were *invented:*

A LIVELY Fancy might almoft imagine, that every Art, as it was
wanted, had fuddenly ftarted forth, addreffing thofe that fought it,
as *Eneas* did his companions—

—*Coram, quem quæritis, adfum.*   VIRG.

AND yet, Fancy apart, of this we may be affured, that, tho' *the*
particular Inventors may unfortunately be forgotten, THE INVEN-
TIONS THEMSELVES *are clearly referable to* MAN; *to that fubtle, and*
active Principle, HUMAN WIT, or INGENUITY.

LET me then fubmit the following Query——

IF the HUMAN MIND be as truly of *divine* Origin, as every *other*
part of the Univerfe; and if every *other* part of the Univerfe bear
teftimony to its *Author:* do not the INVENTIONS above mentioned
give us reafon to affert, *that* GOD, IN THE OPERATIONS OF MAN,
NEVER LEAVES HIMSELF WITHOUT A WITNESS?

C H A P. XV.

Opinions on PAST *Ages, and the* PRESENT—*Conclusion arising from the Discussion of these Opinions*—CONCLUSION OF THE WHOLE.

Part III. AND now having done with THE MIDDLE AGE, we venture to say a word upon THE PRESENT.

Every Past Age has in its turn been *a Present Age.* This indeed is obvious, but this is not all; for every *Past* Age, when *present*, has been the object of *Abuse.* Men have been represented by their *Contemporaries* not only as bad, but degenerate; as inferior to their predecessors both in *Morals* and *bodily* Powers.

THIS is an Opinion so generally received, that VIRGIL (in conformity to it) when he would express FORMER times, calls them simply BETTER, as if the Term, *better*, implied *former* of course.

Hic genus ANTIQUUM *Teucri, pulcherrima proles,*
Magnanimi Heroes, nati MELIORIBUS *annis.*

Æn. vi. 648.

THE same opinion is ascribed by HOMER to old NESTOR, when that venerable Chief speaks of those Heroes, whom he had known in his youth. He relates some of their names; *Pirithous, Dryas, Cæneus, Theseus*; and some also of their exploits; as how they had extirpated the savage *Centaurs*—He then subjoins

———— κείνοισι

——————— κείνοισι δ᾽ ἂν ὔτις,
Τῶν δι νῦν βροτοῖ ἐισιν ἐπιχθόνιοι, μαχέοιϕο.   Ἰλ. Α. 271.

———— *with thefe no one*
Of earthly race, as men ARE NOW, *could fight.*

As thefe Heroes were fuppofed to exceed in *ftrength* thofe of the
Trojan War, fo were the Heroes of *that* period to exceed thofe, *that*
came after. Hence, from the time of the *Trojan* War to that of
Homer, we learn that *Human Strength* was *decreafed* by a complete
half.

THUS the fame *Homer*,
——— ὁ δὲ χερμάδιον λάϐε χειρί
Τυδείδης, μέγα ἔργον, ὃ ὓ δύο γ᾽ ἄνδρε φέροιεν,
Οἷοι νῦν βροτοί εἰσ᾽· ὁ δέ μιν ῥέα πάλλε κ᾽ οἶος.   Ἰλ. Ε. 302.

Then grafp'd Tydides in his hand a ftone,
A Bulk immenfe, which not TWO MEN *could bear;*
As Men are NOW, *but he* ALONE *with eafe*
Hurl'd it———

Virgil goes farther and tells us, that not TWELVE MEN of *his*
time (and thofe too *chofen* ones) could even carry the ftone, which
Turnus flung.
Vix illud LECTI DIS SEX *cervice fubirent,*
Qualia NUNC *hominum producit corpora tellus:*
Ille manu raptum trepidâ torquebat in hoftem.   Æn. xii. 899.
                                                        THUS

Part III.   Thus *Human* ſtrength, which in Homer's time was leſſened to
half, in Virgil's time was leſſened to *a twelfth*. If *Strength*
and *Bulk* (as commonly happens) be *proportioned*, what *Pygmies*
in *Stature* muſt the Men of *Virgil's* time have been, when their
ſtrength, as he informs us, was ſo far diminiſhed? · A Man *only
eight times* as *ſtrong* (and not, according to the Poet, *twelve times)*
muſt at leaſt have been between five and ſix feet *higher*, than *they*
were.

But we all know the Privilege, claimed by Poets and Painters.

'Tis in virtue of this Privilege that Horace, when he mentions
the moral Degeneracies of his *Contemporaries*, aſſerts that " *their*
" *Fathers were worſe than their Grandfathers; that they were worſe
" than their Fathers; and that their Children would be worſe than they
" were;".* deſcribing no fewer, after the Grandfather, than *three
Succeſſions of Degeneracy.*

> *Ætas parentum,* pejor *avis, tulit*
> · *Nos* nequiores, *mox daturos*
> *Progeniem* vitiosiorem.   Hor. Od. L. iii. 6.

We need only aſk, were this a fact, what would the Romans
have been, had they *degenerated in this proportion* for five or ſix
Generations more?

Yet Juvenal, ·ſubſequent to all this, ſuppoſes a ſimilar *Progreſſion*; a Progreſſion in Vice and Infamy, which was not *complete*,
till his own times.

Then

THEN truly we learn, *it could go no farther.*
 Nil erit ULTERIUS, *noſtris quod moribus addat*
 Poſteritas, &c.
 Omne IN PRÆCIPITI *vitium ſtetit,* &c.   Sat. i. 147, &c.

BUT even JUVENAL it ſeems was miſtaken, *bad* as we muſt allow his times to have been. Several Centuries after, without regard to *Juvenal,* the *ſame* Doctrine was inculcated with greater zeal than ever.

WHEN *the Weſtern Empire* began to decline, and *Europe* and *Africa* were ravaged by *Barbarians,* the Calamities *then* happening (and formidable they were) naturally led Men, who felt them, to eſteem *their own Age the worſt.*

THE Enemies of *Chriſtianity* (for *Paganiſm* was not then extinct) abſurdly turned theſe Calamities to the diſcredit of the *Chriſtian* Religion, and ſaid the times were ſo unhappy, becauſe the Gods were diſhonoured, and the ancient Worſhip neglected. OROSIUS, a *Chriſtian,* did not deny the melancholy facts, but, to obviate an objection ſo diſhonourable to the true Religion, he endeavours to prove from Hiſtorians, both *ſacred* and *profane,* that Calamities of *every ſort* had exiſted in *every age, as many* and *as great,* as *thoſe* that exiſted *then.*

IF OROSIUS has reaſoned right (and his Work is an elaborate one) it follows that the *Lamentations* made *then,* and made ever *ſince,* are no more than *natural Declamations incidental to Man;*

VOL. II.4 EDeclamations

Part III. Declamations *naturally* arising, let him live at any period, from
the *superior efficacy of prefent Events* upon *prefent Senfations*.

There is a *Praife belonging to* the Past *congenial* with *this
Cenfure; a Praife* formed from Negatives, and beft illuftrated by
Examples.

Thus a Declaimer might affert, (fuppofing he had a wifh, by
exalting *the eleventh* Century, to debafe *the prefent)* that " in the
" time of the Norman Conqueror we had *no* Routs, *no* Ridottos,
" *no* Newmarkets, *no* Candidates to bribe, *no* Voters to be bribed,
" &c." and ftring on Negatives, as long as he thought proper.

What then are we to do, when we hear *fuch Panegyric?*—Are
we *to deny* the Facts?—That cannot be—Are we *to admit* the
Conclufion?—That appears not quite agreeable.—No method is
left but to compare Evils with Evils; *the Evils* of 1066 with
thofe of 1780; and fee whether the *former* Age had not *Evils of
its own,* fuch as the *prefent* never *experienced,* becaufe they do not
now *exift.*

' We may allow, the Evils of the *prefent* day to be *real*—we may
even allow, that a much *larger* number might have been added—
but then we may alledge evils, by way of return, felt in those *days*
feverely, but now *not* felt at all.

" We may affert, we have not *now,* as happened *then,* feen our
" Country conquered by foreign Invaders; *nor* our Property taken
" from

Ch. XV.

" from us, and diſtributed among the Conquerors; *nor* ourſelves,
" from Freemen debaſed into Slaves; *nor* our Rights ſubmitted
" to *unknown* Laws, imported, without our conſent, from foreign
" Countries."

SHOULD the ſame Reaſonings be urged in favour of Times, *nearly*
as remote, and other Imputations of *Evil* be brought, which, tho'
well known *now*, did not *then* exiſt; we may ſtill retort that—" we
" are *no longer* NOW, as they were THEN, ſubject to *feudal* Oppreſ-
" ſion; *nor* dragged to War, as they were *then*, by the petty
" Tyrant of a neighbouring Caſtle; *nor* involved in ſcenes of blood,
" as they were *then*, and that for many years, during the unin-
" tereſting diſputes between A STEPHEN and A MAUD."

SHOULD the ſame Declaimer paſs to *a later* period, and praiſe
after the ſame manner the reign of HENRY THE SECOND, we have
then to retort, " *that we have now* NO BECKETS." " Should he proceed to RICHARD THE FIRST, " *that we have now* NO HOLY WARS"
—*to* JOHN LACKLAND, and his Son, HENRY, " *that we have now*
" NO BARONS WARS"—and with regard to BOTH of them, " that,
" tho' we enjoy at this inſtant all the benefits of MAGNA CHARTA,
" we have *not* been compelled to purchaſe them at the price of our
" blood."

A SERIES of Convulſions brings us, in a few years more, to the
Wars between the Houſes of YORK and LANCASTER—thence,
from the fall of *the Lancaſter Family*, to the calamities of *the York
Family*, and its final deſtruction in RICHARD THE THIRD—thence

Part III. to the oppreſſive Period of his *avaricious* Successor; and from Him to *the formidable* reign of HIS RELENTLESS Son, when *neither* the Coronet, *nor* the Mitre, *nor* even the Crown could protect their wearers; and when (to the amazement of Poſterity) thoſe, by whom *Church Authority* was *denied,* and thoſe, by whom it was *maintained,* were dragged *together to Smithfield,* and burnt *at one and the ſame ſtake.* [*]

THE reign of his Successor was *ſhort* and *turbid,* and ſoon followed by the *gloomy* one of a BIGOTTED WOMAN.

WE ſtop here, thinking we have inſtances enough. Thoſe, who hear any portion of theſe *paſt* times, *praiſed for the invidious purpoſe above mentioned,* may anſwer by thus *retorting* the Calamities and Crimes, which *exiſted* AT THE TIME *praiſed,* but which NOW *exiſt no more.* A true Eſtimate can never be formed, but in conſequence of ſuch a *Compariſon;* for if we drop *the laudable,* and alledge *only the bad,* or drop *the bad,* and alledge *only the laudable,* there is no Age, whatever its real character, but may be made to paſs at pleaſure either for *a good one,* or *a bad one.*

IF I may be permitted in this place to add an obſervation, it ſhall be an obſervation founded upon *many* years experience. I have often heard Declamations againſt the *preſent* Race of Men; Declamations againſt them, as if they were *the worſt of animals;* treacherous,

---

[*] Some of theſe unfortunate men *denied the King's Supremacy,* and others, *the real Preſence.* See the Hiſtories of that Reign.

treacherous, falfe, felfifh, envious, oppreffive, tyrannical, &c. &c. Ch. XV.
This (I fay) I have often heard from grave Declaimers, and have
heard the Sentiment delivered with a kind of Oracular Pomp.—
Yet I never heard any fuch Declaimer fay (what would have been
fincere at leaft, if it had been nothing more) " I prove my affertion
" by an example, where I cannot err; *I affert* MYSELF *to be the*
" *Wretch, I have been juft defcribing.*"

So far from this, it would be perhaps dangerous to afk him, even
in a gentle whifper— *You have been talking, with much Confidence,
about certain profligate Beings.—Are you certain, that* YOU YOURSELF
are not one of the number?

I HOPE I may be pardoned for the following Anecdote, altho'
compelled in relating it, to make myfelf a party.

" SITTING once in my Library with a friend, a worthy but melan-
" choly man, I read him out of a Book the following paffage —

" *In our time it may be fpoken more truly than of old, that Virtue is*
" *gone; the Church is under foot; the Clergy is in error; the Devil*
" *reigneth, &c. &c.* My Friend interrupted me with a figh, and
" faid, *Alas! how true! How juft a picture of the Times!* — I afked
" him, *of what Times?* — *Of what Times,* replied he with emotion,
" *can you fuppofe any other but* THE PRESENT? *Were any* BEFORE
" *ever fo bad, fo corrupt, fo, &c.?* — *Forgive me* (faid I) *for ftopping you*
" —THE TIMES, *I am reading of, are* OLDER *than you imagine; the*
                                          " *Sentiment*

Part III. " *Sentiment was delivered above four hundred years ago; its Author* " Sir John Mandeville, *who died in* 1371 *."

As *Man* is by nature a *focial* Animal, Good Humour feems an ingredient highly neceffary to his character. 'Tis the Salt, which gives a feafoning to the Feaft of Life; and which, if it be wanting, furely renders the Feaft incomplete. Many Caufes contribute to impair this *amiable* Quality, and nothing perhaps more, than *bad Opinions of Mankind.* *Bad Opinions of Mankind* naturally lead us to Misanthropy. If thefe bad opinions go *farther*, and are *applied to the Univerfe*, then they lead to fomething worfe, for they lead to Atheism. The melancholy and morofe Character being thus infenfibly formed, Morals and Piety 'fink of courfe; for what Equals have we to love, or what Superior have we to revere, when we have *no other* objects left, than thofe of *Hatred*, or of *Terrour* †?

It

---

* See *this Writer's own Preface*, p. 10, in the large *Octavo Englifh Edition* of his *Travels*, publifhed at London, in 1727. See alfo of thefe *Philolog. Inquiries*, p. 553.

† Misanthropy is fo dangerous a thing, and goes fo far in fapping the very foundations of Morality and Religion, that I efteem the laft part of *Swift's Gulliver* (that I mean relative to his *Hoyhnms* and *Yahoos*) to be a worfe Book to perufe, than thofe which we forbid, as the moft flagitious and obfcene.

One abfurdity in this Author (a wretched Philofopher, tho' a great Wit) is well worth remarking—in order to render *the Nature of* Man, *odious*, and *the Nature of* Beasts *amiable*, he is compelled to give Human *Characters* to his Beasts, and Beastly *Characters* to his Men—fo that we are to *admire* the Beasts, *not for being Beafts*, but *amiable* Men; and *to detest* the Men, *not for being* Men, *but detestable* Beasts.

Whoever has been reading this *unnatural* Filth, let him turn for a moment to a *Spectator* of Addison, and obferve the Philanthropy of that *Classical Writer*; I may add the *fuperior* Purity of his *Diction* and his *Wit*.

Ch. XV.

It fhould feem then expedient if we value our *better* Principles, nay, if we value our own *Happinefs*, to withftand fuch *dreary* Sentiments. 'Twas the advice of a wife Man—*Say not Thou, what is the Caufe, that* THE FORMER DAYS WERE BETTER THAN THESE? *For thou* DOST NOT INQUIRE WISELY *concerning this* *.

Things Prefent make Impreffions amazingly fuperior to *things Remote*; fo that in objects of every kind, we are eafily miftaken as to their *comparative* Magnitude. Upon the Canvafs of *the fame* Picture *a near* Sparrow occupies the Space of *a diftant* Eagle; *a near* Mole-hill, that of *a diftant* Mountain. In the perpetration of *Crimes*, there are few perfons, I believe, who would not be more fhocked at *actually feeing a fingle* man *affaffinated* (even taking away the Idea of *perfonal* danger) than they would be fhocked *in reading the Maffacre of Paris.*

THE *Wife Man*, juft quoted, wifhes to fave us from thefe Errors. He has already informed us—*The thing, that* HATH BEEN, *is that,* which SHALL BE; and THERE IS NO NEW THING *under the Sun. Is there any thing whereof it may be faid,* SEE, THIS IS NEW? IT HATH BEEN ALREADY *of old time, which* WAS BEFORE US.—He then fubjoins the Caufe of this *apparent* Novelty—things *paft*, when they return, appear *new*, if they are *forgotten*; and things *prefent* will appear fo, fhould they too be *forgotten*, when they return †.

THIS

---

* *Ecclefiaftes*, Chap. vii. y. 10.

† See of the fame *Ecclefiaftes, chap. the firft,* v. 9, and *chap. the fecond,* v. 16.

 .Th is *Forgetfulness* of *what is similar in Events which return* (for in every returning Event *such Similarity exists*) is the Forgetfulness of a Mind uninstructed and weak; a Mind ignorant of that great, that Providential Circulation, which never ceases for a moment thro' every part of the Universe.

It is not like that *Forgetfulness*, which I once remember in a man of Letters, who, when at the conclusion of a long life, he found his Memory began to fail, said chearfully — " *Now I shall have a plea-* " *sure, I could not have before; that of reading my* old Books, *and* " *finding them all* new."

There was in this *Consolation* something *philosophical* and *pleas-* ing. And yet perhaps 'tis a *higher* Philosophy (could we attain it) not to forget the Past; *but* in Contemplation of the Past to view the Future, so that we may say on the *worst* Prospects, with a becoming Resignation, what Æneas said of old to the Cumean Prophetess,

> — *Virgin, no Scenes of Ill*
> *To me, or* new, *or* unexpected *rise;*
> *I've seen 'em* all; *have seen, and long* before
> Within myself *revolv'd 'em in my mind* *.

In such a Conduct, if well founded, there is not only *Fortitude*, but *Piety :* Fortitude, which never sinks, *from a conscious Inte-*
grity;

---

* Æn. VI. 103, 104, 105.

grity; and PIETY, which never refifts, by referring all to *the Divine* Ch. XV.
Will.

But left fuch Speculation, by carrying me *above* my fubject, fhould
expofe a Writer upon *Criticifm* to be himfelf *criticized*, I fhall here
conclude thefe PHILOLOGICAL INQUIRIES.

APPENDIX

DIFFERENT PIECES.

The First, containing an Account of the Arabic Manuscripts, belonging to the Escurial Library in *Spain*.

The Second, containing an Account of the Manuscripts of Livy in *the same Library*.

The Third, containing an Account of the Manuscripts of Cebes, in the Library of the King of France, at *Paris*.

The Fourth, containing some Account of Literature in Russia, and of its *Progress* towards being civilized.

A P P E N D I X.

PART THE FIRST:

An Account of THE ARABIC MANUSCRIPTS, belonging to *the Efcurial Library in Spain.*

THIS Account is extracted from *two fair Folio Volumes,* to *the Firſt* of which Volumes *the Title* is conceived in the following words:

BIBLIOTHECÆ ARABICO-HISPANÆ ESCURALIENSIS, *five Librorum omnium MSS, quos Arabicè ab auctoribus magnam partem Arabo-Hifpanis compofitos Bibliotheca Cænobii Efcuralienfis complectitur,*
RECENSIO *et* EXPLANATIO:
Opera et Studio MICHAELIS CASIRI,
Syro-Maronitæ, Prefbyteri, S. Theologiæ Doctoris, Regis a Bibliothecâ, Linguarumque Orientalium Interpretatione;
CAROLI III. REGIS OPT. MAX. *auctoritate atque aufpiciis edita.*
TOMUS PRIOR.
MATRITI,
Antonius Perez de Soto imprimebat
Anno MDCCLX.

THIS

APPENDIX.

THIS Catalogue is particularly valuable, becaufe not only each Manufcript is enumerated, but its *Age* alfo and *Author* (when known) are given, together with large *Extracts* upon occafion, both in *the original Arabic*, and in *Latin*.

FROM THE FIRST VOLUME it appears that the ARABIANS cultivated every fpecies of PHILOSOPHY and PHILOLOGY, as alfo (according to their Syftems) JURISPRUDENCE and THEOLOGY.

THEY were peculiarly fond of POETRY, and paid great honours to thofe, whom they efteemed good Poets. Their *earlieft* Writers were of *this* fort, fome of whom (and thofe much admired) flourifhed many centuries before the time of *Mahomet.*

THE ftudy of their Poets led them to the Art of CRITICISM, whence we find in the above Catalogue, not only a multitude of *Poems*, but many works upon *Compofition, Metre,* &c.

WE find in the fame Catalogue TRANSLATIONS of ARISTOTLE and PLATO, together with their *Lives*; as alfo Tranflations of their BEST GREEK COMMENTATORS, fuch as ALEXANDER APHRODISIENSIS, PHILOPONUS, and others. We find alfo *Comments of their own*, and *original* Pieces, *formed on the Principles of the above Philofophers.*

THERE too may be found TRANSLATIONS OF EUCLID, ARCHIMEDES, APOLLONIUS PERGÆUS, and the other ancient *Mathematicians*, together with THEIR GREEK COMMENTATORS, and many original Pieces of their own upon *the fame Mathematical fubjects.* In the ARITHMETICAL Part they are faid to follow DIOPHANTUS, from whom they learnt that ALGEBRA, of which they are *erroneoufly* thought to have been *the Inventors.*

THERE we may find alfo the works of PTOLEMY *tranflated,* and many

many original Treatifes of *their own* upon the fubject of Astronomy.

It appears too, that they Studied with care the important Subject of Agriculture. *One large Work* in particular is mentioned, compofed by a *Spanifh Arabian*, where every mode of *Culture*, and every fpecies of *Vegetable* is treated; Pafture, Arable, Trees, Shrubs, Flowers, &c. By this work may be perceived (as *the Editor* well obferves) *how much better* Spain was cultivated in *thofe* times; and that *fome fpecies of Vegetables* were *then* found there, which are *now* loft.

Here are many Tracts on the various Parts of Jurisprudence; fome ancient Copies of the Alcoran; innumerable Commenta-ries on it; together with Books of Prayer, Books of Devotion, Sermons, &c.

Among their *Theclogical* Works, there are fome upon the Princi-ples of the Mystic Divinity; and among their *Philofophical*, fome upon the Subject of Talismans, Divination and Judicial Astrology.

The First Volume, of which we have been fpeaking, is ele-gantly printed, and has *a learned Preface* prefixed by the Editor, wherein he relates what he has done, together with the affiftance he has received, as well from the Crown of *Spain* and its *Miniflers*, as from *learned Men*.

He mentions *a fatal Fire*, which happened at *the Efcurial*, in the year 1670; when *above three thoufand* of thefe valuable Manufcripts were deftroyed. He has in this Volume given an account of *about fourteen hundred*.

The

APPENDIX:

THE SECOND VOLUME of this valuable Work, which bears *the same Title* with *the First*, was published at *Madrid*, ten years after it, in the year 1770.

IT contains chiefly THE ARABIAN CHRONOLOGERS, TRAVELLERS, and HISTORIANS; and, tho' *national* partiality may be sometimes suspected, yet, as these are accounts given us by the *Spanish Arabians* themselves, there are *many* Incidents preserved, which other writers could not know; Incidents respecting not only *the Successions*, and *the Characters* of the *Arabic-Spanish Princes*, but the *Country* and its *Productions*, together with *the Manners*, and *the Literature* of its then Inhabitants.

NOR are the Incidents in these Volumes *confined* to SPAIN only, many of them relate to *other* Countries, such as the Growth of SUGAR in *Egypt*; the Invention of PAPER there (of which material there are *Manuscripts* in the *Escurial Library* of the year 1180); the use of GUNPOWDER, carried not only to the beginning of the fourteenth Century, but even so far back (if we can believe it) as to the *seventh* Century; the Description of MECCA; the *Antiquity* of the ARABIC LANGUAGE, and the practice of THEIR MOST ANCIENT AUTHORS, *to write in verse*; their Year, *Months, Weeks,* and *Method of Computation*; their Love for POETRY, and RHETORIC, &c.

GREAT HEROES are recorded to have flourished among them, such as *Abdelrehmanus*, and *Abi Amer Almoapheri*.

Abdelrahmanus lived in the beginning of the tenth Century, and *Abi Amer Almoapheri* at its latter end. *The first*, having subdued innumerable Factions and Seditions, reigned at *Corduba* with reputation

tation

tation for fifty years, famed for his love of *Letters*, and his upright adminiftration of *Juftice*. *The fecond*, undertaking the tuition of a young Prince (who was a minor, named *Hefcham*) and having reftored Peace to a turbid Kingdom, turned his Arms fo fuccefsfully againft its numerous Invaders, that he acquired the honourable name of *Almanzor*, that is, THE DEFENDER. (See Vol. 2d of this Catalogue, pages 37, 49, 50.)

Arabian Spain had too its MEN OF LETTERS, and thofe in great numbers; fome, whofe Fame was fo extenfive, that even *Chriftians* came to hear them from remote Regions of *Europe*. But this has been already mentioned, p. 502, 503, of thefe Inquiries.

PUBLIC LIBRARIES (not lefs than feventy) were eftablifhed thro' the Country; and noble Benefactions they were to the Caufe of Letters, at a time when *Books*, by being *Manufcripts*, were *fo coftly* an Article, that few Scholars were equal to the expence of a Collection.

To the Subjects, already treated, were added the Lives of their FAMOUS WOMEN; that is, of *Women* who had been *famous* for their *Literature* and *Genius*.

"Tis fomewhat ftrange, when we read thefe accounts, to hear it afferted, that *the Religion of thefe people* was *hoftile to Literature*, and this Affertion founded on no better reafon, than that *the Turks*, their fucceffors, by being *barbarous* and *ignorant*, had little value for *accomplifhments, of which they knew nothing*.

THESE SPANISH ARABIANS alfo, like their Anceftors *in the Eaft*, were great HORSEMEN, and particularly fond of HORSES. Accounts are preferved both of HORSES and CAMELS; alfo of their

APPENDIX:

Coins of the *two Races* of *Caliphs*, the *Ommiadæ*, and the *Abbaſſadæ*; of the firſt *Arabic* Conqueror of *Spain*, and the Conditions of *Toleration*, granted to the *Chriſtians*, whom he had conquered.

It farther appears from theſe *Arabic* Works, that not only Sugar, but Silk was known and cultivated in Spain. We read a beautiful Deſcription of Grenada, and its Environs; as alſo Epitaphs of different kinds; ſome of them approaching to *Attic* Elegance.

When that pleaſing Liquor Coffee was firſt introduced among them, a Scruple aroſe among *the Devout* (perhaps from feeling its *exhilerating Quality*), whether it was not *forbidden by the* Alcoran, under the article of Wine. *A Council of Mahometan Divines* was held upon the occaſion, and *the Council* luckily *decreed for the Legality of its uſe.* (See Vol. 2d of this Catalogue, p. 172, 173.)

The *Conceſſions* made by, *the Arabian Conqueror of Spain* to *the Gothic Prince*, whom he ſubdued, is a ſtriking Picture of his *Lenity* and Toleration. He neither depoſed the *Gothic Prince*, nor plundered *his People*, but, on payment of a moderate Tribute, ſtipulated not to deprive them either of their *Lives* or *Property*, and gave them alſo their *Churches*, and a *Toleration* for their *Religion*. See this curious Treaty, which was made about the year 712 of the *Chriſtian Æra*, in the *ſecond Vol. of this Catalogue*, p. 106.

When the *Poſterity* of theſe *Conquerors* came in their turn to be conquered, (an Event, which happened *many Centuries afterward*) they did not experience that Indulgence, *which had been granted by their Forefathers.*

The

*The conquered Moors (as they were then called) were expelled by
thousands; or, if they ventured to stay, were exposed to the Carnage
of a merciless Inquisition,—*

————*pueri, innuptæque puellæ,*
IMPOSITIQUE ROGIS JUVENES *ante ora parentum,*

IT appears that many of these ARABIC-SPANISH PRINCES were
men of *amiable Manners,* and great Encouragers both of *Arts* and
Letters, while others, on the contrary, were *tyrannic, cruel,* and
sanguinary.

THERE were usually *many* Kingdoms existing *at the same time,*
and these on every occasion *embroiled one with another;* not to
mention much *internal Sedition* in each particular state.

LIKE their *Eastern* Ancestors, they appear *not to have shared the
smallest Sentiment of* CIVIL LIBERTY; the difference as to good
and *bad* Government seeming to have been *wholly* derived, *according
to them,* from the *Worth* or *Pravity* of the Prince, who governed.
See p. 498 of these Inquiries.

THE Reader will observe, that the Pages *referring to Facts,* in
the *two Historical Volumes* of these Manuscripts, are *but seldom*
given, because whoever possesses those Volumes (and without them
any Reference would be useless) may *easily find* every Fact, by
referring to the copious and useful *Index,* subjoined to the *second*
Volume, which *Index* goes to the *whole* Work.

[596]

A P P E N D I X.

<hr>

PART THE SECOND:

Concerning the Manuscripts of LIVY, *in the* ESCURIAL LIBRARY.

IT having been often afferted, that AN INTIRE AND COMPLETE COPY OF LIVY was extant in THE ESCURIAL LIBRARY, I requefted my Son, in the year 1771 (he being at that time Minifter Plenipotentiary to the Court of *Madrid*), to inquire for me, *what Manufcripts of that Author were there to be found.*

HE procured me the following accurate Detail from *a learned Ecclefiaftic,* DON JUAN DE PELLEGEROS, *Canon of Lerma,* employed by *Monfr.* DE SANTANDER, his *Catholic Majefty's Librarian,* to infpect for this purpofe the *Manufcripts* of that valuable Library.

THE Detail was in *Spanish,* of which the following is a Tranflation.

AMONG *the MSS. of* THE ESCURIAL LIBRARY are the following Works of T. LIVY.

1ft. THREE LARGE VOLUMES, which contain *fo many Decads,* the *1ft, 3d, and 4th* (one *Decad* in each *Volume*) curioufly written

on

on Parchment, or fine Vellum, by *Pedro de Middleburgh*, or of *Zeeland* (as he ftiles himfelf).

The Books are truly magnificent, and in the Title and Initials curioufly illuminated. They bear *the Arms* of the Houfe of *Borgia*, with a *Cardinal's Cap*, whence it appears that they belonged either to Pope *Calliftus the third*, or to *Alexander the fixth*, when Cardinals.

2d. Two other Volumes, written by the fame Hand, one of *the firft Decad*, the other of *the third*; of the fame fize, and beauty, as the former. Both have the fame *Arms*, and in the laft is a Note, which recites: *This Book belongs to D. Juan de Fonfeca, Bifhop of Burgos.*

3d. Another Volume of the same size, and fomething *more ancient*, than the former (being of the beginning of the fifteenth Century) containing *the third Decad entire*. This is alfo well written on Parchment, tho' not fo valuable as the former.

4th. Another of the first Decad, *finely written* on Vellum. At the end is written as follows—*Ex centum voluminibus, quæ ego indies vitæ meæ magnis laboribus hactenus fcripfiffe memini, hos duos Titi Livii libros Anno Dni. 1441. Ego Joañes Andreas de Colonia feliciter, gratiâ Dei, abfolvi*—and at the end of each book—*Emendavi Nicomachus Fabianus.*

In the laft leaf of this Book is *a Fragment* either of *Livy himfelf*, or of fome Pen, capable of *imitating him*. It fills the whole leaf, and the Writer fays, it was in the Copy, from which he tranfcribed.

It

It appears to be a Fragment of the latter times of *the second Punic War.*

5th. ANOTHER LARGE VOLUME in Parchment, well written, of the same Century, viz. the fifteenth, containing *three Decads.* 1. *De Urbis initus.* 2. *De Bello Punico.* 3. *De Bello Macedonico.* In this *laft Decad* is wanting a part of the Book. *This Volume is much* efteemed, being full of *Notes* and *various Readings*, in the hand of *Hieronimo Zunita*, its former poffeffor.

6th. ANOTHER VERY VALUABLE VOLUME, containing *the firft Decad,* equal to the former in the elegance of its Writing and Ornaments. This alfo belonged to *Hieronimo Zunita*; the age the fame.

7th. LASTLY, there is ANOTHER OF THE FIRST DECAD alfo, written on Paper, at the beginning of the fifteenth Century. This contains nothing remarkable.

IN all, THERE ARE TEN VOLUMES, and ALL NEARLY OF THE SAME AGE.

HERE ends *the Account of the* ESCURIAL MANUSCRIPTS, given us by this *learned Spaniard*, in which Manufcripts we fee *there appears no part of* LIVY, *but what was printed in the early Editions.*

THE *other* Parts of this Author, which Parts *none of the Manufcripts here recited give us,* were *difcovered* and *printed afterwards.*

As to *the Fragment* mentioned in the fourth article, (all of which Fragment is there tranfcribed) it has, *tho' genuine,* no peculiar rarity,

rarity, as it is to be found in all *the latter printed* Editions. See particularly in *Crèvier's Edition of Livy, Paris,* 1736, Tome 2d, pages 716, 717, 718, beginning with the words *Raro fimul hominibus,* and ending with the words *increpatis rifum effe,* which is *the whole Extent* of the *Fragment* here exhibited.

From this *Detail* it is evident, that NO INTIRE COPY OF LIVY IS EXTANT IN THE ESCURIAL LIBRARY.

[600]

A P P E N D I X.

PART THE THIRD:

GREEK MANUSCRIPTS OF CEBES, *in* THE LIBRARY OF THE KING
OF FRANCE.

THE PICTURE OF CEBES, one of the moſt elegant *Moral Alle-
gories* of *Grecian* Antiquity, is ſo far connected with *the
middle Age*, that the ingenious *Arabians* of that time thought it
worth tranſlating into ARABIC.

IT was alſo tranſlated from *Greek* into *Latin* by *Ludovicus
Odaxius*, a learned *Italian*, ſoon after *Greek* Literature revived
there, and was publiſhed in the year 1497.

AFTER this it was often printed, ſometimes *in Greek alone*, ſometimes *accompanied* with more modern *Latin* Verſions. But the
Misfortune was, that the *Greek* Manuſcripts, from which *the Editors*
printed, (that of *Odaxius* alone excepted) were all of them defective
in their *End or Concluſion*. And hence it followed that *this Work*
for *many years* was publiſhed, Edition after Edition, *in this defective
manner,*

HAD its *End* been loſt, we might have lamented it, as we lament
other loſſes of the ſame kind. But in the preſent caſe, to the ſhame

of

of Editors, we have THE END PRESERVED, and that not only in
the *Arabic Paraphrase*, and *the old Latin Translation of Odaxius;*
but, what is more, even in the ORIGINAL TEXT, as it stands in
two excellent Manuscripts of the King of France's Library.

FROM thefe MSS. it was publifhed in a neat 12mo. Edition of
Cebes, by *James Gronovius,* in the year 1689; and after him by the
diligent and accurate *Fabricius,* in his *Bibliotheca Græca,* Tom. I.
p. 834, 835; and, after *Fabricius,* in a fmall octavo Edition, by
Thomas Johnfon, A. M. printed at *London,* in the year 1720.

WHOEVER reads the Conclufion of this Treatife will find fufficient
internal Evidence to convince him of *its Authenticity,* both from
the purity of the Language, and *the Truth,* as well as *Connection of
the Sentiment.*

HOWEVER, *the Manufcript* authority refting on nothing better
than the perplexed account of that moft obfcure and affected writer,
James Gronovius, I procured a fearch to be made *in the Royal
Library at Paris,* if fuch Manufcripts were there to be found.

UPON Infpection of no lefs than FOUR MANUSCRIPTS OF CEBES,
preferved in *that valuable Library,* No. 858, 2992, 1001, 1774, it
appeared that in THE SECOND, and in THE THIRD, THE END OF
CEBES was PERFECT and INTIRE, after the manner in which *it
ftands in the printed Editions* above mentioned.

THE End of this fhort Effay is to prove, that the *Genuinenefs of
the Conclufion thus reftored* does not reft merely on fuch authority,
as that of *James Gronovius,* (for *Fabricius* and *Johnfon* only follow
Him) but on *the authority of the beft Manufcripts, actually infpected
for the purpofe.*

A P P E N D I X.

PART THE FOURTH:

Some Account of LITERATURE IN RUSSIA, *and of its* Progress *towards being* CIVILIZED.

THE vast Empire of RUSSIA, extending far into *the North,* both in *Europe* and *Afia,* 'tis no wonder that, *in such a Country,* its *Inhabitants* should have remained so long *uncivilized.* For *Culture of the finer Arts* it is neceffary there should be *comfortable Leifure.* But how could fuch *Leifure* be found in a Country, where every one had enough to do, to fupport his family, and to refift the Rigour of an uncomfortable Climate? Befides this, to make *the finer Arts flourifh,* there muft be *Imagination*; and *Imagination* muft be enlivened by the *Contemplation of pleafing Objects;* and that *Contemplation* muft be performed in a manner *eafy to the Contemplator.* Now, who can contemplate with eafe, where the Thermometer is often many degrees below *the freezing point?* Or what object can he find *worth contemplating* for thofe many long months, when all the Water is Ice, and all the Land covered with Snow?

It

If then the Difficulties were so great, how great must have been the *Praise* of those *Princes* and Legislators, who dared attempt *to polish mankind* in so unpromising a Region, and who have been able, by their *perseverance*, in some degree to accomplish it?

Those, who on this occasion bestow the highest praises upon Peter the Great, praise him, without doubt, as he justly deserves. But if they would refer the *Beginning* of this work to *Him*, and much more its *Completion*, they are certainly under a mistake.

As long ago as the time of our *Edward the 6th*, Ivan Basilowitz *adopted Principles of Commerce*, and granted peculiar privileges to the *English*, on their discovery of a *Navigation* to *Archangel*.

A sad scene of sanguinary Confusion followed from this period to the year 1612, when a Deliverer arose, Prince Pajanky. He, by unparalleled fortitude, having routed all the Tyrants and Impostors of the time, was by the *Bojars* or *Magnates* unanimously elected *Czar*. But this Honor He, with a most disinterested magnanimity, declined *for himself*, and pointed out to them Michael Fedorowitz, of the house of *Romanoff*, and by his mother's side descended from *the ancient Czars*.

From this period we may date the first appearances of a *real Civilizing*, and *a Developement* of the Wealth and Power of *the Russian Empire*. Michael reigned thirty-three years. By his wisdom, and the mildness of his character, he restored Ease and Tranquillity to subjects, who had been long deprived of those inestimable Blessings;--he encouraged them to *Industry*, and gave them an example of the most *laudable* behaviour.

4 H 2

His

APPENDIX.

His fon ALEXIUS MICHAELOWITZ was fuperior to his Father in the Art of *Governing* and found *Politics.* He promoted *Agriculture;* Introduced into his Empire ARTS AND SCIENCES, of which he was himfelf a lover; publifhed *a Code of Laws,* ftill ufed in the Adminiftration of Juftice; and greatly improved *his Army,* by mending its difcipline. This he effected chiefly by the help of *Strangers,* moft of whom were *Scotch. Lefley, Gordon,* and *Ker,* are the Names of Families ftill *exifting* in this Country.

THEODORE or FÆDOR fucceeded his Father in 1677. He was of a *gentle Difpofition,* and weak Conftitution; fond of *Pomp* and Magnificence, and in fatisfying this paffion *contributed to polifh his fubjects* by the introduction of *foreign Manufactures,* and *Articles of Elegance,* which they foon began to adopt and imitate. His delight was in *Horfes,* and he did his country a real fervice in the beginning and eftablifhing of thofe fine breeds of them in the *Ukraine,* and elfewhere. He reigned feven years, and having on his death-bed called his *Bojars* round him, in the prefence of his Brother and Sifter, IVAN and SOPHIA, and of his half Brother PETER, faid to them; " *Hear my laft fentiments; they are dictated* " *by my love for the ftate, and by my affection for my people—the* " BODILY *Infirmities of* IVAN *neceffarily muft affect his* MENTAL " *Faculties—he is* INCAPABLE *of ruling a Dominion like that of* " RUSSIA—*he cannot take it amifs, if I recommend to you to fet him* " *afide, and to let your approbation fall on* PETER, *who to a* ROBUST " CONSTITUTION *joins great* STRENGTH OF MIND, *and marks of* " A SUPERIOR UNDERSTANDING."

Theodore dying in 1682, PETER became *Emperor,* and his brother IVAN remained contented. But SOPHIA, *Ivan's fifter,* a Woman of great Ambition, could not bring herfelf to fubmit.

THE

THE Troubles, which enfued; the imminent Dangers, which Peter efcaped; his Abolition of that *turbulent* and *feditious Sol-diery,* called *the Strelitz; the Confinement* of his half-fifter *Sophia* to a Monaftery; all thefe were important Events, which left Peter in the year 1689 with no other competitor, than the mild and eafy Ivan; who, dying not many years after, left him sole Monarch of all the Russias.

THE Acts at home and abroad, in Peace and in War, of *this ftupendous and elevated Genius,* are too well known to be repeated by me. Peter adorned his Country with *Arts,* and raifed its Glory by *Arms;* he created a *refpectable Marine;* founded *St. Peterfburgh,* a new Capital, and that from the very ground; ren-dering it withal one of *the firft Cities in Europe* for Beauty and Ele-gance.

To *encourage Letters* he formed Academies, and invited *foreign* Profeffors not only to Petersburgh (his *new* City) but to his *ancient* Capital Moscow; at both which places *thefe Profeffors* were maintained with *liberal Penfions.*

As a few *Specimens of Literature* from *both* thefe Cities have recently come to my hand, I fhall endeavour to enumerate them, as I think it relative to my fubject.

1. Plutarchus περὶ Δυσωπίας, κỳ περὶ Τύχης.— *Gr. Lat. cum animadverfionibus Reifkii et alior.—fuas adjecit Chriftianus Fridericus Matthæi. Typis Univerfitatis Mofquenfis, an. 1777, 8vo.*

2. Plutarchi *libellus de Superftitione, et Demofthenis Oratio funebris, Gr. Lat. cum notis integris Reifkii et alior.—fuas adjecit Chrift.*

Chrift. Frider. Matthæi—Typis Cæfareæ Mofquenfis Univerfitatis, an. 1778, 8vo.

3. LECTIONES MOSQUENSES, *in two Volumes,* 8vo. *bound together,* and printed at *Leipfic,* an. 1779—they contain various Readings in different Authors, and fome entire pieces, all in *Greek,* collected from the Libraries of *Mofcow,* and publifhed by *the fame* learned Editor.

4. ISOCRATIS, DEMETRII *Cyd. et* MICHAEL GLYCÆ *aliquot Epiftolæ, nec non* DION. CHRYSOSTOMI *Oratio—Græc.—Typis Univerfitatis Cæfareæ Mofquenfis—*8vo.—*By the fame learned Editor.*

5. GLOSSARIA GRÆCA MINORA, *et alia Anecdota Græca—a Work, confifting of two Parts, contained under one Volume, in a thin Quarto, by the fame able Profeffor, printed at Mofcow by the Univerfity Types, in the years* 1774 *and* 1775. *A Catalogue of the feveral pieces in both Parts is fubjoined to the end of the fecond Part— Among the Pieces in the firft Part are, Excerpta ex Grammaticâ Niceph. Gregoræ; ex Gloffario Cyrilli Alexandrini; Gloffarium in Epiftolas Pauli; Nomina Menfium;—thofe of the 2d Part are chiefly Theological.*

6. NOTITIA CODICUM MANUSCRIPTORUM GRÆCORUM BIB-LIOTHECARUM MOSQUENSIUM, *cum variis Anecdotis, Tabulis Æneis, Indicibus locupletiffimis—edidit Chrift. Fridericus Matthæi— Mofquæ, Typis Univerfitatis, an.* 1776.

This Publication, on a large Folio Paper, is as yet *incomplete,*
only

only fixty Pages being printed off. It ends, *Partis primæ Sectionis primæ Finis.*

7. An Ode to the present Empress, Catharine, in *ancient Greek and Ruffian.*

8. An Ode on *the Birth-day* of Constantine, fecond fon to the *Grand Duke*, in *ancient Greek* and *Ruffian*—printed at *Peterfburgh*, and as we learn from the Title, ἐν τῇ Ἀυ͗οκρατορικῇ Ἀκαδημίᾳ τῶν Ἐπιϛημῶν, *in the Imperial Academy of Sciences.*

9. An Ode to Prince Potemkin, *ancient Greek and Ruffian,* and printed (as before) an. 1780.

10. An Ode, confifting of *Strophe, Antiftrophe,* and *Epode, ancient Greek* and *Ruffian,* made in 1779, in honour of the Empress, the Great Duke and Duchess, and Alexander and Constantine, their two *Sons,* Grandfons to the Emprefs.

This *Ode* was *fung* in the *Original Greek by a large number of Voices,* before a numerous and fplendid Court in one of the Imperial Palaces.

As I have a Copy of this *Mufic,* I cannot omit obferving, that it is a genuine Exemplar of *the Ancient* Antiphona, fo well known to *the Church* in very remote ages. On this Plan *two complete Choirs* (each confifting of Trebles, Counters, Tenors, and Bafes) *fing againft each other,* and *reciprocally anfwer;* then *unite* all of them; then feparate *again,* returning to *the alternate Refponfe,* till *the Whole* at length concludes in *one general Chorus.* The *Mufic*

of

of this Ode may be called *purely Vocal,* having *no other accompany-ment* but that of *an Organ.*

The Compofer was no lefs a man than the celebrated PAESIELLO, fo well known at prefent, and fo much admired, both in *Italy* and elfewhere, for Mufic of a very *different* Character, I mean his truly natural, and pleafing *Burlettas.*

THOSE, who are curious to know more of *this Species of Mufic,* may confult the valuable *Gloffary* of SPELMAN, under the word ANTIPHONA, and the ingenious *Mufical Dictionary* of ROUSSEAU, under the Word ANTIENNE.

11. A SHORT Copy of *Greek Elegiac Verfes,* printed at *Peterf-burgh,* in the year 1780, and addreft to Prince POTEMKIN, with this *fingular* Title,

'Επίγραμμα ἐπὶ τῆς παμφαῦς κỳ χαρμοσύνη. ΓΟΡΓΕΙΟΦΟΡΙΑΣ, τῆς κοινο-τέρως ΜΑΣΚΑΡΑΔΟΣ καλυμένης, ἣν κ. τ. λ.

THUS *Englifhed*——*A Poem, on the fplendid and delightful* FESTI-VITY, WHERE THEY WEAR GORGONIAN VISORS; *more commonly called* A MASQUERADE; *which Prince* POTEMKIN *celebrated,* &c. &c.

A *better Word* to denote A MASQUERADE could hardly have been *invented,* than the Word here employed, Γοργειοφόρια. In attempting to tranflate it, that I might exprefs ONE Word, I have been com-pelled to ufe *many.*

12. A TRANSLATION of *Virgil's Georgics* from *the Latin* Hexa-meters into GREEK HEXAMETERS, by the celebrated EUGENIUS, fa-

mous

mous for his Treatise of *Logic*, published a few years since in *ancient Greek* at *Leipsic*. He was made an Archbishop, but chose to resign his dignity. He is now carrying on *this Translation* under the protection of *Prince Potemkin*, but has as yet gone no farther, than to the end of the *First Georgic*.

The Work is printed on a large Folio Paper, having the *Original* on one side, and the *Translation* on the other. Copious Notes in *Greek* are at the bottom of the several Pages.

Take a short Specimen of the Performance.

Continuo, ventis surgentibus, aut freta ponti
Incipiunt agitata tumescere, et aridus altis
Montibus audiri fragor; aut resonantia longe
Littora misceri, et nemorum increbrescere murmur. Gcor. I. 356.

Ἀυτίκα, ἐγρομένων ἀνέμων, πορθμοῖς ἐπὶ πόντε
Ἄλς τε σαλευομένη οἰδαίνει, κ᾽ κορυφαὶ δὲ
Οὔρεος ἄκραι τραχὺ βοῶσιν· ἀτὰρ μακρόθεν γε
Ἀκταὶ τ᾽ εἰνάλιοι ῥα βρέμονται, κ᾽ αἰγιαλοὶ τε
Σμερδαλέοι πνοιῆσι δὲ μυκάτ᾽ αἷα κ᾽ ὕλη.

Of these various *printed* Works, *the first six* were sent me by the learned Scholar above mentioned, *Christianus Fridericus Matthæi*, from *Moscow*; *the* last six I had the honour to receive from Prince *Potemkin* at *Petersburgh*.

Besides the *Printed Books*, the learned Professor at *Moscow* sent me a curious *Latin Narrative* in *Manuscript*.

In it he gives an account of a fine *Manuscript* of Strabo, belonging to the *Ecclesiastical Library* at *Moscow*.—He informs me, this

APPENDIX:

MS. is in *Folio*; contains 427 Leaves; is beautifully written by one, whom he calls a learned and diligent fcribe, at the end of the fifteenth or beginning of the fixteenth Century; and came, as appears by a memorandum in the Manufcript, from *the celebrated Greek Monaftery* at Mount *Athos*.

He adds (which is worth attention) that almoft all the *Greek Manufcripts*, which are now preferved at *Mofcow*, were originally brought *thither* from this *Monaftery*; and that, in the laft Century, by order of *the Emperor Alexius Michaelowitz*, and *the Patriarch Nico*, by means of the *Monk Arfenius*. So early in this Country did a Gleam of Literature fhew itfelf.

He ftrongly *denies* the Fact, that there is any other MS. of STRABO befides this either at *Mofcow*, or at *Peterfburgh*.

Of the *prefent MS.* he has been fo kind as to fend me COLLATIONS, taken from the *firft* and *fecond* Book.

After this he mentions THE UNPUBLISHED HYMN OF HOMER UPON CERES, and THE FRAGMENT of another by the fame Poet UPON BACCHUS; both of which, fince I heard from him, have been publifhed by RUNKENIUS at *Leyden*, to whom *my Correfpondent* had fent them from *the Mofcowan Library*.

He has been generous enough to fend me Copies of all the Books he has publifhed, for which valuable Donation I take this public opportunity of making my grateful acknowledgments.

With regard to *all the Publications* here mentioned, it is to be obferved, that thofe from PETERSBURGH are faid to be printed in the *Imperial Academy of Sciences*; thofe from Moscow, by *the Types of the Imperial Univerfity*; each place *by its ftile* indicating its *Eftablifhment.*

IN

In justice to my Son, *his Majesty's Minister to the Court of Russia,* it is incumbent upon me to fay, that all this Information, and all thefe Literary Treafures have been procured for me by *his* Help, and thro' *his* Intereft.

I must not conclude without obferving (tho' perhaps it may be a *Repetition)* that the Efforts to Civilize this country *did not begin from* Peter the Great, but were *much older.* A fmall Glimmering, like the firft Day-break, was feen under Czar Ivan, in the middle of the *fixteenth Century.*

This Dawn of Civilizing became more confpicuous *a Century afterwards,* under Czar Alexius Michaelowitz ; of whom, as well as of his fon Theodore or Fædor we have fpoken already.

But under the Great Peter it burft forth, with all the fplendor of a Rifing Sun, and (if I may be permitted to continue my Metaphor) has continued ever fince to afcend towards its Meridian.

More than fifty years have paft fince the Death of Peter ; during which period, with very little exception, *this vaft Empire has been governed by* Female Sovereigns only. All of them have purfued more or lefs the Plan of their great Predeceffor, and none of them more, than the illustrious Princess, who *now* reigns.

And fo much for Literature in Russia, and for its Progress towards being civilized.

ADVERTISEMENT.

It was propofed, as mentioned in p. 299 of this Work, to have joined a few Notes to the Pieces contained in the preceding Appendix; but, the Work growing larger than was expected, the Notes, as not being effentially Parts of it, have been omitted.

One Omiffion however we beg to fupply, becaufe it has happened thro' Inadvertence. Befides the Arabic Tranflations from the Greek, mentioned in the Appendix, Part the Firft, there are alfo Tranflations of HIPPOCRATES GALEN, *and the old Greek Phyficians, whom the Arabians, as they tranflated, illuftrated with Comments, and upon whofe Doctrines they formed many Compofitions of their own, having been remarkably famous for their Study and Knowledge of* MEDICINE.

INDEX

TO THE

PHILOLOGICAL INQUIRIES.

ALEX-

NICEPHORUS,

PIERCEFIELD,

V.

FINIS.

Dépôt légal, 4ᵉ trimestre 1971